CELESTIAL
GEOMETRY

CELESTIAL GEOMETRY

UNDERSTANDING THE ASTRONOMICAL MEANINGS OF ANCIENT SITES

KEN TAYLOR

WATKINS PUBLISHING

LONDON

TO THE SUN AND MOON OF EVERY CHILD OF EARTH – OUR PARENTS

CELESTIAL GEOMETRY
KEN TAYLOR

First published in the UK and USA in 2012 by
Watkins Publishing
Sixth Floor
Castle House
75–76 Wells Street
London
W1T 3QH

Conceived by Ken Taylor, created and designed by
Watkins Publishing

Managing Editor: Sandra Rigby
Senior Editor: Fiona Robertson
Designer: Tim Foster
Picture Research: Julia Ruxton
Commissioned Artwork: David Atkinson and Tim Foster

British Library Cataloguing-in-Publication Data:
A CIP record for this book is available from the British
Library

Library of Congress Cataloging-in-Publication Data
available

ISBN: 978-1-78028-386-9
10 9 8 7 6 5 4 3 2 1

Typeset in Gotham and DIN
Colour reproduction by XY Digital
Printed in China by Imago

Notes
Abbreviations used throughout this book:
CE Common Era (the equivalent of AD)
BCE Before the Common Era (the equivalent of BC)

Distributed in the USA and Canada by
Sterling Publishing Co., Inc.
387 Park Avenue South, New York, NY 10016-8810

For information about custom editions, special sales,
premium and corporate purchases, please contact
Sterling Special Sales Department at 800-805-5489 or
specialsales@sterlingpub.com.

CONTENTS

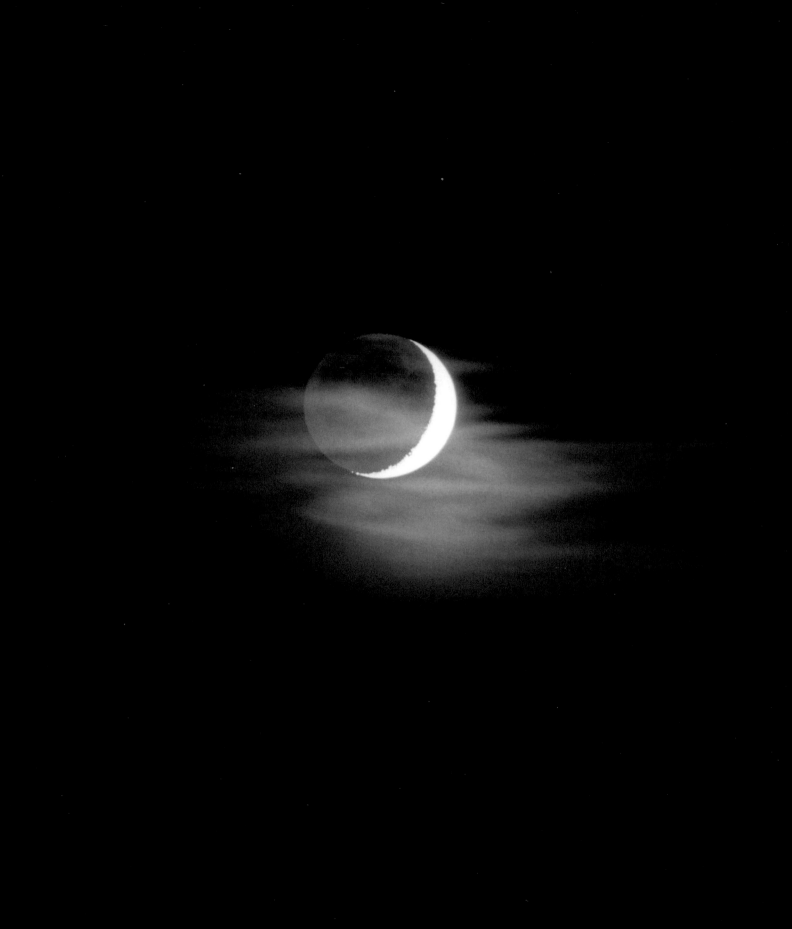

INTRODUCTION

Archaeoastronomy – the study of ancient astronomy – has been something of a buzzword in academic circles for a couple of decades, but the word is still unfamiliar to many people. It was coined in 1969 for a multi-disciplinary subject that includes not only archaeology and astronomy, but also subjects as diverse as geology, climatology and engineering, as well as history, art and religion. Mustering consensus from authorities in such disparate fields takes a considerable amount of time, and is the main reason archaeoastronomy has been rather slow to develop, although it is currently making rapid and exciting progress.

The way the sun impacts on us through the rhythm of our daily lives and the changing seasons has been recognized for millennia. An action as ordinary as placing a pot plant on a sunny windowsill is in tune with the same fundamental forces of the solar system that inspired the choreography of ritual at Stonehenge. We are not so distant from our forebears who first gazed into the heavens, learned its celestial geometry and applied its wisdom to their lives. Astronomy gave us a new perspective on time – knowing the cycles of the sun and moon allowed us to look into the future with confidence, providing a stable framework in an otherwise chaotic world.

Today we live secure in the knowledge that the sun will always rise in the morning, and the moon and stars won't fall from the sky, but these facts have only been understood in the last few centuries. Before the laws of gravity and motion were discovered, people really had no idea what kept the sun on track and held the stars aloft. These mysteries were the stuff of legend, and the heavens were the abode of gods. It may seem absurd to us that our ancestors thought the sun travelled over the sky in a chariot and back under the Earth in a boat, to re-emerge in the dawn sky. Yet the intense energy that sinks below the Earth to be magically reborn is an evocative symbol of human death and resurrection or reincarnation. The name of the Roman sun god Sol Invictus ("the unconquered sun") capitalizes on this powerful metaphor, and there is no gainsaying the influence such religious metaphors have wielded through the millennia.

If we scoff at the old, mythological explanations of natural forces, we must also admit that our finest scientists today still don't understand how dark matter is holding our galaxy together, nor how dark energy is tearing the visible universe

Moon at sunset Within the brighter crescent moon is the shadowy shape of a full moon – the interplay of light and shadow creates the perceived lunar phases.

apart. Some of the most recent cosmological theories are just as ingenious yet outlandish as the old myths, such as the idea that our universe sparked into being when two pre-existing membranes touched each other (this contemporary idea is reminiscent of the ancient Chinese concept of the creative fusion of two primordial essences – yin and yang).

Many early observations and experiments were conducted so long ago that not even their myths survive. But the Earth soaks up history like a child absorbs language, and monuments of stone can endure the passage of aeons. Now that archaeologists are learning to recognize the telltale signs of ancient observatories, archaeoastronomy is set to move from strength to strength.

Exploring the world

Around 10 percent of the sites featured in these pages are of such global importance they are listed by UNESCO as World Heritage sites; these include popular tourist destinations such as the sacred healing centre of Stonehenge, the tomb pyramids of Giza, the temple-pyramids of Central America and the spiritual microcosm of Angkor Wat. But many of the sites in this book are off the beaten track and offer a more intimate yet still eloquent experience of ancient astronomy. A structure that was carefully aligned to an astronomically significant point on the horizon frequently enshrines important clues to the beliefs of the people who built it and the priests or shamans who officiated there. Archaeoastronomy is giving us a new appreciation of previously enigmatic megalithic stone rows, circles

The sun chariot This bronze sculpture found at Trundholm in Denmark has been dated to *c.* 1400 BCE and shows the sun borne across the sky in a horse-drawn chariot.

and rectangles; of temples of all shapes and sizes dedicated to the sun, moon and stars. The east-facing Kilclooney dolmen, constructed in County Donegal, Ireland, around 5,000 years ago, is one of the many burial mounds that had internal passages designed to catch the light of the morning sun – as if in the hope that those warming rays could revivify the dead.

Although our sun is a star, to the casual observer there is no similarity: the sun is uniquely bright and rules the day, while stars are innumerable tiny points of light that only show themselves at night. As a result, many temples and tombs were aligned with the sun's seasonal progress, yet stars have few proven alignments. As we have always related to the sun, moon and stars in very different ways, this book gives each topic its own chapter, each one ending with a selection of stories about their respective celestial gods and goddesses.

The moon, which is so similar to the sun in shape and apparent size (at full moon at least) that it is often thought of in sexual terms as the sun's spouse, occupies the smallest chapter. This is not because the moon's influence was deemed of little consequence. The big temples were usually created by patriarchal cultures who favoured the sun as their patron and often used solar imagery, such

Symbol of renewed life
The huge megaliths used to make the Kilclooney dolmen in Ireland were, like the stones of other ancient burial chambers, positioned so that the rising sun would flood the dark interior with light.

9

as the halo or radiating crown, to bolster the prestige of a ruler who was frequently also the greatest priest. From Augustus, for example, Roman emperors held the title *Pontifex Maximus* ("greatest pontiff"). In such circumstances, women tended to embrace the lunar mysteries in more homely ways that left no grand monuments.

Few archaeoastronomical sites have been excavated in modern times, so little is yet known of the rituals that took place in the calendrical observatories, built by the first farmers to chart and celebrate the turning seasons, or even of the rites of the grand temples and awe-inspiring tombs. Sometimes it is the small objects that amaze and intrigue us most: the Antikythera mechanism, for instance, is so ancient and yet so complex that some believe it must be an alien artefact. This corroded set of gear wheels was found in 1900 off the coast of the Greek island of Antikythera, but it was not until 2006 that X-rays and advanced photography revealed it had once not only functioned as a planetarium, with miniature planets, moon and sun propelled around a backdrop of the zodiac, but also accurately portrayed the phases of the moon, and even predicted eclipses. This unparalleled device was made around 150 BCE.

Some finds, though small in size, have ignited major controversies. These include pieces of bone and antler, dating to around 25,000 BCE, with carved markings that have been claimed as a means of counting and recording the nights in the lunar month. Opinion is divided on the interpretation of these markings, as they could have been simply decorative, or used for counting something else. Examples include the Isturitz Baton and the Blanchard Bone Plaque from France, and the Ishango Bone from the Democratic Republic of Congo.

Ancient astronomy (*Right*) The Antikythera mechanism, found in the Aegean Sea, was used more than 2,000 years ago to model the movement of stars and planets and predict eclipses.

Tracking the moon (*Far right*) The Ishango Bone from the Democratic Republic of Congo (viewed here from all sides) has been claimed as a possible lunar calendar created more than 20,000 years ago.

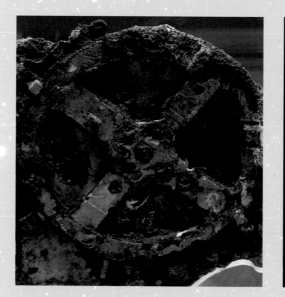

Birth and rebirth

The modern science of archaeoastronomy is the inheritor of the observations of the eclectic antiquarians of the 17th and 18th centuries, such as John Aubrey who in 1678 remarked on the sunrise alignments of English churches, and William Stukeley who noted the midsummer sunrise at Stonehenge in 1724. However, the academic respectability of archaeoastronomy suffered from the over-enthusiasm of some 19th- and early 20th-century advocates, whose claims often said more about their personal beliefs than about the sites they investigated. A site surveyed in the 1950s by engineer and pioneering archaeoastronomer Alexander Thom is still hotly debated today. He claimed that the row of three large stones at Ballochroy, on the western coast of the Kintyre peninsula, Scotland, was an astronomical observatory with high-precision alignments. Thom pointed out that looking along the flat face of the broad but thin 11ft (3.3m) central stone directed the gaze to a mountain on the Isle of Jura where the sun set on the midsummer solstice in around 1600 BCE. He also noted that the three stones stood in a straight line that pointed toward the point where sunset would have taken place on the midwinter solstice at the same period.

Difficulties arose from several inconvenient facts: another of the three stones was also broad and thin, but its surface did not point toward any notable astronomical event; the row itself was quite wide, so a range of alignments could be extended from it, and all but one would miss the winter solstice; and in any

Contested alignments

Alexander Thom believed the stone row at Ballochroy, Scotland, to be aligned to the setting of the summer solstice sun behind the Isle of Jura, yet archaeoastronomers now think that the evidence for this claim is not conclusive.

case, a heap of stones over an ancient burial would have blocked the view to the horizon. However, the fact that both claimed alignments were viable for the same period of the Bronze Age, which tallied with the approximate date of the monument, meant it was at least possible that this was a low-precision observatory.

Amid all this uncertainty, many academics sought to avoid any risk of professional embarrassment by adopting a stance of dismissive scepticism. Archaeoastronomy came to be treated as a fringe subject, relegated to the same category as ley lines and lake monsters. It faced the intellectual backlash provoked by popular books such as Erich von Däniken's *Chariots of the Gods* (1968), which sought to reinterpret ancient ruins and religious documents as evidence of visits by aliens from other worlds (see page 226).

In 1981 the International Astronomical Union held a landmark conference in Oxford, England, bringing delegates together to exchange ideas on approaches to archaeoastronomical investigation. This event ushered in a renaissance of the subject, and has been repeated ever since in venues around the globe at intervals of four or five years. Archaeoastronomy and its sister subject ethnoastronomy – the study of astronomical traditions maintained by indigenous peoples into modern times – still face some serious obstacles, such as the difficulty of statistical analysis, but the current impetus to overcome these challenges, including liaising more closely with authorities in related disciplines, is resulting in significant breakthroughs. The beginning of the 21st century is set to be an important period in the history of the subject.

Any exploration of a mystery is bound to be full of false starts, and there will be inevitable excursions along avenues that arrive at an abrupt dead end. Sometimes the investigation will come to within a hair's breadth of success, only to be turned aside by a seemingly insurmountable obstacle that will perhaps, one day, be overcome. Sometimes the vital breakthrough may be accidental – a chance discovery or imaginative insight.

An adventure for everyone

There are many archaeoastronomical societies, some global, some local, that are actively researching all avenues of the subject, and most welcome new members with or without any academic training. Enthusiasm is valued as the key quality that, combined with careful observation, may open a new understanding.

Professional archaeoastronomers tend to be kept busy researching particular issues thrown up by existing evidence, which means they enjoy scant leisure to seek out new sites. People with little or no training may make advances, simply by being in the right place at the right time.

Seeing is not always believing

The human mind is astonishingly good at recognizing patterns – our ability to spot the face of a friend in a crowd (or a predator in a jungle) is remarkable. Our imagination brings sense and order to a chaotic world, but sometimes this ability can turn against us. When confronted with an unfamiliar situation we instinctively conjure our best guess of what's going on, and although this is usually good enough, we sometimes leap to an unsafe conclusion.

Many prehistoric carved stones contain cup marks (also known as cupules), which are primitive carvings that simply consist of shallow depressions, typically around 2in (5cm) across. A stone covered with dozens of cup marks positively invites us to play a game of join-the-dots, and many researchers claim to discover star patterns among them. The problem is that the sheer quantity of possible permutations can easily create false positive identifications.

These stones are geographically widespread, from Europe to Asia and America to Australia, and for every one known of today, there may be many more awaiting discovery. And even those that are known now may become candidates for further investigation – such as the stone in a field at Trefael near Newport, Wales.

For centuries anyone could have seen that this standing stone was covered in random cup marks, but when it was excavated in 2010, and its full complement of more than 75 cup marks revealed, people began to identify patterns that seemed to resemble stars in the constellations of Orion and Cassiopeia, as well as the stars Sirius and Polaris.

Sky map at Trefael? Some believe the carvings on this heavily marked stone found in Newport, Wales, to represent a section of the night sky, including the constellations Orion and Cassiopeia and the stars Sirius and Polaris.

Such claims attract a good deal of interest from the media, but rarely receive academic acceptance because the correlation between the stones and the stars is generally poor. The shapes of the constellation are skewed, constellations are positioned incorrectly in relation to each other, some stars may be missing or extra ones added, and large and small cups bear no relation to bright or dim stars. Surely, no one who could undertake the extraordinary task of creating so many neat round hollows in a prominent local rock, a rock that family, friends and neighbours would know, would make such a mess of a star chart?

Even a stone with a good match could be the product of chance, and anyone claiming a positive identification will face a difficult challenge convincing professional archaeoastronomers. However, other explanations for these cup marks are equally unsatisfying, with many classified simply as "abstract".

If, however, an indisputable example of a cup-mark star map were to be uncovered, it could be as important to archaeoastronomy as the Rosetta Stone was to Egyptology. Because different stars rise and fall as the seasons turn, the stars can be read as the storybook of the year. It is easy to imagine prehistoric people sitting together and swapping stories as campfire sparks shimmered into the heavens. Seasonal tales of hunting, love and death would become linked with the stars that shone down on the tellers. Newborn myths would begin to populate the sky with the primordial constellations. Discovering which star groups might have been recognized in prehistoric times could unlock many mysteries of megalithic art, architecture and custom.

The bigger picture

When the first farmers noticed the sun's regular cycle of movements, they found they could use it to create a calendar. Just two sticks of wood could set up a sighting line pointing to a spot on the horizon where, for example, the sun rises at midsummer. But wood rots and even the holes in the ground where the sticks stood would eventually fill with soil and become difficult to detect. A modern visitor would struggle to find any evidence of that ancient calendar. Even if the sticks were replaced by stones, and even assuming they remain standing, it could still be difficult to identify them among a scatter of other relics. Two stones will always form a straight line, and must point to the horizon. That some of these alignments will mark a significant date in the calendar by chance alone is inevitable.

Archaeoastronomers must find ways to sift through vast amount of artefacts and other evidence, and identify those that were consciously created to mark a relationship with the heavens. Statistics is a useful tool that enables the analysis of a great number of comparable sites. Such surveys can reveal the pivotal calendar dates, such as the solstices, that really mattered to people living in those communities. Recent large-scale surveys include a study of the orientation of Iron Age roundhouses in Britain and Eire, whose single entrances tend to face the rising sun.

Lists of alignments and tables of data may show us the astronomical dates that were important to people, but not how they affected people's everyday lives. Some ancient cultures have living descendants who still preserve some traditional lore, often in the form of stories or rituals, making ethnoastronomy a valuable investigative technique. The beliefs of the ancient Anasazi (Ancestral Puebloans), for example, are reflected in the memories of the modern Pueblo and Zuni communities. But we must always be careful about drawing inferences, because this is where our own preconceptions are most likely to misguide us – our imagination is a wonderful tool for filling in the gaps between observations, and the fewer the facts, the more creative we tend to become.

Much academic research has focused on prominent sites such as the magnificent pyramids of South America and Egypt. But archaeoastronomy is a surprisingly homely subject that can involve each of us at a personal level. In some respects, archaeoastronomy is like gravity: it is only when we pause and think about it that we begin to feel its influence and discover it is actually all-pervading.

Ancient rituals, new understanding

Many aspects of our daily lives are dictated by the astronomy of our planet and the ordinary yellow star around which it revolves. When we raise a hand to shield our eyes from the noonday sun, we are performing a ritual salute that is far older than our species. When we gaze at a sunset, or relish the sun's dawning warmth on our skin, we are in touch with astronomical forces that have shaped every aspect of our being. It is no wonder our forebears raised observatories and temples to honour and understand these marvels of nature. And it is not surprising that we seek out these places, to take our turn standing in their footsteps.

Many ancient religious sites are beside holy springs, rivers or lakes, or on sacred mountains, and although landscape shrines are not normally classified as archaeoastronomical, perhaps they should be. To an astronomer, there is no fundamental distinction between one planet or moon in a solar system and another. And all the springs, rivers, lakes, seas, mountains and valleys that we have ever deemed special are part of the best-known yet often least appreciated astronomical object of all – our home planet, Earth.

Archaeoastronomy opens a window on the past, offering us an insight into the hopes and aspirations of our predecessors, as well as revealing many of their fears in their struggle to survive. But it also has relevance today. For example, the Armed Forces Memorial at the National Memorial Arboretum at Alrewas in Staffordshire, UK, which opened in 2001, incorporates an astronomical alignment. At 11am on 11 November (Armistice Day) – the time and date when hostilities ceased on the Western Front at the end of World War I in 1918 – sunlight enters the memorial through a slit in the encircling wall, shines through a portal in a statue (symbolically, a door to a better world) and illuminates the central wreath, commemorating those who have died in armed service since 1 January 1948.

When we talk in terms of the "light of reason" or "fear of the dark", we are echoing the thoughts of those ancients who supplicated the god of the sun for prophesy, or propitiated the moon for protection against nightmares. The Western stereotyping of men as solar and women as lunar may have done immeasurable harm (not least in the infamous witchcraft persecutions), and stands a stark warning against literal interpretations of myths.

The development of a complex system of knowledge, combining astronomy with spiritual values and psychological truths, occurred at many places independently, but with the same key building blocks. Our planetary system is special in that the full moon and sun appear to be exactly the same size in the sky, producing total eclipses in which the sun and moon unite in an awe-inspiring spectacle (see pages 128–9). Our solar system also includes some very suggestive celestial geometry, such as the pentagram or five-pointed star drawn by the return appearances of the planet Venus (see page 160) – a characteristically human shape, referring to

Modern alignment At 11am on the 11th day of the 11th month, sunlight pierces the wall of the Armed Forces Memorial at Alrewas, Staffordshire, England, commemorating those who have died in armed service since 1 January 1948.

the head and the four limbs. Natural coincidences such as these are more than enough to have inspired our species to develop a sophisticated intellectual – even metaphysical – approach to the cosmos. Observing the wonders of the sky, it is perhaps inevitable that people would begin to imagine a creator who set them in motion. Such a creator would sit very comfortably in the heavens, holding court among the imperishable stars. So pervasive has celestial mythology become that an alien visitor could suppose sacred astronomy is Earth's fundamental religion.

Our modern astronomers and physicists are the latest explorers that express our species' unbounded curiosity, striving to understand the universe and our place within it. This is as important a task today as it was at any time in the past, and may become even more vital as we learn more about the existence of life forms inhabiting the vastness of space. We may know that the sun is not actually a deity crossing the sky in his chariot, yet the true wonders of the universe may prove to be even more fantastic. By tracing the beginnings of humanity's observation of the heavens, archaeoastronomy finds ever more to inspire us to continue our exploration.

Day turned to night These dramatic time-lapse images capture the overwhelming experience of a total solar eclipse, photographed from the Pacific Ocean on 22 July 2009 over 6.5 minutes.

INTRODUCING ASTRONOMY

This book explores sites from around the world designed by our ancestors to record and make sense of the celestial bodies they observed in the heavens, and to provide a focus for their ceremonies. Although it is not essential to understand every aspect of astronomy in order to appreciate the expertise of ancient societies, an overview of our solar system, and of the Earth's relationship to the sun and moon, will provide a useful context for interpreting the significance of the sites examined in this book.

Today, we know that our sun is a fairly ordinary, middle-aged star emitting vast quantities of radiation that we see and feel as light and heat. It is the spinning heart of the solar system, which includes transient objects such as comets and meteorites, as well as the more stable planets.

Only the planets Mercury and Venus are closer to the sun than the Earth, and from our perspective they never appear to stray far from the sun. Sometimes we see these planets rise as "morning stars" shortly before dawn; at other times they appear in the dusk sky as "evening stars". Between these two extremes, they seem to disappear from view, as they are engulfed in sunlight. A milestone in any culture's astronomy is the time when the morning and evening appearances of Mercury and Venus are recognized as belonging to the same celestial bodies. As the brightest object in the heavens after the sun and moon, Venus was venerated around the world (see pages 160–1 and 222–3).

Only one of the group of inner planets appears to wander around the whole sky: Mars. The inner planets have rocky surfaces, whereas the outer planets are gaseous: Jupiter, Saturn, Uranus and Neptune (the latter two were not identified as planets until modern times). Still further away from the sun, Pluto was classified as a planet when it was discovered in 1930, but in 2006 it was downgraded to a dwarf planet like others in the outreaches of the solar system.

Of the true stars in the sky, if we discount the sun, the brightest appears to be Sirius. This pre-eminence made it of interest to cultures from ancient Egypt to the indigenous peoples of North America (see pages 176–7). Although Sirius is only 25 times as luminous as our sun, it is one of our closest stellar neighbours, just 8.6 light years away.

Similarly, the most prominent star cluster, the Pleiades, also attracted much attention from ancient astronomers in many culturally separate traditions (see pages 180–81). The brightest of this cluster of around 500 stars is Alcyone, 40 times more luminous than Sirius, but much further away and so fainter.

The spinning Earth

Just three key aspects of the Earth's relationship with the sun underpin most ancient solar alignments: the Earth's 365-day orbit around the sun; the Earth's daily rotation on its axis; and the tilt of this axis at 23.4° from the vertical relative to the plane of the ecliptic – the plane on which all the planets orbit the sun, and where they originally formed from a disk of loose material spinning around our star. It is this tilt that gives us our seasons (see pages 22–3).

Early cultures such as that of ancient Greece imagined that the stars were fixed on a sphere rotating around the Earth, and this model is still helpful to us. Astronomers determined that the Earth's north pole pointed to the celestial north pole, and that the Earth's equator could have a corresponding celestial equator. Just as any position on Earth can be described by its longitude and latitude, so the position of a star on the celestial sphere has coordinates of right ascension (RA) and declination (dec).

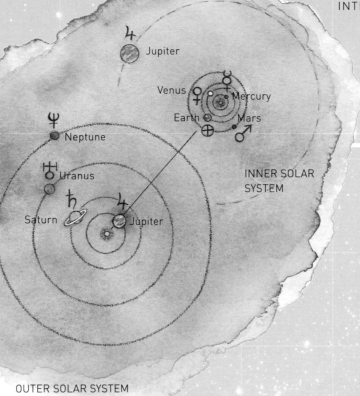

Jupiter

Venus   Mercury

Earth   Mars

Neptune

INNER SOLAR
SYSTEM

Uranus

Saturn   Jupiter

OUTER SOLAR SYSTEM

Our planetary neighbours
The sun and moon and five
planets that are visible to the
naked eye – Mercury, Venus,
Mars, Jupiter, Saturn – have
captivated our imagination
since ancient times. Uranus,
although faintly visible, was
not recognized as a planet
until 1781 and Neptune not
until 1846. In this artwork,
each planet is accompanied
by its astrological symbol.

Because of the Earth's tilt, the sun's annual
journey across the heavens doesn't follow the line of
the celestial equator. Instead, its path oscillates north
and south of the celestial equator, bringing summer
to the Earth's northern and southern hemispheres
as it does so. These movements culminate in the
summer solstice, the longest day of the year, and the
winter solstice, the shortest day. Halfway between one
solstice and the next, the sun crosses the celestial
equator, marking the two equinoxes, when the hours of
daylight and night are equal (see pages 48–9).

If we gaze out into the midnight sky, each night the
stars will appear to move slightly across the sky as the
Earth travels a little farther around its yearly orbit. A
star rises four minutes earlier each night. But viewed
from some locations, some stars never appear to rise
or set: they are ever-present. These circumpolar stars
are seen to revolve around the sky without passing
below the horizon. For an observer at either pole, the
visible stars are circumpolar. At the equator, no stars
are circumpolar (see pages 168–9).

The tilt of the Earth's axis is a legacy from the
formative phase of the solar system, probably caused
by our planet's collision with another massive object.
This collision also created the debris that coalesced
into our closest neighbour, the moon. Viewed from
Earth, the full moon is a close match to the apparent
size of the sun, and this coincidence is dramatically
evident during every solar eclipse (see pages 128–9).
The moon received plenty of attention from ancient
astronomers, its phases being used as a convenient
way of marking time. Some cultures even discovered
the so-called lunar standstills, which are the moon's
equivalent of the solstices, even though the full
standstill cycle takes an impressive 18.6 years to
complete (see pages 134–5).

Our solar system is only a tiny part of our galaxy,
the Milky Way, which contains hundreds of billions of
stars, and there are hundreds of billions of galaxies in
the universe. As we gaze at the night sky, this thought
can bring us closer to the profound sense of awe with
which our ancestors must have viewed the heavens.

1 THE SUN – LIGHT OF OUR LIVES

The heat we feel on a summer's day comes from a distance of 93 million miles (150 million km) – compared to the heat of a bonfire just a few paces away, solar energy is literally astronomical. The sun's heat draws up water from the oceans and drives our weather; its light enables plants to grow our food. Our very lives have always depended on the power of our local star – the sun.

INTRODUCING THE SOLSTICES

Observing the apparent movements of the sun, the star that governs so much of what happens in our world, became particularly important when people began to settle and adopt an agricultural way of life. Knowing what came next in the cycle of the seasons enabled farmers to judge when to sow and reap, and when to trade their surplus crops.

This agricultural revolution occurred in different cultures at different times, probably beginning in the Middle East early in the 10th millennium BCE, and concluding in western Europe in the 3rd millennium BCE. This period is known to archaeologists as the Neolithic Age (New Stone Age) and many monuments of the time incorporated astronomical alignments to the sun, so much so that British archaeologists often call the middle Neolithic the "Age of Astronomy".

The obliquity of the ecliptic

The Earth does not stand upright as it spins around the sun on its yearly orbit, but leans over slightly. This tilt of the Earth's axis of about 23.4° from the vertical is known as the "obliquity of the ecliptic". The Earth's axis is an imaginary line running through the centre of the planet, connecting the north and south poles and extending out into space – in the northern hemisphere it famously points toward Polaris, making this star a traditional navigational aid.

The tilt of the Earth's axis is constant throughout the year. As our planet revolves around the sun, part of its surface is sometimes tilted toward the sun, while at other times the same area is tilted away from the sun – creating summer and winter respectively. In the northern hemisphere, the day with most sunlight is on or around 21 June – the summer solstice. (This is the day of the winter solstice in the southern hemisphere.) Six months later the positions are reversed.

The nearer we are to the poles, the more extreme is the relative difference between day and night at the height of summer and in the depths of winter. In fact, each pole has 24 hours of daylight at midsummer (the "midnight sun" or "white nights") and 24 hours of night at midwinter.

"Solstice" means "sun standstill". As the seasons turn, each day the rising and setting sun appears to move a little way along the horizon. As winter becomes summer in the northern hemisphere, for example, the sun's positions on the horizon move north, until the Earth's tilt is aligned directly with the sun and

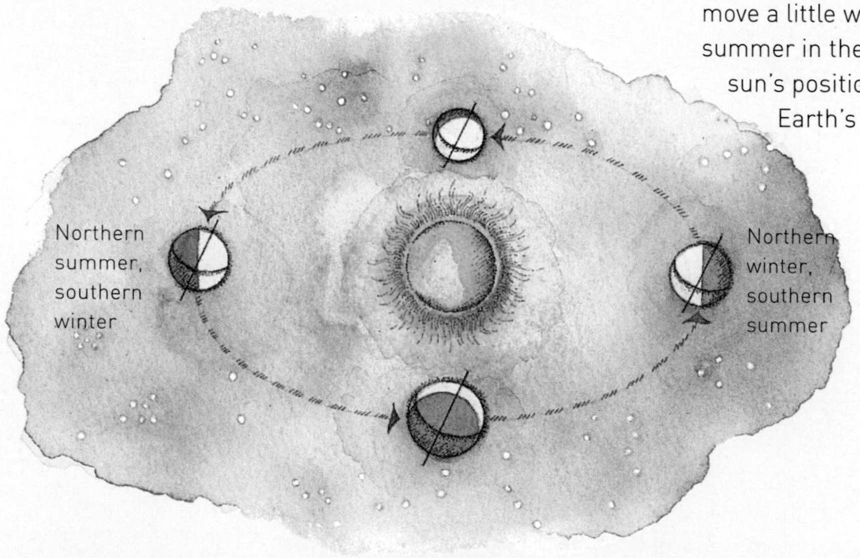

Northern summer, southern winter

Northern winter, southern summer

The obliquity of the ecliptic This diagram shows how the Earth's axis remains oriented in the same direction as the planet circles the sun. As our planet moves through its yearly cycle, we receive more or fewer hours of sunlight depending on whether our hemisphere is tipped toward or away from the sun – we experience this phenomenon as the seasons.

Land of the midnight sun At the fishing village of Reine, Norway, a settlement within the Arctic Circle, the Earth's tilt toward the sun means that from late May until mid-July the sun never sets.

the sun's march along the horizon stops. The next day it reverses course, toward the south and winter.

Halfway between the solstices are the two days when everywhere on Earth has equal periods of daylight and night-time. These are the spring (vernal) and autumnal equinoxes (see pages 48–9).

Many complicated systems are triggered by the single fact of the tilt of Earth's axis. Global weather patterns, for example, are powered by the difference between the summer heat and winter cold simultaneously occurring on opposing hemispheres, as winds and tidal currents continually seek equilibrium. Another atmospheric phenomenon, the aurorae, is also affected by Earth's tilt. The aurorae tend to produce their most spectacular nocturnal lightshows around the equinoxes when the Earth's magnetic field links with the interplanetary magnetic field. There is an auroral zone around each of Earth's magnetic poles in which the northern

lights and southern lights are relatively common, but geomagnetic storms can bring these fascinating beauties into temperate latitudes.

Dating ancient sites

Astronomers have calculated that the obliquity of the ecliptic is changing very gradually in a cycle lasting 41,000 years. The most recent maximum is thought to have occurred around 8500 BCE (approximately 24.5°), and the next minimum is due around 12000 CE (approximately 22.5°). With our current obliquity of 23.4°, Earth is close to the mid-point in this cycle.

Around 2500 BCE the obliquity of the ecliptic was approximately 24°, so the summer solstice sun would have risen slightly further north of east – and, similarly, set a little further north of west. A precise understanding of this change in the angle of the Earth's tilt enables archaeoastronomers to attempt to date sites by their solar (and lunar) alignments.

STONEHENGE ENGLAND

A World Heritage site, this stone circle in the English county of Wiltshire is arguably the best-known archaeoastronomical site in the world. It is famous for an alignment to the rising sun at midsummer, yet this explanation of the position of the huge sarsen stones is now thought to be mistaken or at best only partially correct. For a full picture of the site, we must consider not only the midsummer sunrise but also move half a year and half a day later – and look in the opposite direction, to the setting sun at the winter solstice.

Although ruined, the stone circle of Stonehenge remains impressive, particularly the megalithic blocks of sarsen sandstone that were hauled to the site from some 19 miles (30km) to the north around 2450 BCE. The site dates back to as early as 7500 BCE and may originally have been a centre of lunar ritual (see pages 140–41). However, around *c.* 2550 BCE, when the bluestones were brought to Stonehenge from the Preseli Mountains of Wales, the site's axis was shifted by 4°, onto an alignment with the midsummer sunrise.

Around 2450 BCE Stonehenge was remodelled again, when the great sarsen stones were assembled into a ring of 30 uprights. The same number of stones were placed horizontally on top of the uprights, forming a continuous hoop of stone 98ft (30m) in diameter, raised about 13ft (4m) above the ground.

Inside this ring were the "trilithons": five pairs of larger stones, each pair supporting a single lintel between them. They were arranged in a horseshoe shape and the tallest, the Great Trilithon, stood at the apex, some 24ft (7m) high. The open end of the horseshoe was to the northeast, facing the main entrance – a causeway across a bank and ditch. This bank and ditch encircle the whole complex except for a narrow entrance at the south, but are unusual because a defining feature of henge-type monuments

is a ditch inside a bank; whereas at Stonehenge the ditch is outside the bank (as at a castle or fort).

For centuries midsummer has been celebrated at Stonehenge. In 1223, for example, the Bishop of Salisbury protested about the "vile and indecorous games" that took place there around the solstice. In 1724 the antiquarian William Stukeley wrote that the sarsen stones were oriented to the northeast, where the sun rose on the summer solstice. He also noted that the gap between the uprights of the stone circle was much larger at this point than elsewhere. And so, generations of pilgrims and sightseers have since gone to Stonehenge to stand inside the circle and gaze outward – toward the rising sun.

Outside in A fresh perspective has revealed the importance of midwinter sunset to the builders of Stonehenge.

A new approach

It was also William Stukeley who first noticed the Avenue. This processional way, 70ft (21m) wide at its junction with the encircling ditch, is contemporary with the sarsens, and leads to the causeway from the northeast. Viewed from inside the circle, the Avenue runs straight until it dips down out of sight of the stones, then curves around to the River Avon, a total journey of 1¾ miles (2.8km).

The sarsen circle and trilithon horseshoe are now believed to have been designed to be viewed from the outside. It is thought the elite would have gathered at

the head of the Avenue on the winter solstice to watch the sun set through the stones. Setting over the top of the largest of the bluestones, which stood in front of the narrow gap between the columns of the Great Trilithon, the sinking orb would have been perfectly framed – as if entering a stone-lined grave.

The standing stone known as the Heel Stone was put in place before the erection of the sarsen stones of the circle and horseshoe, before the Avenue and perhaps even before the bluestones, and it once stood beside another megalith (which was removed long ago). The Heel Stone and the other megalith were positioned outside the northeast causeway where, viewed from the centre of the site, they flanked the sun as it rose on the summer solstice. So, although modern visitors may be mistaken in thinking the sarsens to be part of the summer solstice alignment, they are correct in looking to the Heel Stone for the solstice sunrise.

Conflicting claims

Many people journey to Stonehenge to walk in the footsteps of those who built it, and they look to the horizon and especially to the solstice sun, seeking inspiration. The best-known organized gatherings are those of the druids, whom the 17th-century antiquary John Aubrey claimed to be the builders of Stonehenge and who have been associated with summer solstice ceremonies at the site since the late 19th century. However, the history of these modern druids is only a few centuries old, and even the original druids, described by Julius Caesar in Book VI of the *Gallic Wars* (53 BCE), were as distant from the architects of Stonehenge as we are from them today.

In the current era there are many branches of Druidism, and they meet separately to celebrate a variety of seasonal events at Stonehenge and at other megalithic sites such as Avebury, as do many other pagan groups and individuals. Colourful ritual activities and alternative music festivals add vibrancy to the landscape, providing something special for the mainstream tourists.

THE ENIGMA OF AVEBURY

Part of the World Heritage site that includes Stonehenge is the megalithic monument at Avebury, famed as the largest prehistoric stone circle in the world. The circle is 1,100ft (335m) in diameter and its stones were erected around 2600 BCE, along with an encircling henge (a ditch inside a bank). This henge and stone circle enclose a smaller circle and an adjacent, horseshoe-shaped arc of stones (some suppose this is actually another circle), which are both some 300 years older than the great circle. A further century earlier, around 3000 BCE, three towering stone slabs were erected where the horseshoe would later stand, framing a rectangular space with one open side, termed a cove. Only two stones are left standing of this structure. At midsummer sunrise, sunlight streamed into this cove through its open side.

With nearly 100 stones in the large circle, and at least half as many again in the internal structures, there is vast scope for accidental alignments at Avebury. This has led to ingenious attempts to decipher and interpret the monument in terms of complex geometry and astronomy, but most archaeologists remain unconvinced. Aubrey Burl, for example, declared himself surprised at how few astronomical alignments were built into this massive site. Alignments at Avebury appear to focus on the local landscape of hills, valleys and watercourses.

Megalith at Avebury

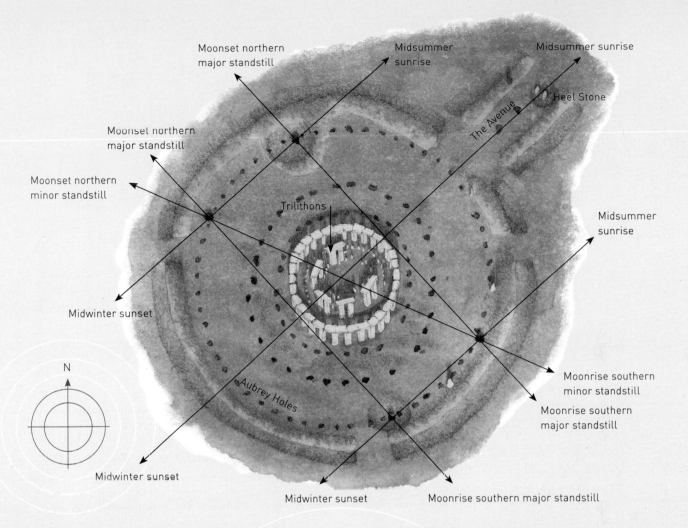

Moonset northern major standstill

Midsummer sunrise

Midsummer sunrise

Heel Stone

The Avenue

Moonset northern major standstill

Moonset northern minor standstill

Trilithons

Midsummer sunrise

Midwinter sunset

N

Aubrey Holes

Midwinter sunset

Moonrise southern minor standstill

Moonrise southern major standstill

Midwinter sunset

Moonrise southern major standstill

Despite differing approaches to spirituality, these groups agree in many key respects. For instance, they tend to be free thinkers, yet they choose to bind themselves to the Earth's seasonal and cosmic cycles. They also share the conviction that we are each responsible for our role in finding a *better way*.

Part of the attraction of Stonehenge lies in the precision of its alignments to the solstices, the turning points in the sun's movements, and many visitors come here seeking to draw on such cycles of renewal in their own lives. Some visitors talk of being healed by their experiences, which is all the more significant in light of the findings of an archaeological excavation that took place here in 2008, which suggested that Stonehenge was an ancient centre of

Multiple alignments The Station Stones (shown with red dots), set up *c*. 2550 BCE, mark the site's orientation to midwinter sunset and midsummer sunrise, and to major lunar events.

healing. Analysis of skeletal remains revealed that the reputation of Stonehenge was potent enough to draw pilgrims not only from Bronze Age Britain but from as far afield as central Europe.

A rival claim to the healing hypothesis is that the site was a cremation centre, and possibly a ritual platform from which the dead could be guaranteed a successful journey into the afterlife. This tradition continues as English Heritage (which looks after Stonehenge) allows the supervised scattering of ashes (although not in the stone circle itself).

KARNAK EGYPT

The World Heritage site Karnak is probably Egypt's best-known ancient site, apart from the pyramids at Giza, and may be the largest ancient man-made religious site in the world. Its ancient name was Ipet-isut ("most chosen of places"). The cluster of linked temples and sacred lakes stands on the east bank of the River Nile and covers an area more than 1 mile north to south, and about ¹/₂ mile wide (1.6 x 0.8km).

This sacred site formed part of the ancient Egyptian capital of Thebes, and its ruins are located 400 miles (650km) south of the Nile delta, about 2 miles (3km) north of the modern settlement of Luxor. The centre of the complex, and the original principal focus of ritual and worship, is the precinct of the sun god Amun-Re (also spelled Amen, Amon and Ammon).

Like most Egyptian temples, the precinct faces the River Nile. Directly opposite, on the river's western side, lies the royal necropolis – the Valley of the

Kings. The precinct of Amun-Re contains a central alignment of temples and ceremonial gateways (pylons) that forms a ritual axis pointing toward those highly significant locations. Victorian physicist and pioneering archaeoastronomer J. Norman Lockyer believed this axis was also aligned with the direction of the summer solstice sunset. Using the mathematics of astronomy to wind back the effects of the gradual change in the obliquity of the ecliptic (see pages 22–3), he calculated that the date of the solar alignment (and therefore the foundation of the temple) was around 3700 BCE. His date fitted reasonably well into the accepted chronology of Egypt's ancient past.

Death and rebirth of the solstice alignment
However, Egypt's chronology was dramatically revised early in the 20th century and we now know the initial phase at Karnak began around 1900 BCE, early in the

Midsummer sunset

River Nile

Precinct of Amun-Re

Quay

N

Hall of Thutmose III

Temple of the Hearing Ear

Gate of Nectanebo

Re-Horakhty Temple

Midwinter sunrise

East–west alignment J. Norman Lockyer's discovery of the alignment to the summer solstice sunset was refuted by archaeologists. However, Gerald Hawkins later confirmed the precinct's orientation to the winter solstice sunrise, on the same east–west axis.

Temple of the creator god The largest precinct at Karnak was dedicated to the worship of Amun-Re, the god who combined the sun's dual aspects of hidden and revealed, night and day.

Twelfth Dynasty. Lockyer was proved wrong. At this new date, the dying rays of the summer solstice sun could not have penetrated the main axis of the Amun-Re temple complex because the sun's disc would already have set behind the hills on the western bank of the Nile. Armed with this evidence, conventional archaeologists dismissed Lockyer's theories wholesale, but in their haste to banish astronomy from their field they overlooked the crucial fact that the summer solstice sunset lies on the same alignment as the winter solstice sunrise (with allowances for horizon height) – which Lockyer noted was indicated by a window in the main temple.

In the 1960s, Gerald Hawkins re-evaluated the alignment of the temple of Amun-Re at Karnak, and not only confirmed Lockyer's winter solstice window, but also noticed another window in the Hall of Thutmose (Tuthmosis) III that aligned with the midwinter sunrise. This temple contains an inscription showing the pharaoh in front of the very window that allowed the dawning sun's light to flood in at the

rebirth of the year, and the associated inscription praises the face of Amun-Re, greatest of gods.

A 2005 survey of the complex by M. Shaltout and J.A. Belmonte shows that a structure built by Hatshepsut, mother of Thutmose III, was aligned so the midwinter solstice sun would rise between two large obelisks of rose-coloured granite. Hatshepsut, who reigned c. 1472–1458 BCE, is renowned for having herself declared pharaoh (king) in her own right – an unprecedented feat for a woman of her era.

It is possible that the site of Luxor–Karnak was chosen because here the Nile flows perpendicular to the rising winter sun, allowing temples to be aligned to both the Nile and the winter solstice sunrise.

The processional path of the temple of Amun-Re at Meroe, some 550 miles (900km) south of Karnak in modern-day Sudan, lies on the very same alignment, so that the rays of the rising midwinter sun enter the sun god's own temple. Devotion to Amun-Re was widespread and many temples were dedicated to him, so many similar alignments are expected to be found.

Ritual axis The temple precinct of the sun god Amun-Re at Karnak lies on an east–west axis, oriented to both sunrise at midwinter and to the great River Nile. Directly opposite this site, on the other side of the Nile, lies the royal necropolis of the Valley of the Kings.

THE ANCIENT TEMPLES OF MALTA

The Republic of Malta, an archipelago with two main islands in the Mediterranean, south of Italy, is one of the world's smallest countries. The first settlers arrived from Sicily *c.* 5200 BCE, and a thousand years later the famous period of temple building began.

The word "temple" must be used with a degree of caution here, as the sites have not produced the unequivocal evidence of worship that some archaeologists require. But, as no alternative theory has been generally accepted as entirely plausible, we will probably continue to call them temples for some years yet. The figurines of obese women that are associated with some of the sites may indicate a fertility cult of the Mother Goddess, a suggestion supported by the often femininely curvaceous outlines of the temples themselves.

More than 40 megalithic temples have been found on Malta, some containing stones weighing more than 30 tons (30.5 tonnes). Most are in poor condition, but seven have been granted World Heritage status.

While the design of temples changed during the millennium over which they were built, a typical temple had several distinctive features, beginning with an entrance framed with large stones. From here, a straight, stone-lined passage led to a pair of semicircular chambers (one each side of the passage) and then continued through an internal entrance (perhaps with an ornate altar on either side)

Fertility cult Rounded figurines found on Malta echo the outlines of the ancient temples there, and may indicate a cult of the Mother Goddess.

Temples of Ggantija These two temples may be the world's oldest free-standing religious structures.

into another pair of chambers. The passage then culminated in a final, central end or head chamber.

Although the temples are roofless today, there is some evidence that the chambers (at least) had corbelled roofs. The whole structure was surrounded by a roughly circular stone wall with a concave segment at the entrance; these walls of grey-white coralline limestone slabs reflect both sun- and moonlight well. The gap between the outer wall and the temple chambers was filled with rubble.

The alignment of straight passages has been carefully investigated. Of the temples whose passage axis can be measured with a reasonable accuracy, two-thirds point to the arc of horizon that is too far south to contain either the rising or setting of sun or moon. This has led researchers to suppose that they are oriented toward stars, asterisms or constellations,

such as the Southern Cross. Such theories are difficult to substantiate because there are so many stars to choose from, and their rising and setting positions shift gradually over time thanks to the movement of the Earth's axis in a 26,000-year cycle known as the precession of the equinoxes (see pages 220–21). Some researchers have claimed that there is a significant cluster of orientations toward the southeast, marking the position of the moon shortly after it has risen at its far southern standstill (see pages 134–5). But, as we shall see below, an alternative solar explanation suggests that this lunar event is merely fortuitous.

The Giant's Tower

The two adjoining temples of Ggantija ("giant's tower") may be the oldest free-standing religious buildings in the world (older temples have been excavated, such

Altars at Ggantija These ancient structures were erected without the use of metal tools.

as Göbekli Tepe, Turkey, 9000 BCE). They are on Malta's northern island, Gozo, and were built around 3500 BCE. Both temples face the southeast, and each contains a central passage giving access to five semicircular chambers (four to the sides and one at the end).

The southern temple is the largest in Malta, with a passage 85ft (26m) long flanked with stones up to 20ft (6m) tall. This passage is aligned to the winter solstice sunrise, the light from which illuminates the altar deep in its interior.

Mnajdra

The Mnajdra temple complex is perched on the southern coast of the largest island, Malta, and is composed of three adjoining temples. The northern temple is the earliest and smallest of the three, and

may be contemporary with Ggantija. The southern temple dates to *c*. 3000 BCE, while the middle temple is more recent, but was still built before 2500 BCE.

The southern temple has a central passage around 50ft (15m) long. It has only four chambers, lending it the appearance of butterfly wings. Where the fifth, end chamber might be, there is instead a broad altar shelf flanked by a pair of massive slabs. The easterly alignment of this temple allows the light of the equinoctial sunrise to shine directly through the entrance, along the passage and onto this central altar.

The passage leads from the entrance into the first pair of chambers, and from here the internal entrance to the second pair is flanked with an arrangement of large, upright slabs that jut out into the first chambers. More slabs form L-shapes on either side of the internal entrance. From these a thin strip of the horizon is visible between the stones of the entrance. The architecture is such that these small segments of horizon are precisely those where the sun rises at the winter and summer solstices – each sunrise casting a strip of light directly onto one of the slabs.

This arrangement of marking both ends of the sun's annual journey across the horizon is reminiscent of the design of the Nebra Sky Disc (see page 36) and the entrance of Angkor Wat in Cambodia (see page 210) – but of course the similarity is due to the global nature of the sun's passage, not to any direct cultural contact.

AN ANCIENT MYSTERY

Mnajdra's solar orientation has not gone unchallenged. Around 3000 BCE the first appearance of the star cluster known as the Pleiades in the eastern sky before dawn (their heliacal rising) was also due east, and some researchers have suggested that this asterism, not the sun, was the original point of interest.

However, the solar interpretation of ancient temples throughout the Maltese islands has been reasserted by further research into the alignments of the internal slabs and altars to the side of the central passages. All the temples on both islands whose passages were oriented to the southeast were surveyed by Klaus Albrecht in 2001, and in each case the dawning winter solstice sun was found to illuminate the left-hand altar stone.

These temples are complex structures, created over a long period of time, and many uncertainties exist about their original use. It may be that we will never find convincing answers to the puzzles of their astronomical alignments. However, as the techniques of archaeoastronomy are refined, and the experience and understanding of researchers broadens and deepens, perhaps one day a consensus will develop.

Alignments at Mnajdra
(*Right*) The southern temple of the Mnajdra complex (pictured *below*) is aligned to sunrise at the winter and summer solstices, when light illuminates slabs beside the internal entrance to the second pair of chambers. This temple is also aligned to the equinoxes, when the rising sun lights up the central altar.

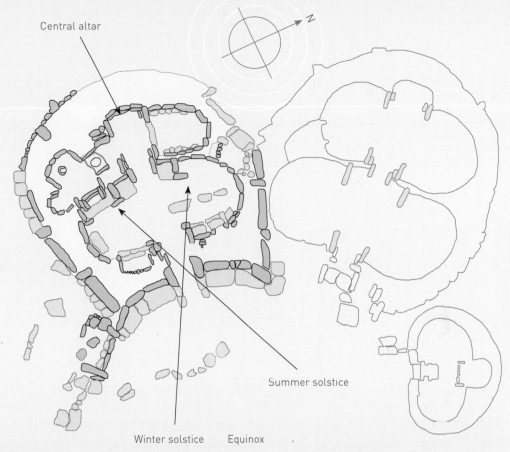

Central altar

Summer solstice

Winter solstice   Equinox

THE NEBRA SKY DISC GERMANY

In 1999 two men using metal detectors to scour the site of a prehistoric settlement in Saxony-Anhalt, Germany, unearthed a hoard of Bronze Age artefacts. Buried in the ditch surrounding the enclosure, the cache included swords, axes, wire spiral bracelets and a disc of corroded bronze 13in (32cm) in diameter, weighing around 4lb 6oz (2kg) and inlaid with thin, beaten gold. Rather than reporting this valuable find to archaeologists, who could then have excavated the site properly and perhaps discovered vital new information about the deposition, the men tried to sell the treasures illegally. Fortunately, the trade was intercepted, and in 2002 the archaeoastronomical find of a lifetime was restored to public safekeeping, becoming known as the Nebra Sky Disc.

Golden sunlight

The artefacts were hidden around 1600 BCE on top of the Mittelberg hill in the south of the Ziegelroda Forest, close to the modern settlement of Nebra. Seen from this ancient site, the summer solstice sun sets behind the Brocken Mountain, and this alignment is particularly significant in view of the two bands of gold that once curved around sections of the Sky Disc's perimeter (only one band survives).

When the rim of the disc is seen as a representation of the site's encircling horizon, the two bands of gold correspond to the range of points at which the sun rises and sets throughout the year. Each golden arc measures 82.5° – the range over which the sun travelled between solstices at this latitude at this time in the Bronze Age. The ends of the gold bands mark the points where the solstice sunrises and sunsets occur.

The solstice bands were added after, and in one case on top of, the 32 small gold spots that represent stars. Seven of these form a distinctive cluster confidently identified as the Pleiades. The identification of the large gold disc and crescent seems obvious at first – the sun and moon, respectively – but their relative positions can't portray anything ever seen in the sky because the illuminated crescent is on the wrong side of the sun disc.

Perhaps the gold crescent signifies a solar eclipse during which the stars become visible in the day. Or it may be that the crescent and disc both represent the phases of the moon, or a lunar eclipse. It is even possible that these symbols were intentionally ambiguous and their combined meaning embraced all of these possible interpretations, giving the design a remarkable versatility.

Mystery surrounds the oddly striated arc of gold that seems to point to both the disc and crescent. Many suggestions have been made to explain it, including a rainbow, the arcing path of the sun across the sky, and even a boat in which the sun is borne across the sky or makes the underground crossing from its western setting to its eastern resurrection.

Although the gold solstice bands have been satisfactorily explained, solutions to the many puzzles presented by the Nebra Sky Disc still await consensus among researchers. In recognition of the importance of this remarkable object, an exhibition centre has been built near the site of its discovery and an observation tower has been erected at the site itself. From here visitors may view the sun as it sets behind the Brocken Mountain each summer solstice.

Sky map The disc appears to show the sun, moon and stars. The ends of the two gold bands at the rim (only one survives) marked the points on the horizon where sunrise and sunset occurred at the two solstices.

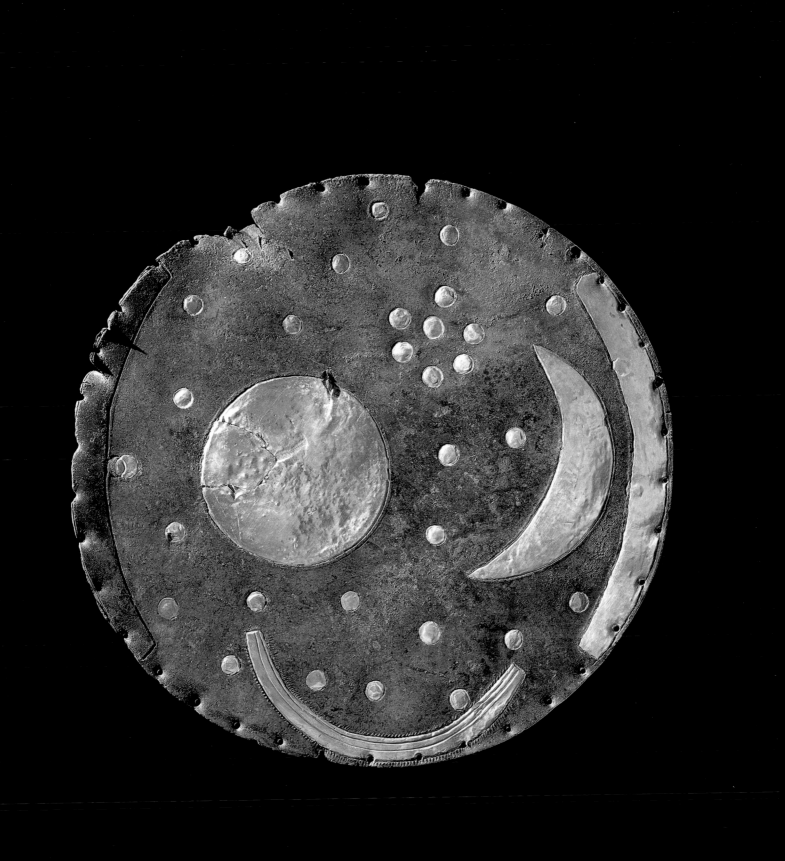

THE GOSECK CIRCLE GERMANY

Goseck, in the Burgenlandkreis district of Saxony-Anhalt, is the site of a remarkable prehistoric ceremonial centre dubbed the Sonnenobservatorium ("sun observatory"), which has been claimed as the oldest solar observatory yet discovered in Europe.

Located on flattish, low-lying terrain, the reconstructed wooden-post fences of Goseck's two concentric circles are surrounded by a ditch inside a bank some 240ft (73m) in diameter. While a ditch outside a bank indicates a defensive barrier against an external threat, the ditch inside a bank found at Goseck may indicate a desire to contain something within the circle rather than prevent something from entering. There are three main entrances in the perimeter bank, creating causeways that archaeologists interpret as entrances to the enclosed, sacred space. These are located to the southeast, southwest and just to the east of polar north. The northern entrance presents something of a puzzle and its alignment has yet to be satisfactorily explained.

Solstice alignments

Following its discovery on aerial photographs in 1991, the site was excavated in 2002, revealing holes for the wooden posts that had once stood closely ranked in two concentric circles, with gaps aligned to the causeways. At dawn on the winter solstice, an observer at the centre of the circle could have gazed through the southeastern gap in the palisades and across the causeway to the point on the horizon where the sun rose. That same evening, the view to the southwest would have framed the sun as it set.

In 2005 the circles were reconstructed using some 2,000 oak posts 8ft (2.5m) high. The site was officially reopened to the public with a dramatic procession by torchlight on 21 December, the winter solstice.

Winter solstice A spotlight simulates sunset during the inauguration of the reconstructed site on 21 December 2005.

This early Neolithic structure is geographically close to the source of the Nebra Sky Disc (see page 36), lying just 15½ miles (25km) to the southeast of Mittelberg, but the Goseck Circle was created some 3,000 years earlier, around 4900 BCE. Some 130 human generations separate them, but the same fascination for the solstices is enshrined in both designs. The similarity highlights the extent of serious prehistoric interest in calendrical observation and astronomy.

The clear focus on the winter solstice may indicate a cult related to the symbolism of the sun's lowest point, the place from which things can only get better. As at Stonehenge, the ceremonies at Goseck may have incorporated an element of healing and perhaps fertility, as well as celebration of the year's turning.

There are thought to be at least 250 sites in Germany, Austria and the Czech Republic that have similar features to the Goseck Circle, such as a ring ditch, but very few have yet been explored archaeologically. They may prove to be a rich source of astronomical alignments.

Europe's oldest solar observatory Goseck's reconstructed wooden fence (*above*) is 8ft (2.5m) high, with a diameter of 240ft (73m). The site is aligned with sunrise and sunset at the winter solstice through its two southern entrances (*right*), but the function of the northern entrance remains a mystery.

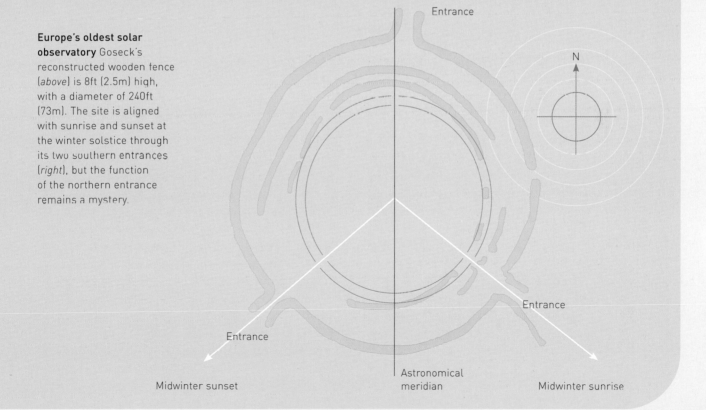

Entrance

N

Entrance

Entrance

Midwinter sunset

Astronomical meridian

Midwinter sunrise

DIE EXTERNSTEINE GERMANY

The Externsteine is a tall blade of rock jutting above a small lake in the Teutoburg Forest, some 3³/₄ miles (6km) south of the city of Detmold in northwestern Germany. Weathering has split the ridge into five separate pillars, the tallest of which is 123ft (37.5m) high. The massive outcrop is famous for its rugged grandeur.

The site's most notable archaeoastronomical feature is in the so-called chapel carved into the rock on a ledge on top of the tallest pillar. Served by staircases and a bridge from another pinnacle, the walled space, now open to the sky, would originally have been difficult to reach. A circular window measuring 20in (50cm) in diameter has been cut into the northeast wall, and frames both the summer solstice sunrise and the moon at its northernmost rising.

The chamber is not large, so the range of possible alignments is restricted. Because the row of natural pillars is oriented in a line toward the southeast, any opening in the side wall would face northeast – the general direction of the rising midsummer sun. How important this solar alignment was to the people who created the awe-inspiring sanctuary at the Externsteine is a matter of conjecture. Opinions range from the sunrise being the whole point of the chapel's existence, to its being mere chance, another aspect of the spectacular natural setting. Of course, the view from the chamber would only have been accessible to the elite few who had access to it.

Legend has it that the site was used for pagan worship from prehistoric times until 782 CE, when the ruler Charlemagne officially abolished the indigenous religion to encourage people to convert to Christianity. However, there is no archaeological evidence for a major shrine here dating to that period. It is widely assumed that the steps and chapel date to the late 8th century, and were carved from the rock by Christian monks seeking solitude and an elevated perspective on life.

Dual alignments The chapel window is aligned to the midsummer sunrise and to the moon at its most northerly rising.

Clash of cultures

The famous 12th-century bas-relief here, called *Descent from the Cross*, is a carving of Jesus being taken down from the cross. The sculpture has several pagan elements, including a figure standing on – and dramatically bending – what many believe to be an *irminsul*, the tree or pillar that stood at the heart of Saxon paganism. Such an element is suggestive of Christianity crushing the ancient native religion. At the top of the carving are, on the left, a weeping sun and, on the right, a weeping moon. While these probably represented heavenly grief at Christ's suffering, some choose to interpret them as nature grieving over the destruction that would be wrought in Christ's name.

Die Externsteine is a popular venue for neo-pagans interested in commemorating ancient Teutonic ways. Both summer and winter solstices are celebrated annually with colourful festivals that brighten the night with numerous bonfires. Such occasions offer a particularly atmospheric way to experience this spectacular natural monument, although access to the chapel at dawn is necessarily restricted.

Pagan site Its scenery (*top*) ensures the site's continuing popularity for pagans; the Christian victory over paganism may be commemorated in *Descent from the Cross* (*above*).

THE NAZIS' SACRED GROVE

Die Externsteine is less well known than other archaeoastronomical sites in Europe. This may be due to the interest it aroused in the Nazi party during World War II. Wilhelm Teudt, an amateur archaeologist researching ancient German civilization, believed the site to have been a solar temple and wished to have it recognized as a sacred grove. His ideas were supported by Heinrich Himmler, who initiated the Externsteine Foundation in 1933.

Himmler was the head of the Ahnenerbe, which ostensibly was a group dedicated to studying "intellectual ancient history", but in reality was committed to subverting Germanic history for political purposes. The notion of the Externsteine having been a cultural and religious focus for an imagined glorious Aryan past fitted well with the group's aims. The site is still perceived as a nationalist centre by some neo-Nazis.

Protective structures The wall at Barcola, close to Trieste, would have protected people and livestock from attack.

THE *CASTELLIERI* ITALY

In the countryside around the northern extremity of the Adriatic Sea, particularly in northeast Italy and the Istrian peninsula, is a distinctive group of large, fortified enclosures known as *castellieri*. They were usually built strategically on the tops of hills, but sometimes they were also constructed on plains, as in the area of Friuli, in northeast Italy.

With perimeter walls rising to 16½ft (5m), the *castellieri* were clearly defensive structures, and many enclosed an area more than 650ft (200m) across – large enough to protect a village with livestock. They are often associated with a motte, a mound of earth or stones up to 20ft high and 200ft in diameter (6 x 60m). *Castellieri* were constructed over a millennium from *c.* 1500 BCE until the ascendancy of the Roman Empire in the 3rd century BCE.

An archaeoastronomical survey

In the late 1980s an archaeoastronomical assessment was carried out by A.F. Aveni and G. Romano on the remaining well-preserved sites in the Friuli plain. The researchers examined alignments between structures and the orientation of the *castellieri* themselves, which, unlike the *castellieri* of other areas, were frequently roughly square in plan. Their study of 48 pairs of structures identified three alignments to the horizon where the June solstice sun would rise, and seven to the December solstice sunrise. They found that 17 of the *castellieri*'s walls and diagonals (alignments connecting corners) were measurable: one pointed to the spot on the horizon where the June solstice sun would rise, four aligned to the December solstice sunrise and two aligned with the equinox.

The sites surveyed include the *castelliere* of Motte di Godego, a tourist attraction on the boundary of the town of Castello di Godego. Three of its four sides appeared to be aligned to the solstices, with a diagonal alignment to the equinox.

The Motte di Oderzo in the town of Oderzo, a crossroads of the Roman Empire, is a conical mound with an adjacent linear earthwork that appeared to be oriented to the December solstice sunrise.

Independent reassessment of some sites suggests that the alignments are imprecise and not convincing as proof of deliberate orientation toward astronomical events. The archaeoastronomical credentials of these claims remain open to debate.

Veronella Alta

A horseshoe-shaped earthwork known as Veronella Alta, 1,000ft (300m) in length and situated ²/₃ mile (1km) northwest of Veronella, has been acclaimed for an alignment to the December solstice sunrise. This embankment may be all that is left of an originally egg-shaped structure, but it is not the pointed end that points to the sunrise, but a line perpendicular to that axis. This is in contrast to the stone horseshoe at Stonehenge, aligned to the December solstice sun along its central axis (see pages 24–7).

Veronella Alta was classified as a *castelliere* by Aveni and Romano, and also proposed as an official archaeoastronomical site at the UNESCO World Heritage and Monuments of Astronomy conference in 2004.

MACHU PICCHU PERU

High in the Peruvian Andes, nearly 8,000ft (2,500m) above sea level, lies the extraordinary and beautiful Inca citadel of Machu Picchu. It was built around 1450 CE but abandoned just a century later, possibly due to diseases such as smallpox introduced by Europeans. The site along a ridge above the Urubamba river escaped the attention of the Spanish invaders in the 16th century and was forgotten and gradually overgrown, until it was discovered in 1911 by American archaeologist and explorer Hiram Bingham.

The Sun's Tethering Post The obelisk of the Intihuatana is said to symbolize Huayna Picchu (the large peak at right).

Now a World Heritage site, Machu Picchu was built in traditional Inca style, with cleanly carved and polished stone blocks fitted tightly together. Despite using no mortar, the construction was strong enough to withstand major earthquakes. The city has a central square and around 150 structures, including houses, religious sanctuaries, fountains, temples and plazas. Most are still in an excellent state of preservation.

What purpose the settlement served remains essentially unknown. It may have been a royal estate, a religious centre and place of pilgrimage, a garrison or even an agricultural testing centre – the variety of terraces provides a range of microclimates that could

have been used for experimentation with crops. The terraces may have provided enough food for the 800 or so people the site could accommodate.

The Sun's Tethering Post

In common with many ancient cities, Machu Picchu contains a variety of alignments with celestial events. The best-known astronomical feature is the granite monolith known as the Intihuatana – the Sun's Tethering Post. At the solstices, so the legend goes, the priests tied the sun to this stone, so it couldn't stray from its annual course. On the summer solstice (in December), the sun is seen to set behind Mount Pumasillo ("puma's claw"), a mountain associated with crop and livestock fertility and sacred even today.

The Intihuatana's obelisk is said to replicate the shape of Huayna Picchu, prominent from this vantage point (other mountains were similarly honoured elsewhere in the city), reminding us that celestial and terrestrial observances may be combined in a single monument. The pyramid has a variety of carefully carved angles and surfaces that may have been illuminated or shadowed in specific ways on other important dates of the year.

The visit of the sun god

The entrance to the royal mausoleum, a natural cave with internal masonry and carvings that indicate high-status burial, was aligned to face the sunrise on the winter (June) solstice.

The Intimachy, another natural cave, was modified to block out sunlight except on 20 days around the summer solstice, when the rays of the rising sun would enter and illuminate its depths. Boulders at the entrance resemble a condor with wings open as if about to land. To the Inca the condor symbolized the realm of the gods, and the sun god Inti was their chief deity from whom their leader was descended. This design of the portal may have commemorated, and perhaps even assisted, visits by the supreme deity.

Embedded in the landscape Machu Picchu has alignments to surrounding sacred mountains as well as to celestial events.

NAZCA PERU

The Nazca Lines lie in the desert some 285 miles (460km) southeast of Peru's capital city Lima and some 2,000ft (600m) above sea level – one of the most arid and bleak places in the world. These geoglyphs, a World Heritage site, feature images of animals, birds and plants as well as straight lines more than 1 mile (1.6km) long. They were drawn in the sand between 200 BCE and 600 CE by the Nazca people.

Best viewed from the air, the Nazca Lines were created by the removal of the black iron-oxide pebbles that form the surface of the desert to reveal the bright yellow sand underneath. Almost anywhere else in the world such images would have been rapidly eroded by the weather, but this plateau is windless, and rain here is slight. However, in recent decades people and especially their vehicles have caused a significant amount of damage.

In 1939 Paul Kosok of Long Island University visited Nazca and a chance observation of a straight line that appeared to be aligned to sunset on the winter (June) solstice inspired his interpretation of the Nazca Lines as a gigantic and sophisticated astronomical calendar. This idea was embraced by Maria Reiche, who was to devote her long life to the study and conservation of the Nazca geoglyphs.

The lines unravel

In 1968 Gerald Hawkins conducted a computer-assisted statistical analysis of the site and failed to confirm any overall pattern of astronomical alignments. The lines that did appear to lead toward significant celestial events on the horizon could be explained by pure chance. Since then, the interpretation of the Nazca Lines as an astronomical riddle has not been proven. But the idea that the geoglyphs have a cosmic connection has been so widely publicized that it seems set to endure for many decades to come.

The real purpose of these lines, shapes and figures appears to have been concerned with more earthly matters, such as rainfall and the associated agricultural fertility. Many of the lines are directed to higher ground, as if in the hope that by creating a symbolic irrigation canal, real water could be coaxed into the dry valleys. There is, however, likely to be more than one reason why these remarkable geoglyphs were created. For instance, some complexes of radiating lines bear similarities to the ancient Andean system of recording data on knotted strings.

Much speculation has gathered around the Nazca Lines, with interpretations ranging from the utterly implausible (their use as landing fields for alien spacecraft) to the more likely (as ceremonial markings in religious rituals). The large bird and animal figures may have been designed for people to walk around in sacred procession, invoking the power or aid of the creature's spirit. Attempts to match the drawings with constellations and asterisms have been made, but have yet to receive academic acceptance.

Perhaps, though, the linear geoglyphs really did include some deliberate alignments to horizons marking key solar, lunar and even stellar events. Such alignments could have been statistically masked in the Hawkins survey by the other, non-astronomical lines. A new investigation of the orientation of the lines is currently underway at the Faculty of Geoinformatics at the University of Applied Sciences in Reiche's home town of Dresden, Germany.

Nazca pathways Giant drawings of birds and animals may have been used in rituals to draw on the spirits' power.

INTRODUCING THE EQUINOXES

Between the solstices are a pair of days when the sun rises directly due east and sets directly due west, and day and night are approximately equal. Each of these days is called an equinox, meaning "equal night".

The obliquity of the ecliptic, or in other words the tilting of the Earth's axis to the plane of its orbit around the sun (see pages 22–3), means that the sun's apparent path does not follow the celestial equator (the earth's equator projected into the sky). At each of the equinoxes, however, the sun crosses the celestial equator. For example, when it crosses from the southern celestial hemisphere to the northern celestial hemisphere, the start of the northern spring is signalled (this is the astrological First Point of Aries).

Each day, as our planet circles its star, the point on the horizon where the sun rises and sets moves a little. This regular, annual cycle was commemorated in many prehistoric ritual sites, such as temples and tombs, with alignments to the equinoxes and solstices.

Quartering the year

In Chaco Canyon in New Mexico (see pages 50–55) the summer solstice sun rises over a pointed butte or outcrop and illuminates a pictograph at the ancient Anasazi (Ancestral Puebloan) site Wijiji 931. This artwork was almost certainly created within a century or two either side of 1000 CE. Prominent against the yellow rock of the canyon's cliff face, the white painting depicts four straight lines or rays emanating vertically and horizontally from a disc. This symbol apparently depicts the sun quartering the circle of the year with the solstices and equinoxes.

Nearby Wijiji is the smallest pueblo in Chaco Canyon. From here, some 16 or 17 days before the winter solstice, the sun can be seen to rise at the left-hand (northern) side of a distinct notch in the distant skyline. As the days pass, the sun rises further and further into the notch until, at the solstice itself, it rises at the right-hand (southern) side of the notch. Such an alignment would be overlooked as imprecise, but for the Piedra del Sol ("sun's rock") near the modern visitors' centre, which bears a petroglyph of concentric circles. Anyone standing with their back against this symbol will face a prominent, triangular rock over which the sun rises two weeks before the summer solstice.

Perhaps other alignments heralding the approach of the solstices and equinoxes await discovery elsewhere. Such markers may have inaugurated a period of festivity and ritual preparation for the coming of the dates that quartered the year.

Solar calendar at Wijiji The importance of the equinoxes and solstices, which may have been marked by natural notches in the clifftop skyline at Wijiji, is highlighted by a nearby petroglpyh that seems to depict a quartered year.

ZENITH

MERIDIAN

Sun's apparent motion At the equinoxes, sunrise is due east and sunset due west anywhere on Earth (this artwork shows the positions of sunrise and sunset at 51°N in 2550 BCE when the first stones were erected at Stonehenge). In summer, sunrise and sunset are closer to the north; in winter, they are closer to the south.

Midsummer

Equinox

Midwinter

50°

90°

130°

180°

E

S

N

W

SYMBOL OF THE YEAR'S FOUR SEASONS

The solstices and equinoxes provide a convenient calendrical tool that divides the sun's annual cycle into four seasons, just as the cardinal directions quarter the encircling horizon. This basic understanding of our world as divided into four parts is represented in a simple diagram that has become the symbol for our planet, the Earth – an upright cross inside a circle.

In ancient times, before people realized that Earth orbits the sun, this symbol was also used as a symbol for the sun itself. It is sometimes called a sunwheel or solar wheel, and it is also reminiscent of the Celtic cross. The symbol was also associated with the chariot that carries the sun across the sky, such as that of the Indian sun god Surya, which is drawn by seven horses, or that of the Greek sun god Helios, whose four-horse chariot later became associated with the Roman sun god Sol.

CHACO CANYON USA

In the arid desert of northwestern New Mexico, nearly 6,600ft (2,000m) above sea level, lies the deserted ancient settlement of Chaco Canyon. Scorched by blistering heat by day and bitterly cold at night, it is a wonder in itself that people ever lived here.

This remote and inhospitable valley, some 10 miles (16km) long and covering nearly 54 square miles (140 square km), has been designated a World Heritage site. The earliest evidence of human habitation in the area is of nomadic hunter-gatherers

around 2900 BCE, but the first settled farming communities date from around 200 CE. These people are today generally called Anasazi, a Navajo word which means "enemy ancestors" or "enemies of our ancestors", but has come to be regarded as meaning "ancient peoples". An alternative and less controversial name is Ancestral Puebloans.

Around 850 CE, the Anasazi began to build the "Great Houses". These massive buildings, up to five storeys in height, were made of tightly fitting stone masonry, with wooden floors. Rock is readily available in the area, but today the nearest trees are some 70 miles (110km) away. It may have been deforestation,

Enigmatic site We may never know why Pueblo Bonito was built so close to a dangerously unstable cliff face.

PUEBLO BONITO

Many of the structures in Chaco Canyon are astronomically aligned to the sun (some lunar alignments have been proposed, but these remain controversial) and pages 50–55 explore some of the sites relating to the solstices and equinoxes. The largest of the Great Houses is known as the Pueblo Bonito ("beautiful village"). Situated in the central part of the canyon, this semicircular structure covers some 86,000 square feet (8,000 square metres), contains more than 650 rooms accessed from the central courtyard and has 35 circular *kivas*.

The straight boundary of Pueblo Bonito runs east–west, aligned with the equinoxes. The semicircle is bisected by a wall aligned north–south so that at midday the shadow of the wall disappears as the sun moves overhead. On each side of this wall is a large *kiva* (these are not, however, positioned symmetrically).

Pueblo Bonito was built close to the base of the canyon's cliff face, part of which was in danger of collapse. Although there may have been some ancient attempts to buttress the enormous slab of loose rock, there must have been a compelling reason to build this Great House in such a precarious site. Perhaps this spot held some special significance that remains to be discovered. It certainly enjoys a fairly central position among the other sites in the Chaco Canyon.

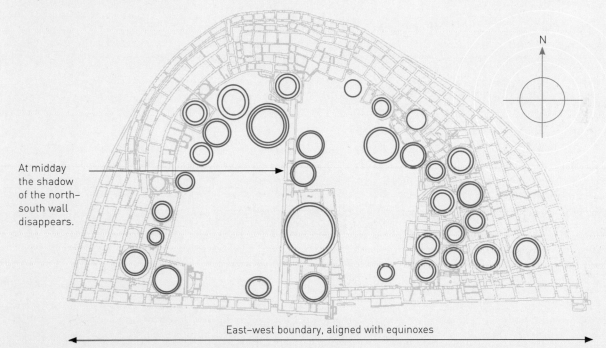

At midday the shadow of the north–south wall disappears.

East–west boundary, aligned with equinoxes

allied with one of the extensive droughts to which the area is prone, that led to the abrupt abandonment of the canyon around 1150 CE.

It is not clear whether the Great Houses were permanent villages or places of pilgrimage overseen by a priestly elite. Usually circular rooms built partially below ground level, *kivas* are believed to have been religious structures devoted to worship and ceremony.

Even today, the site has perfectly clear night skies, and the inhabitants would always have enjoyed a magnificent nightly spectacle and been able to follow the changes in the sky with relative ease. These would have provided a reliable way to regulate their seasonal activities – when to plant, for example, or when to prepare for the start of the cooler winter.

Casa Rinconada
Another of the major monuments in Chaco Canyon, the great *kiva* called Casa Rinconada, is unusual in that it stands alone rather than being part of one of

the Great Houses. It, too, is aligned to the cardinal directions, with entrances to the north and south.

Native creation myths say that the first *kiva* was given a round shape, to reflect the circle of the sky. Still used today by Native Americans for ceremonial purposes, *kivas* are not constructed upward from ground level, but are built with sunken floors so that as people leave and emerge into the open air, they symbolically re-enact the journey of the spirits (*kachinas*) from the hole in the ground (the *sipapu*) that leads to the spirits' home. This symbolism may also extend to representing the emergence of life in the form of plants from below ground and perhaps also to the emergence of a newborn from its mother's womb.

The focus on cardinality at Chaco Canyon seems to be based on observations of the sun (see the Sun Dagger, pages 54–5) rather than, as is often the case, the celestial pole (see pages 168–9). Using such a blueprint for designing buildings may be seen as an attempt to bring the orderly operation of the cosmos down to Earth, reinforcing the value of living in harmony with natural cycles – the surest survival strategy in a challenging environment. This effort was seemingly taken to extraordinary lengths with the creation of the Great North Road (see opposite).

Cardinal alignments The impressive *kiva* of Casa Rinconada was precisely oriented, with entrances at north and south.

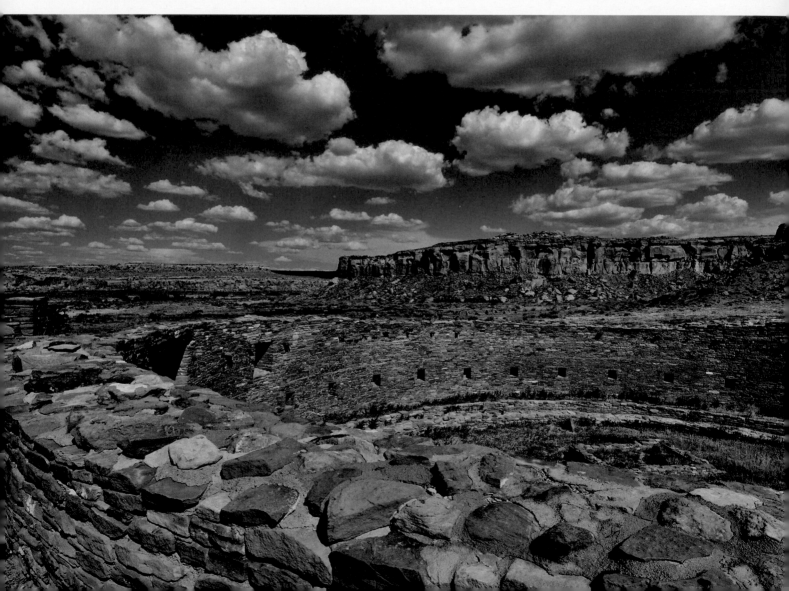

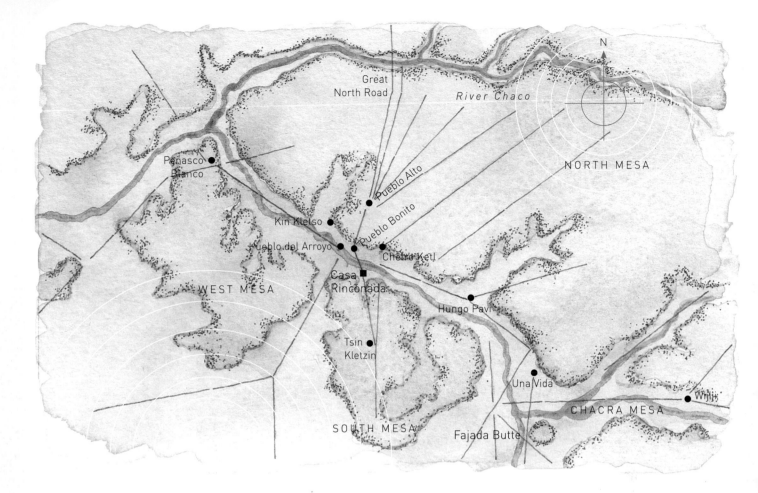

THE CHACO CANYON ALIGNMENTS

This map shows the relative position of the nine Great Houses, the Casa Rinconada and other sites within Chaco Canyon, as well as the mysterious "roads" that can be traced radiating in many directions. The Great North Road, 30ft (9m) wide, is the most impressive of these ancient highways, heading north in an absolutely straight line. The Great North Road deviates for nothing – even cliffs are scaled with narrow, perilous stairs. The road continues for at least 34 miles (55km). The effort involved

in creating this structure indicates the immense importance it had in the minds of its architects.

It is difficult to conceive of this road having anything other than a symbolic or spiritual purpose. North is still considered the way to the spiritual homeland for many indigenous peoples, and life itself is considered to be a road or a path. Whether the intended journey was from Chaco Canyon toward the north, or enabled spirits from the north to visit the Great Houses, we may never know. Perhaps traffic was routinely two-way.

Another feature of this all-embracing interest in the cardinal

directions is that Pueblo Alto and Tsin Kletzin lie on a north–south alignment. Chetro Ketl and Pueblo Bonito (the two largest Great Houses) are situated roughly equidistant on either side of this north–south alignment, and are themselves on an east–west alignment. In addition, both Pueblo Alto and Tsin Kletzin are, like Pueblo Bonito, aligned to the cardinal directions, as is one of the diagonals at Chetro Ketl.

The Sun Dagger

The Fajada Butte is a dramatic outcrop of rock that soars 440ft (135m) from the floor of Chaco Canyon. Two-thirds of the way up this often sheer-sided pinnacle is a ledge on which are the remains of more than 20 dwellings and the ruins of a circular building thought to have been the ceremonial site of a *kiva*. The only access was by a ramp and stairway, the remains of which were discovered at the end of the 20th century, but even with these the climb would have been treacherous.

What makes the Fajada Butte famous is the Sun Dagger. At the foot of the final 40ft (12m) section of the butte were three massive slabs of sandstone, each around 8ft high, 3ft wide and 1ft 6in thick (2.5 x 1 x 0.4m), with a 4in (10cm) gap between each slab. They stood on edge, essentially upright, leaning

against the cliff face. Like many other slabs in the canyon, they were probably deposited there as the result of a natural rockfall, although they may have been rearranged to accentuate the remarkable properties of their position. The slabs are shaded both by the butte and by an overhanging rock, so for most of the year they are in deep shadow, but at certain times they displayed a phenomenon that made them arguably the most famous of all North American archaeoastronomical sites.

The spirals of time

In the triangular niche behind the three slabs, two spiral petroglyphs have been carved into the cliff. The largest spiral curls anticlockwise outward, while the much smaller spiral to the left curls clockwise and has a tail. In 1977 Anna Sofaer discovered that just before noon on the summer solstice a shaft of light struck the top of the larger spiral. As the minutes passed the patch of light elongated downward until at noon it formed a vertical streak slicing through the very centre of the spiral – the blade of the so-called Sun Dagger. Inexorably, the streak of light continued its downward movement until it disappeared off the bottom of the spiral.

At the winter solstice the gaps between the slabs created two identical daggers, which precisely bracketed the spiral. Not only was the spiral's position on the cliff fixed, but its size was also determined by the extremes of summer and winter solstice sunlight.

Solstice lightshow The Sun Dagger (*left*) sliced through the spiral at noon at the summer solstice (*below, left*), while at the winter solstice two daggers appeared, to bracket the spiral's outer edges (*below, right*).

Midsummer, noon

Midwinter, noon

Sunset at Fajada Butte Ruins dating back to the 10th–13th centuries CE indicate that the inhospitable upper reaches of this waterless rock outcrop were once a dwelling place of the Chacoan people.

The small spiral was positioned so that at the equinoxes a dagger bisected it, while another shaft of light lay across the large spiral, as we have seen.

The unusual position of the slabs must have been noticed and the petroglyphs created after at least a year of careful observation. But why the markers were drawn as spirals rather than circles (a more common solar symbol) is unclear, unless it was perhaps to remind the shaman-priest that the cycles of our years have a beginning and an end.

Tragically, in 1989 the slabs slipped out of place, probably owing to erosion caused by the many visitors who made the perilous ascent, and the awe-inspiring light effects can no longer be seen.

A LUNAR SIGNIFICANCE?

In 1979 it was noted that moonlight also illuminated the Fajada Butte petroglyphs. At the moon's minor standstill (see pages 134–5), the right-hand side of the large spiral was brightly lit, while the left remained dark. At the major standstill, moonlight would have just touched its left-hand edge, while the rest of the spiral was in darkness. Such effects may have been coincidental, and substantiating the claims for a lunar component would demand a profound rethink of many other sites relating to this enigmatic culture.

HOVENWEEP USA

A cluster of six Anasazi (Ancestral Puebloan) sites spread over 20 miles (32km) of mesas and canyons along the Utah–Colorado border, Hovenweep has cultural similarities to the early Chaco Canyon site, including architecture and construction techniques. Mostly dating to 1150 and 1200 CE, the impressive and still well-preserved structures were built next to springs on canyon floors and perched on boulders, rock outcrops and canyon overhangs.

These sites possess a variety of plausible alignments to solstice and equinoctial sunrises and sunsets. In the group of structures known as Hovenweep Castle, a room attached to the western

tower has two small openings aligned to the solstice sunsets, as well as inner and outer doors aligned to the setting sun on the equinoxes.

The bridge of light

A frieze of petroglyphs in the canyon below Holly House is remarkably similar to the famous light dagger at Fajada Butte (see pages 54–5). Around 45 minutes after sunrise on the summer solstice, a horizontal streak of sunlight cuts across the left-hand spiral (an Anasazi sun symbol), and just minutes later a similar streak appears at the right-hand spiral. As the sun continues to rise, these two streaks advance toward each other until they meet, creating a bridge of light across both spirals.

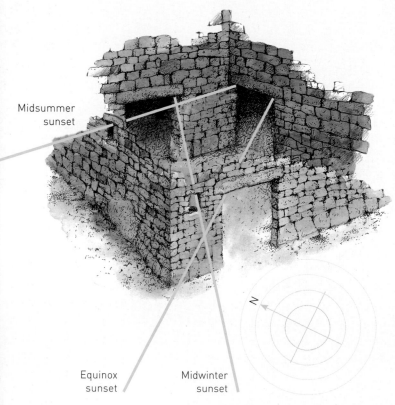

Midsummer
sunset

Equinox
sunset

Midwinter
sunset

Complex solar alignments Two openings in the external walls of a room in Hovenweep's western tower provide pathways for a ray of sunlight at sunset at the summer and winter solstices. An outer and inner door are also aligned to sunset at the equinoxes.

CASA GRANDE USA

Apart from their skill at constructing irrigation canals to make the desert bloom, little is known about the Sonoran Desert people of the Hohokam culture, who lived from about the 1st century to the mid-15th century CE. They built the large, enigmatic structure now known as Casa Grande ("big house") about 36 miles (58km) southeast of Phoenix, Arizona. The house and village were constructed around 1300 CE, and in 1892 this site became the first archaeological reserve protected by the United States government. The ruins are now protected by a roofed shelter.

Little remains of the site and what is still there has suffered from vandalism, but the Case Grande was probably the focus of the village. In plan it is 60 x 40ft (18 x 12m) and around 35ft (11m) high, with four storeys including a small, single-roomed structure on the top. Its walls are aligned to the cardinal directions. The function of this 11-room block are

a mystery, although two odd openings, one circular, one square, on its west wall may align with astronomical events. The square (southerly) opening appears to be aligned to the setting moon at a major standstill, while the round window looks onto the summer solstice sunset.

The uppermost room has a hole in its east wall and another in its west wall. Soon after sunrise, the east hole throws a beam of light onto the west wall. Around the time of the two equinoxes, the beam cast through the east wall aligns with the hole in the west wall.

The floor plan of the building may also symbolize the patterns laid out in ceremonies that consecrated the cornfields around the village. This theory was proposed in 1887 by anthropologist Frank Hamilton Cushing – and has recently been endorsed by the Senior Research Anthropologist at the Museum of North Arizona, David Wilcox.

Desert enigma Many archaeoastronomical theories have been put forward about Case Grande, suggesting, for example, that its floor plan may have represented ritual patterns used to consecrate land for agriculture. Alignments are also proposed from the mysterious circular and square openings on its west wall to, respectively, midsummer sunset and a major lunar standstill.

CAHOKIA USA

The Native American city of Cahokia lies on the fertile Mississippi floodplain some 4 miles (7km) east of St Louis, Illinois. It is known that there was a settlement here by about 700 CE, and that around 1050 it exploded in size, yet the city was practically deserted by 1400. Even the original place name is unknown – the site is named after the Cahokia people who arrived in the area in the late 1600s. It is now a World Heritage site.

City of mounds

The roughly diamond-shaped settlement covers around 6 square miles (15 square km) and at its height

North–south orientation From between the Twin Mounds, a north–south alignment runs through Central Plaza to Monks Mound, the largest earth mound in North America.

was capable of accommodating more than 20,000 people. There are more than 120 mounds, arranged on a grid pattern and aligned to the cardinal directions. Some mounds were burial sites, while others provided a platform for ceremonial purposes. At Cahokia's centre is the largest earth mound in North America – the Monks Mound. Some 100ft (30m) high and containing an estimated 22 million cubic feet (623,000 cubic metres) of earth, this huge mound once supported a temple and/or palace.

Much smaller, at roughly 6ft (2m) high, Mound 72 is presumed to have been the burial mound of a celebrated leader. His body was laid out on a bed of 20,000 shell beads and accompanied by a cache of finely worked arrowheads. More than 250 other skeletons have been found at this

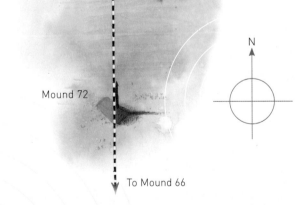

Equinox sunset

Equinox sunrise

Woodhenges

Shrine

Mound 48

Monks Mound

Central • Plaza

Twin Mounds

N

Mound 72

To Mound 66

mound, including four males whose hands and heads had been removed, and a mass grave of more than 50 young women. This mound is skewed to a northwest–southeast orientation roughly 30° north of east, considerably at odds to the majority of mounds at this site. The significance of this alignment is as yet uncertain, but it seems clear that the principal burial had been accompanied by numerous human sacrifices. Some commentators see comparisons with the Natchez people who in the 16th century lived in the Mississippi valley 435 miles (700km) to the south. Many of their practices, dissimilar to those of other local peoples, were similar to those at Cahokia. When their leader Great Sun died, his wives and servants were ceremonially slain to accompany him into the afterlife.

Alignments of the woodhenges

In the 1960s the remains of five circles of cedar posts were discovered to the west of Monks Mound. Most overlapped, suggesting each had been erected once its predecessor was no longer standing. The diameter of the circles varied from around 120 to 233ft (37–71m) and there were 24–72 posts per circle (the largest circle was never completed). While lacking the bank and ditch of a true henge, these circles were dubbed woodhenges. In the 1960s the archaeologist responsible for excavating the holes claimed that three of the posts aligned to sunrise at the winter and summer solstices and to sunrise at the equinox (which rose over Monks Mound). Although still widely cited as evidence of a Native American calendrical monument, these alignments are now regarded by academics as the product of chance alone.

Grid pattern Monks Mound is aligned to both the east–west rising and setting points of the equinoctial sun, and to the north–south alignment that organizes the complex of Cahokia as a whole.

DZIBILCHALTÚN MEXICO

Dzibilchaltún in Yucatán, Mexico, is an ancient, sprawling settlement of more than 8,000 structures, which occupies an area of around 10 square miles (25 square km). The site is located 9 miles (15 km) north of the capital Mérida, and lies within the remains of the Chicxulub crater, which was made by the meteorite that is believed to have been a key event in the extinction of the dinosaurs 65 million years ago. The name means "the place with writing on the stones".

Structures date from at least 500 BCE, and at its peak around 750 CE this large Maya city was home to as many as 40,000 people. The city was still inhabited when the Spanish arrived in the 1500s, but it later fell into ruin and was forgotten.

Temple of the Seven Dolls

The most significant monument so far identified here is the Templo de las Siete Muñecas (Temple of the

Seven Dolls) – so called simply because clay figurines were found at the base during excavation in the 1950s. This temple was built in around 700 CE, yet just two centuries later it was filled with rocks and a larger pyramid was built over it (a not uncommon event in the evolution of such sites).

This building, striking in its solid simplicity and raised off the ground atop a low, flat pyramid, has wide, high entrances in each wall. The entrances to east and west are aligned to the equinoctial sunrise, as are openings in the inner walls, so that the rising sun shines straight through the temple. This illuminates the inside of the temple and creates a deeply impressive spectacle for those watching from outside. It is no wonder this twice-yearly event attracts crowds of visitors keen to witness it for themselves.

Apart from its intrinsic beauty, this temple served an important purpose because the equinoxes marked key dates in the agricultural calendar: the spring equinox heralded the time for planting corn, a staple food for the Maya, and the autumn equinox signalled the harvest.

Only the centre of the complex has been investigated to date, and the rest of the site remains enigmatic. In the 16th century, the Spanish invaders removed stones from a number of the original buildings to use in their own constructions, such as the open chapel. The demolition of even part of a site by cultural outsiders was an archaeological tragedy half a millennium ago – and today's tragedy is that similarly irreversible destruction still continues at sites all around the world.

Hidden marvel For centuries the Temple of the Seven Dolls was concealed within a larger pyramid, and was not uncovered until the 1950s.

Equinoctial spectacle At sunrise on both equinoxes, the sun blazes through the temple to amaze the waiting crowd.

With so many sites worthy of excavation and conservation, it can be a challenge even to raise funds for a thorough survey of the ruins. A casual glance at Dzibilchaltún shows a wide variation in the orientation of the buildings, making more alignments almost inevitable. Only careful examination of the site as a whole will establish whether such alignments were deliberate, or merely the product of chance, but the Temple of the Seven Dolls gives a clear indication of the importance of astronomy to the livelihood of the local people.

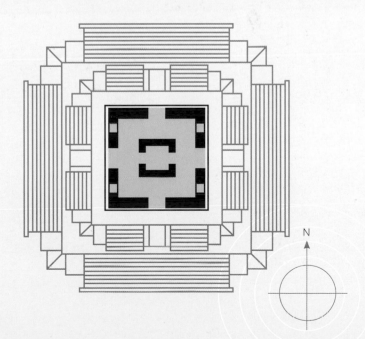

Agricultural calendar Aligned east–west to commemorate the equinoxes, rites at the Temple of the Seven Dolls would probably have signalled the times for planting and harvesting.

CHICHÉN ITZÁ MEXICO

Roughly 65 miles (105km) east of the Yucatán capital Mérida lies Chichén Itzá, a significant focus of modern pilgrimage for people interested in Maya astronomy. They are drawn in particular by a spectacular light effect that takes place on both equinoxes at the pyramid of Kukulcan (also known as El Castillo).

At the heart of Chichén Itzá, the nine-tiered step pyramid of Kukulcan is 79ft (24m) high. A staircase runs up the centre of each of the pyramid's four sides; at the top is a two-storey temple. The 91 steps of each staircase, added to the top platform (4 x 91 + 1), total the 365 days of the Maya year (see page 106). The square base of the pyramid is oriented to all four solstice directions: the northwest face is aligned to midsummer sunset; the southeast face to midwinter sunrise; and the diagonals to midwinter sunset and midsummer sunrise.

The equinox hierophany

What draws visitors in their thousands is an effect of light and shadow on the northern staircase at the equinoxes – the so-called "equinox hierophany" (holy appearance). Onlookers see the setting sun cast a shadow from the terraces of the northwestern corner of the pyramid onto the western side of the balustrade of the northern staircase. At the climax of the display, the sun illuminates a continuous zigzag running from the top of the pyramid to its base, where the balustrade terminates in the head of an enormous snake that is also bathed in sunlight. In this way the sun creates the luminous body of the divine Kukulcan – the feathered serpent. Kukulcan is the Maya name for the Aztec deity Quetzalcoatl, who was strongly associated with the planet Venus (see pages 160–61 and 223–4).

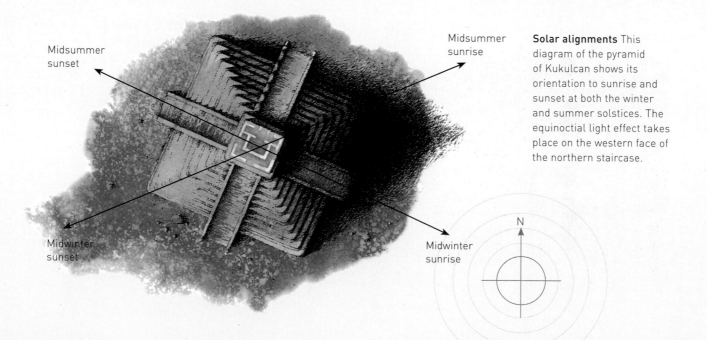

Midsummer sunset

Midsummer sunrise

Midwinter sunset

Midwinter sunrise

Solar alignments This diagram of the pyramid of Kukulcan shows its orientation to sunrise and sunset at both the winter and summer solstices. The equinoctial light effect takes place on the western face of the northern staircase.

N

The pyramid of Kukulcan
This impressive nine-tiered pyramid is topped with a double-storey temple approached by a steep staircase on all sides (*above*). At both equinoxes, in a spectacular lightshow, the serpent deity Kukulcan is seen rippling down the western face of the northern staircase, his head illuminated at the staircase's base (*left*).

UAXACTÚN GUATEMALA

The Maya site of Uaxactún lies in the Petén rainforest of northern Guatemala, 12 miles (20km) north of the prominent Maya city of Tikal. Inhabited from the 1st millennium BCE onward, the settlement reached its height between 330 and 880 CE, yet by 900 it was practically deserted.

·Recent advances in the decipherment of Maya writing systems indicate that the original name of this site was probably Siaan K'aan ("born in heaven"). The name Uaxactún was coined by the American Sylvanus Morley, who rediscovered the city in 1916, and means "eight stones" (the pronunciation "wah-shack-tun" is also a play on the name of the American capital, Washington). The ruins extend for approximately 2$\frac{1}{2}$ x 1$\frac{1}{2}$ miles (4 x 2.3km), and are largely unexplored.

Temple of the Masks (*Above*) An observer standing on this staircase at a solstice or equinox would see the rising sun marked by one of the three Group E temples.

Sunrise alignments (*Below*) The plan shows positions on the Temple of the Masks for viewing sunrise at midsummer, midwinter and the equinoxes; the elevation shows how the sun might have appeared rising behind a temple on these dates.

Sunrise viewing points

Among the pyramids, plazas and temples is an intriguing complex of buildings given the name Group E. These comprise three small temples on top of a roughly 600ft (180m) long platform oriented north–south. To the west is a small step pyramid known as the Temple of the Masks. To an observer standing on this pyramid, the dawn sun at the equinox appears to rise directly over the central temple on the platform: two standing stones between the two structures mark the alignment. On the winter solstice the sun appears from the vantage point of the Temple of the Masks to rise from the southernmost corner of the platform's southern temple, while at the summer solstice it rises from the northernmost corner of the north temple. (This effect is almost exactly the same as the sunrise alignments at the main entrance to Angkor Wat – see page 210.)

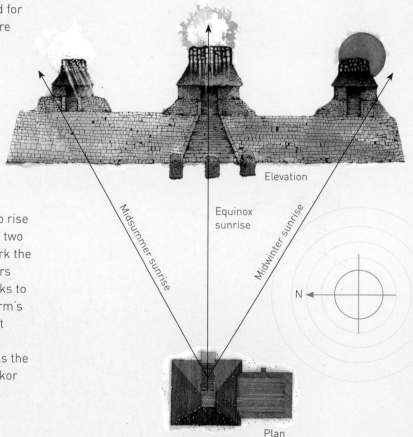

Midsummer sunrise

Equinox sunrise

Midwinter sunrise

Elevation

N

Plan

Harsh landscape The stones of Wurdi Youang are set in the dry terrain of the Wathaurong Aboriginal people.

WURDI YOUANG AUSTRALIA

Indigenous Australians have a wealth of stories about the spirits of sun, moon and stars (the kindling of the sun from the yolk of an emu's egg is one example) and intriguing rock art such as at Ku-ring-gai Chase National Park (see pages 130 and 188). However, very few Aboriginal sites with clear astronomical features have been located, probably due to the harsh environment that dictated a nomadic hunter-gatherer lifestyle, making the construction of lasting monuments less likely. This way of life, which had been practised for at least 40,000 years, was annihilated by the colonial settlers, and much of the verbal and ceremonial lore that had been passed down from generation to generation now seems lost. It is therefore all the more important to try to understand the archaeological heritage of what is the most ancient, consistent human culture on our planet.

Cardinal orientation

On arid grassland near Little River, some 22 miles (35km) southwest of Melbourne, Victoria, is the site of Wurdi Youang, a protected Aboriginal Heritage Site traditionally belonging to the Wathaurong Aboriginal people. Wurdi Youang is a roughly egg-shaped circle of 100 or so basalt stones, with its 165ft (50m) axis aligned east–west. It is one of several stone circles in the area, many with clear orientation to the cardinal directions. It has not been possible to date the circle.

At the western end, 33ft (10m) to the west of the three largest stones, is a cluster of five stones, three of which are aligned on the east–west axis, with the

other two sited on each side. In 2003 John Morieson noted that the row of three stones aligns with the equinox sunset, and that the two outliers align with sunset at midwinter and midsummer. It is possible that the three large boulders in the circle itself also relate to these three alignments.

In 2010 astrophysicist Ray Norris and others published their observation that, when viewed from the sharp, eastern end of the egg, the stones of the circle align to sunset on the winter and summer solstices. This adds up to persuasive evidence that Wurdi Youang's builders deliberately commemorated solar dates that were of real importance to them.

Sunset alignments From the western end of the circle at Wurdi Youang, alignments have been noted to the equinox, midwinter and midsummer sunsets. Similar alignments have been found from the circle's eastern end.

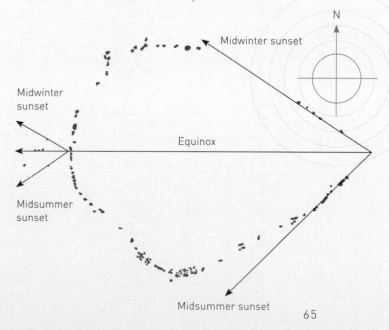

Midwinter sunset

Midwinter sunset

Equinox

Midsummer sunset

Midsummer sunset

N

KARAHUNJ ARMENIA

A former republic of the Soviet Union, Armenia lies to the east of Turkey, within the Caucasus Mountains. On a hilltop near the town of Sisian in the south of the country stands a complex of Neolithic megaliths that were erected in or by the 3rd millennium BCE and have been dubbed "Armenia's Stonehenge". This name is regarded as unhelpful by archaeologists, who see obvious dissimilarities between the sites.

The complex is named after the nearby settlement of Karahunj, 1 mile (1.6km) south of the town of Goris, but it used to be called Ghoshun Dash ("stone army"). However, with *kara* meaning "stone", and "hunj" sounding similar to "henge", the modern name has stuck. The site contained more than 200 basalt standing stones, of which some 150 are still in place, ranging from 2–9ft (0.6–3m) in height. At the heart

of the complex is an egg-shaped circle of some 40 stones, about 140ft (43m) in diameter, aligned to the cardinal directions with its point toward the east.

Sighting tubes and periscopes?

On each side of this egg of standing stones, running directly to the north and south, is a row of stones extending like wings from a bird's body. Each row is around 670ft (205m) long and each one bends some 130ft (40m) from the end, sweeping due west. These two symmetrical rows have attracted the attention of archaeoastronomers because more than 80 of the stones have been pierced (about 50 remain intact). The holes, 1½–2in (4–5cm) in diameter, are positioned in thinner parts of the megaliths, usually near the top – but some holes are still up to 8in (20cm) long. Their narrow diameter and reasonable length mean some of these holes or tubes could align with relatively high precision to a distant target, such as the horizon.

Sighting tubes The pierced stones at Karahunj may have been oriented to the solstices, or to stellar events as yet unknown.

Armenia's Stonehenge A total of 150 stones remain standing at this impressive yet relatively unknown site.

Several holes align to the point where the sun rises at midsummer, and several to where it sets later that day. However, most do not point toward other solstice or equinox positions, or even toward lunar standstill events. Also, most are tilted to point slightly above the horizon. Three holes that penetrate the stone halfway, and then change course abruptly to point straight upward, have been interpreted as possible Stone Age periscopes. Polished obsidian placed at the angle could have reflected starlight from the zenith.

Controversy

The astronomical interpretation of the tilted holes is highly controversial: with so many holes, some are bound to be oriented toward points on the paths of the brighter stars arcing through the sky. Claims that these were deliberate alignments have been met with scepticism, pending a thorough survey. A further obstacle to the acceptance of these theories by the archaeoastronomical community is the mystery of how the holes were made. And as yet there is no explanation for why – when the standing stones are profoundly weathered and often covered with ancient lichens – the holes appear polished and pristine.

Whatever the origin and nature of the holes, Karahunj's overall alignment to the cardinal directions gives it credentials as a site of major archaeoastronomical significance.

THE CRUCUNO RECTANGLE FRANCE

Now and again patterns emerge in the relationship between the Earth and the sun – not only patterns that repeat through time, such as the seasons, but also actual geometric patterns. The cross formed by the four cardinal points is the best known of these, as it is the same all over the globe, but there are also other geometric solar patterns that are restricted to a particular latitude. One of these is expressed in the Crucuno rectangle, which occurs at a latitude of 47° 38' and is situated less than 3 miles (5km) northwest of the famous megalithic site of Carnac in Brittany, France (see pages 84–5).

The Crucuno rectangle is also megalithic, with its 22 remaining stones averaging around 5ft (1.5m) in height. The short sides of the rectangle are aligned north–south and measure 81½ft (24.9m), while the longer sides are aligned east–west and measure 109ft (33.2m). The length of the long and short sides and the diagonals that split the rectangle into two equal Pythagorean (right-angled) triangles have an

THE MEGALITHIC YARD

Professor Alexander Thom, an engineer and avid field researcher of archaeoastronomy in Britain, discovered that many of the sites he surveyed had similar measurements. They seemed to be composed of multiples of a single unit of just over 2ft 8½in (0.83m), which he called the megalithic yard. In 1970 he visited Crucuno and established that the Pythagorean triangles in the rectangle both measure 30 x 40 x 50 megalithic yards. This remains one of the most impressive pieces of evidence for the megalithic yard.

At nearby Le Manio are three standing stones – the Géant du Manio, the Dame du Manio and the Square Stone – that enthusiasts of the megalithic yard suggest also provide an example of the Pythagorean 3:4:5 triangle, based on distances expressed in megalithic yards:

Lady to Square = 82ft (24.9m) = 20.7my = 3 x 6.9my
Square to Giant = 109ft (33.2m) = 27.5my = 4 x 6.9my
Giant to Lady = 113ft (41.5m) = 34.4my = 5 x 6.9my

The measurements resolve to factors of very nearly 7my, but sceptics regard even this small error as a serious flaw. Many of the sites cited by Thom as evidence for the megalithic yard have been re-examined and the unit of measurement he favoured has been proven not to apply.

Géant du Manio

Ancient geometry At this latitude, the 3:4:5 proportions of the Crucuno rectangle allow the commemoration of sunrise and sunset at both equinoxes and both solstices.

interesting numerical property: they can be expressed as a ratio of 3:4:5. If we say that the short side of the Crucuno rectangle measures three units, then the long side will be four units and the diagonal five units.

At this latitude, a rectangle aligned in this way and of these precise proportions has a remarkable archaeoastronomical feature. Around 1800 BCE, the summer solstice sun would have risen along one diagonal and the winter solstice sun would have risen along the other. On these days, the sun would also have set along the opposite diagonal. The simple design at Crucuno therefore exactly incorporates not only the cardinal points but also the rising and setting of the sun on all four major solar events: both equinoxes and both solstices.

It is uncertain that the builders realized the neat mathematical properties of their rectangle – it is simply inherent in the solar alignments here. But

some claim they sought out this site, knowing it was the only latitude at which they could build a rectangle whose measurements expressed the special 3:4:5 dimensions. Archaeoastronomer Alexander Thom believed such Pythagorean triangles to be incorporated in the design of many British and European megalithic monuments. His idea of an ancient unit of measurement called the megalithic yard is the principal (but controversial) evidence for this idea.

Some researchers see the proportions of this ancient site as simply coincidence heaped upon coincidence. However, others regard the Crucuno rectangle as proof that there really was a mathematically sophisticated elite who roamed freely across tribal boundaries and exercised their authority to build monuments based on a mixture of astronomy and sacred geometry.

ELEUSIS GREECE

The ancient Greek myth of Persephone is among the most famous of all the descriptions of the cycle of the seasons. The myth begins with the maiden Persephone blithely collecting flowers in a meadow, where she is abducted by Hades and taken into the underworld. The story ends with her rescue, but she is doomed to return below the earth to her captor for part of each year.

Persephone embodies all the colour and vitality of spring and summer, and her disappearance from the world takes away these qualities, leaving only the decay and desolation of autumn and winter. The great earth mother Demeter reflects her daughter's dual lifestyle with an endless cycle of rejoicing for her presence and mourning for her absence.

Although many commentators regard this simply as an agricultural myth, the fact that the tale of Persephone lies at the heart of the Eleusinian Mysteries suggests some deeper meaning. The Eleusinian Mysteries were arguably the most well respected of all the mystery schools – secret sects whose tiered teachings were revealed in full only to carefully chosen candidates.

The cult centre at Eleusis was less than 12 miles (20km) west of Athens, and as the city grew in prosperity and political importance, so the Eleusinian Mysteries thrived. The cult is thought to have spread from Minoan Crete and taken root at Eleusis around 1500 BCE. It endured until the late 4th century CE, when it was outlawed by a branch of Christianity that embarked on wholesale persecution of paganism and which condemned the ancient idea of Christ as a Gnostic saviour as espoused by the mystery schools. It is remarkable that so little is known of such long-lived teachings, but Eleusinian initiates, like many others, were sworn to secrecy and it seems this silence was reverently upheld.

The darkness and the light

The myth of Persephone divides the year into two parts: a period of light and warmth when she is above ground and a period of darkness and cold when she is incarcerated below. It is highly appropriate that her story was celebrated at the autumn equinox – a time when not only was the year changing from one period to the next, but the day too was divided into two equal halves.

The Athenian festival calendar began each year with the first sighting of the new crescent moon

Triptolemus of the Mysteries Detail of a vase painted in Greece in c. 460 BCE, depicting Triptolemus with the goddess Demeter. According to myth, it was to Triptolemus that Demeter imparted the secret rites of the Eleusian Mysteries.

The Rape of Persephone This fresco by the Italian Renaissance artist Luca Signorelli in Orvieto Cathedral depicts Hades' abduction of Persephone, a popular theme in Western art.

following the summer solstice. The third full moon of the year marked the start of the 10-day festival of the Greater Mystery at Eleusis, and this method of fixing its date ensured it fell as close to the autumn equinox as possible. The long festival incorporated feasting and fasting, and culminated in the ritual tipping of two libation jars – one to the east, the other to the west. This was another clear indicator of the significance of the equinox, the date at which the sun rises and sets at these cardinal points.

Many scholars accept that the myth of Persephone and Hades would have been interpreted among select initiates as a divine message of personal salvation: the ability to enter the underworld of the dead and then leave it – to live again. Just as the seasons swing around, and as night follows day, the soul could survive the extinction of life in the body and be reborn at the start of a new cycle of life. Today, we might interpret this myth in a different way: people who feel buried in a rut of unhappiness (Hades) may find a way to freedom and renewed life. Liberation from the psychological problems that prevent people from fulfilling their potential as human beings seems always to have been a key element of the Mysteries.

Holding this commemoration at the time of the autumn equinox, when Persephone is about to begin anew her lonely sojourn, could have reminded initiates to try to keep from following in her footsteps. It was also, as the two jars indicated, a good point to remember that although hard times may come, the spring equinox would surely arrive in due course and darkness be left behind.

INTRODUCING SOLAR BURIAL

Megalithic tombs – literally, tombs built with "large stones" – are common from Iberia in the south of Europe to the Orkney Islands in the north: a distance of some 1,250 miles (2,000km). Their construction began early in the 5th millennium BCE, during the Neolithic Age (New Stone Age) and continued for more than a thousand years.

Architectural details vary from place to place and time to time, but there is an underlying consistency. Archaeologically, megalithic tombs were communal burial places that served the needs of all the local people and, astronomically, they were strongly associated with the rising sun.

Their simplest form is often termed a dolmen ("table stone") or cromlech ("arched stone") – Breton and Welsh words, respectively. A dolmen can be just three large stones, usually slabs: two are set upright in the ground to act as parallel walls supporting the roof stone. Often, another upright stone is set to make an enclosed chamber. These tombs were probably covered with a layer of soil, which has since eroded away, exposing the stone framework.

With parallel walls and open end, a simple dolmen can be oriented to a narrow sector of the horizon, but complex tombs such as passage graves can achieve a much more precise alignment. The entrance to a passage grave leads into an internal passage or corridor that penetrates deep into the earthen mound of the tomb. Sometimes there is a single chamber at the end, although pairs of chambers may open on each side. It is the long, straight passage that allows investigators to measure the alignment with a high degree of accuracy.

Death and rebirth

Solar alignments may have been intended to bring the sun's fertility into the tomb to nourish or revivify the

Dolmen de Mané-Groh This relatively sophisticated four-room tomb was constructed in France c. 4000–3,500 BCE.

ancestors, so the spirits of the great and the good buried there could be reborn into the community. If so, this tradition may have a remarkably long pedigree.

Chantal Jègues-Wolkiewiez surveyed caves that contain paintings from the Palaeolithic Age (Old Stone Age) such as Lascaux (see pages 200–203). Of the 130 sites she investigated, 122 were found to have entrances oriented to a solstice horizon. Perhaps these caves were selected so the sun's light could penetrate the womb of Mother Earth, enabling her to reproduce the painted animals within, to populate the world outside.

Ballykeel portal tomb Like other dolmens, this tomb at Ballykeel, Ireland, would have once been covered with earth that has since fallen away to reveal a dramatic stone tripod.

STATISTICAL CLUSTER OF SOLAR ALIGNMENTS

Mathematical probability is a key tool in determining whether a site's alignments are coincidence or deliberate design. This bell-curve graph is based on work by David Le Conte and shows the direction of the alignments of more than 1,500 Neolithic tombs in Iberia and parts of the Causses, southern France. The great majority of tombs were aligned toward sunrise, and the most popular dates (shown by the apex of the bell curve) were either a few weeks after the autumn equinox or a few weeks before the spring equinox. A likely explanation for this cluster is that tombs were aligned to face the rising sun on the first day of their construction, with the work commencing in autumn – after the harvest was finished and before the weather deteriorated.

Michael Hoskin and others have also compiled measurements for thousands of these tombs and have reached a clear statistical appreciation of their orientation. For example, in 2008 Hoskin published an overview of more

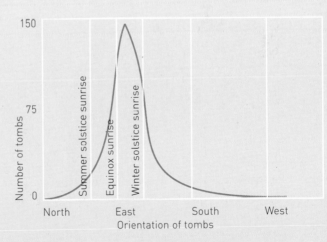

than 1,700 tombs from Iberia to the Channel Islands, 95 percent of which were oriented to face the sun as it was either rising or climbing into the morning sky.

NEWGRANGE, KNOWTH AND DOWTH IRELAND

Inside a crescent of the meandering River Boyne in County Meath in the east of Ireland lies the megalithic complex known as Brú na Bóinne – Palace of the Boyne. This World Heritage site contains one of the earliest known sophisticated astronomical alignments: the Newgrange midwinter sunrise alignment predates the Great Pyramid of Egypt by more than half a millennium.

The three principal monuments in the complex were built in the Neolithic period, around 3200 BCE. Each mound of earth and stone contains stone-lined passages leading to chambers where the bones of the dead were deposited.

By far the most famous site in the complex is the great circular mound of the Newgrange passage tomb, which stands some 45ft high and 290ft across (14 x 88m) on a small hill overlooking the fertile river valley. The outer wall of the mound slopes steeply down, almost vertically, and has been reconstructed with a facing of white quartz stones (found at the site) that reflect light and make it conspicuous from a distance – especially by moonlight. However, this wall is controversial, as modern cement was required to hold the quartz in place.

The spirit's journey

The passage within Newgrange is 63ft (19m) long and culminates in three small chambers, giving the structure a cruciform shape, possibly in commemoration of the four quarters of the year. Each of the small chambers is a tomb where the bones of the dead were deposited. These chambers also contained stone basins each more than 40in (1m) across. Archaeologists have suggested that the basins held the cremated remains of the dead. If so, they may be linked with legends of the inexhaustible cauldron

Cruciform plan The atmospheric interior of Newgrange contains a long passage and three burial chambers.

of the Dagda, a god who had his home in the Brú na Bóinne; and other Celtic myths tell of cauldrons that could resurrect the dead.

It was apparent that the entrance to the mound faced the midwinter solstice sunrise, but initial investigations in the 20th century showed that the rising sun only illuminated part-way along the upwardly sloping floor of the passage. Then, in 1963, a strange feature was discovered in the roof of the passage entrance: a stone-framed aperture or box, 47in long x 39in wide x 35in high (1.2 x 1 x 0.9m), with a lintel carved with lozenges and upright lines. Further investigation revealed that this roofbox, as investigating archaeologist Michael O'Kelly named it, allows the light from the rising winter solstice sun to stream directly into the central chamber at the very

Symbolic art The kerbstones that decorate the exterior of Newgrange mound feature an astonishing array of carvings, the meaning of which we can only guess at today.

back of the mound, flooding it with brilliant winter sunlight for around 15 minutes.

There is only one carving at this point, of three connected spirals. Their original significance is unknown although may relate to ideas of the spirit's journey from life to death and back again in an endless looping cycle. This carving is believed to be the earliest surviving example of this intriguing geometric figure. The accuracy with which the monument was constructed makes Newgrange one of the most famous of all archaeoastronomical sites.

The tomb's orientation must have been worked out in advance of its construction, which implies a deliberate attempt to establish a connection between the ancestors buried in the tomb and the sun's rising on the midwinter solstice – the day that marks the

halting of the sun's descent from autumn into the darkness of winter. At the heart of this alignment is the sun's reappearance at the dawn of a new day – and perhaps the mystery of rebirth.

Neolithic art

A particularly intriguing feature at Newgrange is its kerbstones, thought to have been brought from a quarry some 9 miles (15km) distant. The entire mound was encircled at the base by 97 of these kerbstones, many of which are carved, some in great detail, with spirals, chevrons and lozenges. It has been suggested that the spirals are solar symbols, an idea supported by the kerbstone that lies across the tomb's entrance. A vertical line bisects the top of this kerbstone: to the right is a triple spiral, curling anticlockwise; to the left,

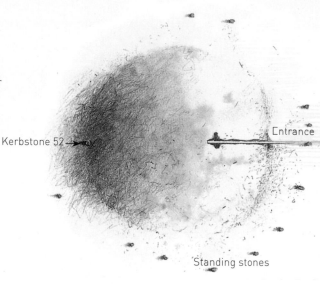

Tomb of the sun (*Left*) Above the entrance kerbstone at Newgrange, itself decorated with solar spirals, is the roofbox through which a ray of the rising sun at midwinter is channelled into the heart of the mound.

Sacred symmetry (*Right*) This plan of the exterior of Newgrange mound shows how the passage into the central chamber is sited on the same east–west axis as Kerbstone 52; this stone's carvings echo those of the entrance stone and may have stellar as well as solar significance.

Kerbstone 52

Entrance

Standing stones

Annual ceremony A plan and elevation show how sunlight enters the mound of Newgrange through the roofbox, to illuminate a triple spiral on the rear wall of the central chamber for just 15 minutes of every year.

ELEVATION

Roofbox

Standing stone

Passage entrance stone

Stone basin

Stone basins

Triple spiral carving

PLAN

N

the spirals curl clockwise. The spiral motif seems to have had special importance to the Newgrange artists.

The mound was also surrounded by a circle of standing stones that may originally have numbered between 32 and 35, set around 35ft (10m) out from the kerbstones. Most of the stones are missing, but on the midwinter solstice the standing stone in front of the entrance cast a shadow on the triple spiral of the entrance kerbstone. And another stone in the circle cast a similar shadow over this triple spiral at the spring equinox.

Intriguingly, the kerbstone at the back of the mound, diametrically opposite the entrance kerbstone, is also bisected by a vertical line. Its other carvings include diamonds and holes as well as spirals; the holes may have stellar significance while the spirals may relate to the sun. With its ancient art, architecture and astronomy, Newgrange is a special site, full of fascinating possibilities.

Knowth

Today, Newgrange is the most visually impressive of the three major mounds at Brú na Bóinne, but Knowth is slightly larger. Sited about ³⁄₄ mile (1.3km) northwest of Newgrange, its main mound contains not just one but two unconnected passages running west–east.

These two passages may be aligned to the equinoxes, although they are accurate enough only to mark the approximate dates, leading some to suspect that the alignment may be accidental. Damage to the mound after it fell into disuse around 2500 BCE may, however, account for some of the apparent inaccuracy.

THE SOLAR SPIRAL

The symbol of the spiral may represent an artist's belief about the sun's movements. If we wanted to represent the sun's motion across the sky at the autumn equinox, we would draw a large arc. A month later the sun would still trace an arc through the sky but it would be a smaller one, so we would draw an arc inside the first one. Each succeeding month the arc would be smaller still and we would draw each arc inside the previous one.

If we believed that the sun travels below ground each night, passing through an underworld, then we might connect the west end of the arc with the east end of the next arc. And if we assumed that this nocturnal journey was also in the form of an arc, then our picture of the sun's movements would become a neat spiral.

Only an observer in the Arctic or Antarctic Circle (66° 33' north or 66° 33' south) would trace a spiral that continues to a dot in the centre at the winter solstice. However, even at the latitude of Newgrange, Knowth and Dowth, such a prospect – a winter that continued to grow ever colder – may well have seemed possible to people without the benefit of modern science. Fear of the world ending in a frozen waste could easily have become enshrined in religious beliefs, and ceremonies conducted at key times of the year may have been employed to ward off such a terrifying fate. Perhaps the Newgrange spirals are maps of a territory into which ancient people were keen not to trespass.

Triple spiral inside Newgrange

Kerbstones with bisecting lines found at the entrances to the two passages at Knowth lend weight to the idea of purposeful planning, as does the position of a tall, thin standing stone outside the entrance to the western passage, whose shadow falls in the middle of the bisected kerbstone at sunset near the equinoxes. The eastern passage ends in a cruciform tomb, as at Newgrange, which may again mark the quartering of the year.

This mound is encircled by carved kerbstones that are strikingly varied in their decoration, and two in particular may have astronomical features. One to the east resembles a sundial with carved rays radiating in a semicircle downward from a central point like the ribs of a fan. Although we have no confirmation of its use as a sundial, many researchers find it a compelling possibility. Another kerbstone to the south-southwest appears to show the phases of the moon throughout the 29-day lunar month (see pages 126–7).

With more than 400 carved stones, Knowth contains nearly half of all megalithic art known in western Europe. The sheer variety of images and

patterns carved into the rocks would reveal much if we could regain an understanding of their meaning.

Dowth

Dowth, 1¼ miles (2km) northeast of Newgrange, is in a poor state of repair, partly from neglect and partly from excavations in the 19th century. Although the mound is much the same size as Knowth and Newgrange, its tomb chambers are smaller and the two passages are shorter at 50ft (15m) or less. The artwork is also less abundant and of lower quality than that at the other two monuments. However, solar and other alignments still appear to have been built into its design.

The two passages in the mound at Dowth are both located on the western side. The most northerly passage has an arm terminating in a small cruciform tomb area with an annex off the right-hand chamber. The curling passage north of the cruciform tomb is relatively recent – a souterrain or refuge dug into the mound probably in the early first millennium CE.

The entrance of the southern passage looks toward Newgrange mound. This passage terminates in a circular burial chamber, which also has a recessed chamber on the right. Stones in this recess are carved with apparently solar icons such as circles, concentric circles and a rayed or segmented circle known to students of megalithic art as a sunwheel (sunwheels also appear outside the mound on Kerbstone 51). This passage has been observed by Anne-Marie Moroney to align to sunset at the midwinter solstice, thus complementing the alignment at Newgrange. When the sun's rays strike the stone at the rear of the passage, its light is reflected into the recess, illuminating the solar imagery, including the segmented circle – a reference, perhaps, to the division of the year into seasons by calendar dates that form the spokes of a solar wheel.

Knowth sundial One kerbstone outside Knowth (artificially illuminated here to make the carvings more prominent) may be an ancient representation of a sundial.

N

To Newgrange and
midwinter sunset

Midwinter alignment The southern passage at Dowth is oriented toward sunset at the midwinter solstice. As at Newgrange, when the rays strike the rear wall of the mound they illuminate solar imagery. The entrance to the northern passage faces roughly in the direction of Knowth, while the entrance to the southern passage faces Newgrange – linking the three sites in a unified sacred landscape.

THE MAKING OF DOWTH

A traditional legend explaining the name Dowth – which simply means "darkness" – was recorded in the early medieval period as one of the Dindsenchas verses that tell of the creation and naming of many places in Ireland, and are believed to incorporate legends from the pre-literate, pre-Christian age of bardic poetry. The legend tells how, following a pestilence, the King of Ireland drew together all the men of his kingdom and set them to build a tower to heaven. Grudgingly they consented, but only to give their labour for a single day. The king's sister was skilled in the magical arts and she cast a spell that made the sun stand still, giving the labourers an endless day in which to build the tower.

It is said that the king was so intoxicated at the sight of his sister's power that he was overpowered by the urge to make love with her. This was their undoing. As her maidenhead was

The mound of Dowth

surrendered to him, so her magic was lost and the sun resumed its natural course. The men returned home, leaving the tower nothing more than the vast mound of Dowth.

This tale combines magic with a possible observation of the behaviour of the sun at the solstices, when the progressive movement of its rising and setting points along the horizon

is halted in the "sun standstill". While the legend in the form we have it is likely to be of Iron Age Celtic origin, it certainly appears to enshrine some of the key themes that interested the Neolithic people who built the passage tomb at Dowth.

MAESHOWE SCOTLAND

The Orkney Islands have around 3,000 Neolithic sites and were a significant centre of culture at that time. The islands were exposed to the extremes of weather from the north Atlantic and the Arctic Circle and to the ravages of invaders from Scandinavia, yet the fertile land and abundant harvest from the sea sustained a thriving community, and there's a savage beauty to the area.

The World Heritage site here is a cluster of monuments that include the coastal settlement of Skara Brae, the passage tomb of Maeshowe and the circles of standing stones known as the Stones of Stenness and the Ring of Brodgar, which were all constructed around 3100 to 2800 BCE.

Maeshowe bears a marked similarity to the slightly earlier tomb of Newgrange (see pages 74–7), as it also has a cruciform tomb. This measures almost 15 x 15 x 12½ft high (4.5 x 4.5 x 3.8m high), at the end of a passage around 30ft (9m) long. Maeshowe is somewhat smaller than Newgrange, at 24ft high and 115ft in diameter (7.3 x 35m), but is still a distinctive feature of the landscape.

The entrance to Maeshowe faces the winter solstice sunset, so that from this perspective the sun was seen for a few days to set into a natural trough between two hills some 9 miles (15km) away on the island of Hoy. The setting sun at this solstice also illuminated the tomb's inner chamber. Inside an alcove off the passage is a block of stone that, while fitting the width of the passage exactly, is a little too short to cover the entrance. Moved in front of the entrance, it would have left a 19in (50cm) slit at the top that, like the roofbox at Newgrange, may have directed the light of the solstice sunset directly into the inner chamber.

Viking graffiti (*Left*) When Maeshowe was excavated in 1861, archaeologists found that they were not the first to have broken into the ancient tomb: the walls were covered with runic inscriptions dating back to the 12th century.

Mound of Maeshowe (*Opposite*) Prominent in the landscape and with a cruciform interior (comprising a long passage with three small chambers leading off the central chamber), Maeshowe is similar in structure to the Newgrange mound.

AN INTEGRATED LANDSCAPE?

A solitary standing stone, just over 10ft (3m) tall and known as the Barnhouse Stone, seems to have been deliberately sited on the winter solstice alignment from Maeshowe, around 2,500ft (760m) away. And there are many other broadly contemporary monuments in this area whose use almost certainly overlapped. Of these, the Ring of Brodgar is one of Britain's largest stone circles at 341ft (104m) in diameter (only the circles at Avebury and Stanton Drew are larger). When it was built, c. 3000 BCE, it had 60 stones, of which 27 are standing today, although many were re-erected in 1906. Like Stonehenge, Brodgar was surrounded by a ditch cut into bedrock, yet the stone was not piled into a protective bank but was mysteriously removed from the site.

Until the 1840s the Ring of Brodgar was known as the Temple of the Sun (with the nearby stone circle of Stenness referred to as the Temple of the Moon). Visitors to Brodgar can find alignments with most solar events on the horizon. However, there are so many stones at Brodgar, and the horizon is so full of notable niches and bumps, that some alignments are bound to occur by chance. For example, viewed from the centre of the circle the winter solstice sunset occurs behind one of the two Hills of Hoy – an

alignment also apparently marked by a burial mound built around a thousand years after the stones were raised. Proving that such alignments were purposeful elements of the circle's original design is difficult. Although the Ring of Brodgar may hold remarkable astronomical secrets, for now they remain tantalizingly out of reach.

The Stones of Stenness circle, which is slightly older, features a pair of stones that precisely frame the funeral mound of Maeshowe. Such alignments hint that these structures may have formed an integrated complex in the landscape, with the entire design locked into an astronomical framework. More significant alignments may await discovery, but until a rigorous investigation includes all the possible markers (rather than just focusing on those with clear alignments and disregarding the rest), the scientific community will not be convinced. Not all these ancient monuments will be astronomically aligned, and until we understand which ones are and which ones are not, we will not be able to see prehistoric astronomy in context.

Ring of Brodgar (*Overleaf*) Many solar alignments have been suggested for this huge stone circle – one of Britain's largest – but for this site proof remains elusive.

CARNAC FRANCE

The massed stone rows of Carnac in Brittany, France, are one of the few archaeological sites that have achieved international fame and been painstakingly investigated by archaeologists and archaeoastronomers alike.

The stone avenues contain more than 3,000 individual stones, the earliest of which may date to the end of the Mesolithic Age (Middle Stone Age) around 4500 BCE. They run in three great swathes from the north of the town of Carnac toward the northeast and the village of Kerlescan. Although they often appear to run in straight, parallel lines, these rows actually have apparently random curves that argue against a design based on astronomical alignments. However, there may be solar significance in the fact that the tallest of the menhirs in all three groups stand at each group's western end.

Many other monuments were constructed in the area, including tombs, some of which do appear to incorporate astronomical features. For example, the Tumulus of St Michael, a burial mound some 395ft (120m) long, is oriented east–west, to the rising sun. On top of its eastern end is a Christian chapel, built in 1663 and also seemingly aligned to the rising sun. The east–west alignment is often found in Christian architecture (see page 88). The townspeople of Carnac used to light a bonfire on this mound each summer solstice, a tradition that survived until the 19th century.

The Kercado passage tomb is less conspicuous, secluded in what is now woodland at the highest part of the locality. Some 82ft in diameter and 16ft high (25 x 5m), the circular mound is partially ringed by the remains of a stone circle. The tomb entrance faces the winter solstice sunrise, which shines into a passage 21ft (6.5m) long. The capstone (roofing slab) is engraved with an image of an axe head, and axe heads, arrowheads and pottery were found in the burial chamber at the end of the passage, indicating a high-status tomb. This tomb is said to date to 4,800 BCE, making it the oldest stone construction still standing in Europe.

Solar alignments The western menhirs in each of Carnac's three main groups of standing stones are taller than the others, suggesting a possible orientation to the setting sun.

A FALLEN GIANT IS ENTOMBED

Three chamber tombs sited around 6 miles (10km) east of Carnac share a common feature: their roofing slabs include part of a single standing stone that may have been one of those that once stood alongside Le Grand Menhir Brisé at Locmariaquer (see page 146). This fallen, broken and recycled stone had distinctive carvings that include an axe and what appears to be a plough pulled by oxen. The three pieces make a perfect match and indicate that the stone would have stood at least 43ft (13m) high – a giant by normal standards, yet dwarfed by Le Grand Menhir Brisé.

One fragment is built into the circular tomb known as the Table des Marchand, which would have been shadowed by these great stones. Its entrance and passage are aligned to admit the light from the rising summer solstice sun. Also part of this close-knit complex at Locmariaquer is the Tomb of Er Grah, an impressive stone burial mound 525ft (160m) long, that appears to be aligned directly with Le Grand Menhir Brisé itself.

The third fragment of the fallen stone is 1¼ miles (2km) away on the island of Gavrinis, where the tomb appears to have been oriented toward the sun shortly after the midwinter sunrise (see page 147).

Table des Marchand

LOS MILLARES SPAIN

***Tholos* tombs** Most of the passage tombs at Los Millares, with their typical beehive-shaped roofs and dry-stone walls, are oriented to the east – the direction of the resurrected sun.

Located 11 miles (17km) from the coastal city of Almería, Andalucía, the settlement of Los Millares is one of the most important megalithic sites in Spain, dating to around 3000–2500 BCE.

At its heart is a fortified citadel on the top of a promontory above the Andarax river. Below this stronghold is a larger village of stone huts, and the entire site is surrounded by a wall averaging 6½ft (2m) thick. This outer wall was heavily fortified with at least 17 towers and bulwarks and two barbican entrances. These impressive defences suggest that the settlement was wealthy (its prosperity was probably founded on copper working), and feared a serious threat to its security.

Outside the settlement is a cemetery of at least 80 passage tombs. These are unlike the megalithic tombs that were being constructed in other parts of western Europe around the same time. Rather than using a small number of very large stones (megaliths), these tombs were built with a great many smaller stones, with a few megaliths to provide an impressive entrance. The passage and burial chamber were constructed using dry-stone walling techniques and had a corbelled roof whose shape inspired the technical name for this type of tomb – *tholos*, meaning "domed". Finally, each tomb was covered with a mound of earth. The tombs were communal and each contained from 30 to more than 100 burials. Grave goods, presumably deposited for the well-being of the deceased, included ostrich eggs, ivory, pottery, bone artefacts and copper and flint tools.

Los Millares is certainly a major megalithic monument and its tombs display an impressive cultural interest in the rising of the sun. With just a tiny handful of exceptions, all the Los Millares tombs face east, their entrances aligned to allow the light of the rising sun to penetrate the passage. However, just two tombs are aligned directly with the midsummer solstice sunrise and only one is aligned with the midwinter sunrise; the great majority ignore these turning points of the year. The few tombs that are not oriented toward sunrise may be aligned with the sun slightly later, as it climbs into the sky.

Despite their apparent ability to align tombs with the solstices, the builders seemed overwhelmingly content simply to catch the morning light, caring little for the particular date of the dawn. However, we cannot discount the possibility that they were working to some formula of which we are unaware. For example, an alignment might reflect the date on which the builders started work, perhaps a set number of days after the death of the tomb's first occupant. Statistical work by Michael Hoskin, Elizabeth Allan and Renate Gralewski has established that the great majority of these tombs are oriented toward sunrise in the winter months, although relatively few are aligned near the winter solstice itself. More discoveries may well await further archaeoastronomical research.

HASHIHAKA KOFUN JAPAN

The official Japanese name for the nation – Nippon ("sun's origin") – is often translated as "Land of the Rising Sun", and was first noted in correspondence with the imperial Chinese court *c.* 600 CE. Chinese influence can be seen in the tombs built in Japan at that time, especially in the painting of star charts (see page 219). Other celestial resonances have also been suggested for these burial sites, particularly the *kofun* or keyhole tombs, which are burial mounds with a circular end from which a splayed wedge extends. Their axis of symmetry may indicate direction. Several *kofun* situated 1–2 miles (1.5–3km) northwest of the city of Nara are roughly aligned north–south, but others exhibit an apparently random placement.

Hashihaka Kofun near Sakurai in Nara Prefecture is 920ft long, 490ft wide and 100ft high (280 x 150 x 30m) and may be the tomb of the semi-legendary Queen Himiko. Pottery found at the site has been dated to *c.* 250 CE, when the queen is thought to have died. This tomb may house an archaeoastronomical treasure such as the star charts that have been found in similar tombs, but it is designated an Imperial Tomb, hence it is protected and excavation is forbidden.

The islet in the lake to the north of Hashihaka Kofun is a *baicho*, a small funerary tumulus built to hold votive items and burial goods apart from the main tomb. From here a protrusion on Mount Miwa is visible over the top of Hashihaka Kofun, marking the point of the midwinter sunrise.

A further alignment runs along the axis of the *kofun*, from its wedge end and over the circular part of the mound, to the summit of a hill 2 miles (3km) away where the sun rises at midsummer. These alignments to the two solstice sunrises could have implied a link between the dead ruler's spirit and the orderly progression of the seasons that make life possible. Such a connection would have made it clear that even after death the ruler continued to be instrumental in the life of the people by maintaining that order.

Cult of the ancestors Prestigious tombs such as Hashihaka Kofun reinforced the authority and power of the ruling elite.

INTRODUCING OTHER SOLAR ALIGNMENTS

Although the solstices and equinoxes quarter the year around the globe, other dates may also be locally significant. Some of the solar alignments that commemorate these dates may appear arbitrary today, but once would have been full of meaning.

Most of the sites in this book are ancient, but astronomical alignments have also been used in more recent times – and churches are a rewarding subject for study. These structures often incorporate an alignment to the solstices or equinoxes, or may feature a more unusual solar orientation.

Church alignments

It is well known that churches often have an eastward orientation. As the rays of the sun poured through their great east windows and shone over the high altar into the face of the congregation, the priest would have been symbolically put in the place of the risen Christ, bringing spiritual illumination to the faithful.

LIGHT FROM THE MARTINSLOCH CAVE

The Tschingelhörner ridge in the Alps of northeast Switzerland is pierced by the Martinsloch, a natural 65ft (20m) cave that is part of a World Heritage site. Twice a year on – or a day either side of – 13 March and 1 October (the variation in date is caused by leap years), the rising sun shines through this tunnel, creating a shaft of light that shines for 3 miles (5km) across the Sernftal valley. It falls to earth in the heart of the ancient village of Elm, striking the roof of the church for just a couple of minutes on each occasion.

Proponents of new religions often build over the sites of older ones, and it would be interesting to know what, if any, pre-Christian activities had taken place here and at the four other alpine sites where similar beams of light pinpoint the location of churches.

However, there is also clear evidence of more specific solar alignments in the siting of European churches. Studies of Austrian and Italian churches have found some to be aligned to sunrise on their patron saint's feast day, while in Hungary 13th- and 14th-century churches appear to favour orientation to sunrise on the solstices and equinoxes.

A popular belief that British churches were oriented to sunrise on the date of their patron saint's holy day was recently tested by Ian Hinton during a 10-year survey of nearly 1,750 medieval churches throughout England and Wales. His conclusions, published in 2006, showed that although the churches all faced roughly eastward, they apparently ignored their patronal sunrises. Four of every five churches were aligned within 15° of true east. But Hinton noted a curious feature: the average alignment of churches in the west of the area studied was nearly 10° north of the average for churches in the east. More work is needed to investigate this puzzle.

Imperial display

The cathedral of Aachen, Germany, is built around the Palatine Chapel raised by Charlemagne in 805 CE. On the summer solstice a ray of sunlight illuminates the head of whoever is seated on the throne, where coronations were celebrated for centuries. At noon on the winter solstice, the light shines on the figure of Christ flanked by the symbols of eternity: alpha and omega, the beginning and the end.

Sanctifying rulers In a dramatic solar effect, a ray of the summer solstice sun illuminates the head of anyone seated on the throne of Charlemagne in the Palatine Chapel, once part of the emperor's Palace of Aachen and for 600 years the site of imperial coronations.

AMARNA EGYPT

The dazzling vision of pharaoh Amenhotep IV, who attempted to sweep away traditions established during nearly two millennia of dynastic rule in Egypt, culminated in failure on a grand scale. He was condemned as a heretic and his name was ordered to be erased from all records so that the memory of him would perish. It was only the discovery and excavation of Amarna during the 19th century that led to his renewed fame as the creator of the city of Akhetaten.

He became pharaoh around 1353 BCE, inheriting a prosperous kingdom. By the fifth year of his reign he had fallen under the influence of the sun god Re, whose icon was the solar orb, or Aten, and he adopted a new name – Akhenaten, "effective for the Aten".

Akhenaten's devotion to the Aten upset the powerful priests whose polytheism involved hundreds if not thousands of deities. His spiritual revolution is often cited as an early example of monotheism and there are similarities between hymns to the Aten and descriptions of Jehovah in writings attributed to Moses, who may have lived at this period. However, although Akhenaten ordered destruction of the names and images of the chief creator deity Amun (after whom he, as Amenhotep, was originally named), he tolerated subordinate gods.

The pharaoh chose the site of his new capital city carefully. Hieroglyphs on boundary markers on the cliffs encircling the area stated that the Aten showed Akhenaten where to build. Now known as Amarna, the city was called Akhetaten – "horizon of the Aten".

Homage to the sun god (*Left*) Akhenaten offers lotus flowers to the Aten, the orb representing the Egyptian sun god, Re.

A great king (*Overleaf*) This colossal statue of Akhenaten was erected at one of the several temples to Aten constructed by the monarch at Karnak.

The iconography of the Amarna period is dominated by the rounded disc or orb of the Aten, from which descend numerous thin rays that often terminate in a small hand holding the hieroglyph of the *ankh* – "life". Akhenaten and his queen Nefertiti are often depicted adoring the Aten, whose rays nourish them. This rayed orb was also a hieroglyph, meaning "shining" or simply "light".

End of the dream

The great spiritual experiment did not last. Akhenaten died in the 17th year of his reign, and was succeeded *c*. 1332 BCE by the young Tutankhaten ("living image of Aten"). He changed his name and reinstated the old worship of Amun. When his tomb was discovered in 1922, he became the most famous of all ancient Egyptians: Tutankhamun. Akhenaten's capital city was abandoned and its great stone buildings were demolished. Even the temples built to the Aten at Karnak were torn down and their ornate sculpture used as rubble in the foundations of other sacred buildings, including an extension of Amun's temple.

THE *AKHET*

The hieroglyph *akhet* means "horizon", and shows the sun rising out of a concave land surface. The axis of the Small Aten Temple at Amarna is aligned to a distinct notch in the eastern horizon 2½ miles (4km) away. The sun rose here, recreating the *akhet* hieroglyph, around 23 February and 24 October. These dates lack astronomical significance, but could have been important to Akhenaten himself (the alignment continues to his tomb). This was surely the *akhet* after which the city was named.

ABU SIMBEL EGYPT

The four statues that front the Great Temple at Abu Simbel together became an international icon in the 1960s when the construction of the Aswan Dam created Lake Nasser, and the rising waters of the Nile threatened to swamp the site. The colossal statues were built around 1265 BCE and all depict pharaoh Ramesses II. Although the figures are seated, they still loom some 72ft (22m) tall. They were carved from living rock, with the temple itself burrowing deep into the sandstone cliff behind them.

In a major feat of modern engineering, the entire temple was extracted from the cliff in blocks, and

Giant among men (*Previous page*) The four monumental statues at Abu Simbel all depict the same man: Ramesses II.

Heart of the Great Temple (*Below*) The sun's rays reach the four statues in the inner sanctuary on 21 February and 21 October – the significance of these dates remains unknown.

hauled some 650ft (200m) further away from the water's edge, where it was reassembled beneath an artificial hill. The same process was applied to the smaller, adjacent temple dedicated jointly to Hathor (goddess of motherhood and love) and Ramesses' principal consort, Nefertari. This temple is aligned to the sunrise at midwinter. The complex of Abu Simbel is a World Heritage site and a popular tourist destination despite its remote location near Egypt's border with Sudan.

The Great Temple

Above the four massive statues of Ramesses the Great is a row of squatting stone baboons, each gazing forward with palms held vertically up as if basking in the warmth of the rising sun. Standing around the feet of Ramesses are smaller statues of his family. At the centre of the facade is a bas-relief of the temple's patron – the falcon-headed sun god Re

New site of the temple When the Aswan Dam was constructed, the Great Temple was moved back from the water but retained the same alignment, meaning that the solar alignment to the inner sanctuary (on 21 February and 21 October) was not disrupted.

in his manifestation as Horakhty ("Horus of the two horizons"; sometimes spelled Harakhty) – beneath which is the entrance to the temple itself. From this point the temple extends some 185ft (56m) into the solid rock. The masons maintained a precise alignment as they created a series of chambers that began as vast pillared halls, but reduced in size until the final sanctuary was reached.

At this furthest extremity, which was directly illuminated by sunshine on only two days each year, lay four further statues. Alongside Ramesses himself are the three most important gods of the period, each of whom is associated with one of the main cult centres of his kingdom: Re-Horakhty of Heliopolis, Ptah of Memphis and Amun of Thebes. Ptah was a

lord of the underworld and the rays of the sun do not quite engulf his statue, allowing him to remain a figure of shadow and mystery.

Mystery also surrounds the dates of this solar alignment – 21 February and 21 October. Although their significance remains unknown, it is thought that the temple itself was created to commemorate the Sed or jubilee of Ramesses in the 34th year of his reign. Gerald Hawkins has calculated the date of the alignment to 1257 BCE, offering a way to bridge the gaps in the historical record. Egyptologists variously suggest the coronation of Ramesses was in 1304, 1290 or even 1279 BCE, a selection that can be refined (assuming that 1257 was indeed the 34th year of the reign) to a single date – 1290 BCE.

DENGFENG CHINA

The Gaocheng Observatory in Henan Province is the oldest of its type in China. It is one of the monuments of Dengfeng, a World Heritage site. Dengfeng lies at the foot of Mount Song, one of the five sacred mountains of Daoism. The Chinese of the Han Dynasty (206 BCE to 220 CE) considered Dengfeng to be the spiritual centre of the world, and even earlier the site was already in use as an observatory.

Better calendars and maps

The monk and scholar I Hsing (Yi Xing, 683–727 CE) was the most notable Chinese astronomer of his age. Between 721 and 725 the court of the Tang Dynasty put I Hsing in charge of a survey to obtain astronomical data to devise a more accurate calendar and predict eclipses. He set up 13 observation stations ranging from Russia to Vietnam, a distance of around

1,550 miles (2,500km). Measurements from the station at Gaocheng (formerly called Yangcheng) were used as the standard against which other data was measured.

I Hsing set up gnomons (sundial blades) 8ft (2.5m) high to measure the sun's noontide shadow on the solstices and equinoxes. Comparing measurements from his 13 stations, he could determine how latitude varied across the kingdom. It was vital for gnomons to be exactly the same height, and to measure the shadows' length on the same date. The gnomon closest to the equator would have the shortest shadow, and the other observation stations would have longer shadows the further north they were situated. From this information I Hsing could calculate the latitude of the 13 observatories, information that was used to help define territorial boundaries.

The observatory we see at Dengfeng today was built in 1276, designed by the astronomer and engineer Guo Shoujing. It stands some 41ft (12.6m) high, with sides over 52ft (16m) wide. The gnomon in this case is a horizontal rather than vertical rod, while the scale is measured on the *shigui*. This is a low structure of 36 square stone blocks, 102ft (31m) long and running due north, on which the shadow of the gnomon is cast by the sun. Two linked channels filled with water created a perfectly level surface for the measurement of the rod's shadow. This technique provided more precise readings than earlier systems with a vertical gnomon.

Shoujing was also tasked by the emperor Kublai Khan to update the calendar. Using the Gaocheng Observatory he calculated the length of the year to an accuracy that would not be equalled by the West until the Gregorian Calendar was instituted more than 300 years later. Shoujing chose the winter solstice of 1280 as the starting date for his new calendar.

Gaocheng Observatory
The shadow cast onto the long scale on the ground was measured when the midday sun was at its height at midsummer, and at its lowest at midwinter.

Sun at noon, midsummer

Sun at noon, midwinter

Shigui

Solstice stele

At the site are replicas of other ancient astronomical devices including the abridged armilla, invented by Guo Shoujing in 1276 CE to determine the position of celestial objects. Other devices include a bowl sundial and the world's first seismograph. A stele or stone column set on a pedestal (with a combined height of 6½ft/2m) was set up in 723 CE by the astronomer Nangong Yue. Only at noon on summer solstice does the stele's shadow stay entirely on the pedestal.

Reading the shadow The shadow cast by the gnomon of the Gaocheng Observatory was measured in the perfectly level surface of the two water channels mounted on the *shigui*.

Pagoda Forest at Shaolin Monastery

MAGIC OF THE MOUNTAINS

The sun is the guiding principle of the type of feng shui (the Chinese art of placement) that is best known in the West, but in the vicinity of the sacred Mount Song another force holds sway. Here it is *luan tou* – the form of the land – that governs the flow of life-nourishing energy, and the dominant feature of the landscape here is the mountains themselves.

According to the lore of *luan tou*, the mountains were raised through the attraction of certain stars, and so terrestrial geology was shaped by celestial characteristics, some mountains becoming rounded and peaceful, others jagged and awe-inspiring. The mountains that dominate the setting of the Shaolin Monastery (5th century CE) and the monk's cemetery of the Pagoda Forest are of a type associated with the star Mizar in Ursa Major (Great Bear). This star is known as Military Arts, and its influence is thought to have especially inspired the famous martial art of Shaolin kung fu that developed here.

CHANKILLO PERU

The solar observatory known as the Thirteen Towers dates back to the 4th century BCE. It is part of a large site at Chankillo, situated around 200 miles (320km) north of Lima, and around 9 miles (15km) from the Pacific coast, in the arid sand and rocky outcrops of the Casma–Sechin river valley.

The Thirteen Towers

This row of squat towers extends for some 1,000ft (300m) along the ridge of a low hill, with one tower positioned on the summit. The 10 towers to the north of the summit are aligned north–south, while the two to the south deviate from this alignment by bending toward the southwest. They are neatly spaced some 16ft (5m) apart.

The name "tower" may give a slightly false impression of these stout, four-sided structures, which are 6½–20ft (2–6m) tall, because they are actually somewhat wider than they are high. A pair

Solar observatory The towers that run along a ridge at the top of the site at Chankillo can be used to mark the yearly progress of the sun.

of staircases leading from the ridge to the top of each tower is positioned on the north and south sides of the towers, allowing a traveller to walk unimpeded up and over the towers from one end of the ridge to the other. Natural weathering and the deliberate quarrying of their stone for other local building projects has degraded the towers, but they still form an impressive archaeoastronomical monument.

A map of the solar year

The site has been known since the 19th century, but until the 21st century no one had studied the Thirteen Towers. In 2007 Ivan Ghezzi (of Peru's National Institute of Culture) and Clive Ruggles (of the University of Leicester, UK) investigated the structures and found that they constituted a comprehensive solar – and possibly lunar – observatory.

At a distance of 750ft (230m) to the east and west of the line of towers are two observation points, on an almost exact east–west alignment, and at the same elevation as the towers. The western observation point is in a passageway running along the outside of a ceremonial building. Here, a door-sized opening

Ancient settlement The site of Chankillo extends over 1½ square miles (4 square km) and includes a temple, a plaza and an administrative complex, as well as the solar observatory itself.

offered the perfect view of the towers, and ritual deposits of shells and pottery were found at the threshold. The eastern observation point was in a small building isolated from the rest of the site. Both these observation points had restricted access, which argues that they were intended for a very limited number of elite observers.

Seen from these viewing stations the towers provide a reference scale, like the divisions of a protractor, against which the movements of the sun can be tracked as its rising and setting points shift a little each day during its annual cycle. From the western observation point the distant Mucho Malo mountain provides an additional marker, equally spaced from the end tower, from which the sun on the winter (June) solstice would have risen.

The sunrises and sunsets that shine through the 12 gaps (or 13 if Cerro Mucho Malo is included) and over the Thirteen Towers would have allowed an observer to chart the solar year with unusual precision. This could have not only helped farmers to gauge when best to plant or harvest, but also fixed the times when sacred rituals should be celebrated to ensure the favour of the gods.

CUZCO PERU

In the foothills of the Andes, at an altitude of 11,200ft (3,400m), Cuzco was raised from a small town to the centre of an empire in the early part of the 15th century CE by Pachacuti Inca Yupanqui. A skilled politician and administrator from a military background, he became ruler of the Inca Empire, which was called Tahuantinsuyu ("four quarters of the world"). The Incan name of this city – Qosqo – embodies the meaning of "centre" and is often translated as "navel". Unlike many Inca sites, Cuzco was not abandoned following the Spanish invasion of the 1530s and much of the ancient city survives.

At the heart of the Inca capital city was the Inti Kancha, the Temple of Inti (the sun god) that is now known as the Coricancha ("golden enclosure"). The courtyard of the Coricancha was graced with life-size statues of gold, and walls and floors were covered in the same lustrous metal. Within the temple was a magnificent statue of Inti facing the rising sun. This, too, was made of gold, and encrusted with emeralds whose beautiful green colour could have referred to the lushness of fertile land.

After the Spanish executed the last Inca king, Atahualpa, in 1533, the priceless Inca art was reduced to bullion. Much of the temple's structure was also destroyed, and the Cathedral of Santo Domingo raised in its place.

Some contemporary chroniclers attempted to record the way of life of the original inhabitants. In doing so, they preserved many clues that still tantalize archaeoastronomers today.

Lost alignments Towers on the hills around Cuzco once marked solar alignments, and were the focus of pilgrimage.

Temple of the sun god The Cathedral of Santo Domingo now occupies the site of the Inti Kancha; some of the stone walls of the original temple were incorporated into the colonial structure and are still visible.

Rays of the sun temple

From these records we learn that the city was divided into two unequal halves: one described as *hanan* ("upstream"), to the northwest, and the other as *hurin* ("downstream"), to the southeast. These halves were themselves each divided into two unequal quadrants known as *suyus*. Each of these quadrants emanating from Cuzco was further split until a total of 40 (some say 41) lines radiated from the Inti Kancha, the temple of the sun god (or the centre of the adjacent plaza).

These conceptual lines or rays were known as *ceques*, and sacred sites called *huacas* were strung along them like beads. The 328 *huacas* ranged from natural sites, such as rocks, springs or trees, to structures such as statues or temples. Each *huaca* was tended by people living along the *ceque*. The locations of the *ceques* have been forgotten, but some researchers suppose that each *ceque* was precisely aligned to an astronomical event on the horizon – solar, lunar or stellar. Just as the king claimed kinship with the sun, so other creatures and occupations had their own earthly ancestors and celestial patrons, and although some *ceques* were probably aligned to significant astronomical events, many were likely to have been laid out with mundane matters in mind. There is even evidence that some *ceques* were not straight but zigzagged across the landscape.

Several chroniclers mentioned towers on the hills around Cuzco, which were the focus of ceremonial races that followed the movements of the sun. Of the remains of 19 *huaca* sites around Cuzco investigated by Steven Gullberg in research published in 2010, 4 were found to have alignments to sunrise or sunset on the solstices, equinoxes or days when the sun was at its zenith (directly overhead) – February 13 and October 30 at this latitude.

CROSS-QUARTER DAYS

In temperate and, especially, arctic latitudes, equinoxes may be seen as dividing the year into two halves, one of light and one of darkness, and the solstices mark the extremes of these halves, splitting the year into four roughly equal parts. These are the quarters of the year, which are strongly associated with Neolithic and Bronze Age megalithic complexes. The cross-quarter days lie at the middle of each quarter, giving a total of eight milestones around the year. These are mainly associated with the Iron Age Celtic calendar and are celebrated by modern Wiccans as the eight sabbats.

The introduction of the cross-quarter days is believed to mark a change of climate in Britain that brought increasingly wet weather. This made growing crops more difficult and unpredictable and led to greater reliance on pastoral farming, with livestock becoming more valuable. Many Celtic myths are based around the movements of livestock, and the cross-quarter days are thought to reflect these new seasonal activities.

Candlemas (1–2 February; the Celtic day began at sunset) is thought to have marked the start of lambing and was a homely festival associated with birth. Beltane (31 April–1 May) marked the movement of cattle away from the home settlement to summer pastures further afield. Lammas (1–2 August) was when the livestock fairs were held. And Samhain (31 October–1 November), at the onset of winter, was when livestock that couldn't be fed through the barren months ahead were slaughtered.

The Iron Age Celts did not build stone circles or even reuse existing ones, so we lack any great megalithic monuments that clearly incorporate astronomical alignments. Consequently, very few archaeoastronomical sites are known from this period.

Stannon stone circle

Even though there is little academic support for alignments to cross-quarter days at Neolithic or Bronze Age monuments, these dates are still celebrated at the stone circle of Stannon on the west of Bodmin Moor, near Camelford in Cornwall, England. This irregular circle is an average of 138ft (42m) in diameter and its tallest stone is around $3^1/_2$ft (1.1m) high.

About $1^1/_4$ miles (2km) northeast of this site is Rough Tor, which appears as a rounded mound on the horizon, with a distinctive semicircular gap right at the top of the mound. The once impressive view of this tor has been marred by the unsympathetic positioning of a spoil heap from nearby china clay works, but the notch is still visible from the stone circle.

One of the tallest of the stones at Stannon is roughly triangular and its apex presents a similar profile to the shape of Rough Tor, with which it is apparently aligned. Some people suppose that when the stone was erected, probably early in the Bronze Age around 2400 BCE, its apex may have had a notch that has since weathered away. Pagans visit Stannon stone circle to watch the May Day sun rise from the hollow of Rough Tor, a spectacle that is repeated during the Lammas festival at the beginning of August, as the sun swings around its annual cycle.

Marking the cross-quarter days From Stannon stone circle the sun may be seen rising from the side of Rough Tor at Beltane (May Day) and Lammas.

THE *SAROEAK* BASQUE COUNTRY

Scattered across the north of Spain, and also in southwestern France although mostly found in the Basque Country, are hundreds of clusters of stone boundary markers, each set positioned in a carefully constructed pattern. Eight stones mark the limits of an area that is called, in the Basque language, a *saroe* (plural *saroeak*). We may imagine these standing stones as marking the corners of an imaginary octagon, but we do not know what shape (if any) their creators had in mind when they constructed them. However, precisely positioned at the centre of each *saroe* is a carved, flat-topped stone.

Saroeak seem to occur in two sizes: the larger has a diameter of around 1,050ft (320m), while the smaller *saroeak* are about half that size. The stones

Central stone Radiating lines on the central pillar align to the cardinal directions, and to the other stones in the *saroe* at Altzusta in northeast Spain.

themselves are modest compared with the scale of their megalithic forebears, the central pillars often only around 20in (50cm) high. These central stones are incised on the upper surface with straight, radiating lines – sometimes four, usually eight and sometimes 16. These lines are equally spaced and accurately aligned to the cardinal directions, and also point directly to the stones that surround them.

There are numerous *saroeak* in the area around the popular coastal resort of Donostia-San Sebastián, which is the capital city of Gipuzkoa, a mountainous province in the Basque Autonomous Community, around 9 miles (15km) from the border with France. Here, nearly 40 *saroeak* have been found in an area of just 15 square miles (40 square km). These include some *saroeak* near the town of Urnieta, which have been excavated. Deposits of burnt wood around the central stone, which is sometimes called the ash stone, allowed archaeologists using

Celestial orientation The circumpolar stars may have been used to align this *saroe* at Altzusta with the cardinal directions.

a carbon-dating technique to date the charcoal to around 200 CE.

It seems that *saroeak* were primarily used to organize communal grazing for animals, although there are records recounting their use as meeting places and as spaces for religious rites. Although other ancient monuments, such as prehistoric tombs, may be sited close outside the edge of a *saroe*, none have been found inside.

The careful orientation of these groups of stones must have been achieved through astronomical observation because magnetic compasses were not available for a millennium after the ash deposits were made at Urnieta. Watching stars circling the north celestial pole was one way to have oriented a *saroe*, but it is also possible that the sun was used to determine the cardinal directions. Such alignments may be achieved by observing the rising and setting points of the sun at the equinoxes or perhaps simply by noting the direction of the shortest shadow cast by a pole planted vertically in the ground.

The use by the *saroeak* of the four cardinal points interspersed with subdivisions is suggestive of the way the year was first quartered by the equinoxes and solstices, and of how these divisions were halved again by the cross-quarter days of the Celtic era. Whatever system was used to create their orientation, *saroeak* present a notable mystery. Perhaps this systematic demarcation of the land was an attempt to bring a sense of cosmic order down from the skies and to institute some measure of symbolic control over the chaos of creation.

SOLAR MYSTERIES OF CENTRAL AMERICA

The indigenous Maya culture of Central America has its roots around 2000 BCE, and reached its classical period of greatest sophistication between 250 and 900 CE. The ruins of its great cities reveal a wealth of fascinating archaeoastronomical features. Many of these sites seem to embody ideas enshrined in the unique Maya calendar that became globally famous in the run-up to 2012 CE.

As we shall see, the astronomical architecture of the Maya ranges from simple alignments to zenith tubes – strange, vertical wells with observation chambers at the bottom. Some vast ceremonial complexes appear to have been deliberately sited where a number of astronomical alignments converged, as if "X" marked the spot.

There is undoubtedly much more to be learned about these enigmatic, ancient almanacs written in stone, but what has already been decoded offers a tantalizing glimpse into a society in which knowledge of astronomy was profoundly revered.

Mesoamerican calendars

The Maya were excellent astronomers and their observations allowed them to determine the *haab*, the 365-day solar year. Primarily related to agriculture, this was divided into 18 months of 20 days each, giving 360 days – the remaining five days lay outside this regular calendar, and were considered perilous.

But the Maya and many other ancient cultures of Mesoamerica also used another calendar, the *tzolk'in*

TIME SOLIDIFIED

The impressive Aztec sun stone is 12ft (3.6m) in diameter and weighs 24 tons (24.4 tonnes). It was positioned on top of the main temple in Tenochtitlan – capital of the Aztec Empire – where Mexico City's cathedral now stands. The stone was buried by Spanish invaders, and rediscovered in 1790.

In the centre is the sun, principal god of all Mesoamerican cultures. Around him are four rectangles, each depicting a god that ended one of the four previous ages (destroyed by jaguars, hurricanes, fire falling from the sky and flood). Between the gods at top and bottom are images of the four cardinal directions, while claws either side of the sun hold human hearts to indicate the necessity of sacrifice to placate the gods and keep the world running smoothly.

Around this central group is a ring of symbols for each of the 20 named days, running anticlockwise from the top. The 18 months of 20 days give the 360 days of the *xiuhpohualli* (the equivalent of the Maya *haab*), and the remaining five that complete the cycle of 365 days are symbolized by dots inside this ring – thought to relate to the traumatic days of sacrifice.

The eight large V shapes represent the sun's rays and divide the calendar into the cardinal and intercardinal directions. In a square at the very top are 13 dots and the symbol of *acatl* (a reed), which give the date that the carving was finished – 1479 CE.

THE *TZOLK'IN*

20 named days cycle	1–13-day cycle
Caiman (*Imix*)	1 ....
Wind (*Ik*)	2 ....
House (*Akbal*)	3 ....
Lizard (*Kan*)	4 ....
Snake (*Chikchan*)	5 ....
Death (*Kimi*)	6 ....
Deer (*Manik*)	7 ....
Rabbit (*Lamat*)	8 ....
Water (*Muluc*)	9 ....
Dog (*Ok*)	10 ....
Monkey (*Chuwen*)	11 ....
Grass (*Eb*)	12 ....
Reed (*Ben*)	13 ....
Jaguar (*Ix*)	1 ....
Eagle (*Men*)	2 ....
Vulture (*Kib*)	3 ....
Earthquake (*Kaban*)	4 ....
Flint knife (*Etznab*)	5 ....
Rain (*Kawac*)	6 ....
Flower (*Ahau*)	7 ....

Each day of the 260-day *tzolk'in* had a name that was composed of two parts. The first was a name from a list of 20 things relevant to daily life, and the second was a number from 1 to 13. These two sequences ran alongside each other from "Caiman 1", the list of names or numbers restarting whenever the list's end was reached (see *left* for the *tzolkin's* first 20 days). In this way, all 260 days had a unique name, the last day being "Flower 13". This artwork (*below*) shows how the two sequences intersect to create the *tzolk'in*, and how the *tzolk'in* itself intersects with the 360-day *tun* year.

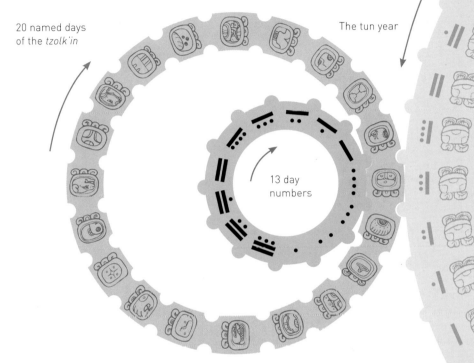

20 named days of the *tzolk'in*

The tun year

13 day numbers

– a 260-day sacred calendar, which consisted of 20 named days and 13 numbered days that intermesh like cogs (see above).

The *tzolk'in* harmonizes with the *haab* after 73 and 52 repetitions respectively. This 52-year count is known as the Calendar Round.

The Long Count
The Maya also used the Long Count, as follows:
• 360 days = 1 year or *tun*
• 400 years = 1 *bak'tun*
• 13 *bak'tun* = 1 Great Cycle of 1,872,000 days (some 5,125 solar years).

Many Mesoamerican cultures believed the world routinely ended at the end of each Great Cycle and was reborn at the start of the next. The last Great Cycle began *c.* 11 August 3114 BCE. Some reckoned that it would end on 21 December 2012 (the calculation is complex because year length changes slightly over the centuries) – hence the abundance of apocalyptic tales. The Maya actually dealt with even greater time spans in their calculations, and the Western Tablet of the Temple of the Inscriptions at Palenque refers to a date that equates with 4772 CE. Clearly, if the Maya happily noted dates so far into the future, they probably did not believe the world was going to end in 2012.

TEOTIHUACÁN MEXICO

Thirty miles northeast of Mexico City lies the massive, ancient city of Teotihuacán, now a World Heritage site. Founded between 200 and 100 BCE, by c. 1 CE the city covered an area of 8 square miles (20 square km). At its height in c. 450 CE it was one of the largest cities in the world, certainly the largest in the Americas. It had a population well in excess of 100,000, its inhabitants dwelling in more than 2,000 apartment compounds.

The people who built Teotihuacán are a mystery to us today, but we know the city was a thriving metropolis for over 600 years before vanishing from history in the 6th century CE. The Aztecs rediscovered the site in the 14th century CE, and believed it to be the cradle of civilization. They called the settlement Teotihuacán, which is usually translated as "the birthplace of the gods", although the Nahuatl scholar Thelma D. Sullivan translates it as "place of those who have the road of the gods".

The city's ceremonial centre contains palaces, plazas, a temple of Quetzalcoatl, the Pyramid of the Sun and the Pyramid of the Moon – this latter being at the north end of a straight thoroughfare some 3 miles (5km) long, now called the Avenue of the Dead.

The Pyramid of the Sun appears to have been the earliest structure built at the site and, in conformity with a frequently observed tradition in Central America, has an alignment to the mountain that is the source of the local water supply. Here, the relevant mountain, to the north of the site, is Cerro Gordo, its peak faced by the north side of the Pyramid of the Sun.

The names of the Pyramid of the Sun and the Pyramid of the Moon are not original to this site, and it is widely assumed the Aztecs named them in reference to their legends, rather than for any intrinsic astronomical properties of the structures. However, the Pyramid of the Sun at least may be aptly named.

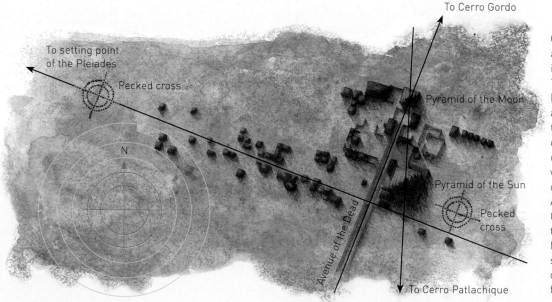

City grid A Pleiades alignment was noted in the 1980s based on "pecked cross" petroglyphs (concentric rings with a cross that was taken to indicate the site's orientation), but the finding of pecked cross petroglyphs without alignments has cast doubt on this famous line. A suggested alignment to Cerro Patlachique through the Pyramids of the Sun and Moon is not perfectly north–south, and it, too, is usually dismissed nowadays as a false positive.

Grand design The view from the Pyramid of the Moon down the Avenue of the Dead to Cerro Patlachique, with the Pyramid of the Sun on the left. So many hills encircle Teotihuacán that we have to be careful not to identify false positive alignments.

The Pyramid of the Sun

The Pyramid of the Sun is the largest at Teotihuacán. Its alignment to the sacred landscape of the water-source mountain is not quite north–south, but about 15° east of north, a feature that is broadly replicated elsewhere in Central America, and which has puzzled many researchers. An analysis of the astronomical alignments of the Pyramid of the Sun published in 2000 by Ivan Sprajc offers an intriguing insight into this mystery, by studying the sides of the pyramid at right angles to those facing the mountain.

If the builders of the pyramid in the 1st century CE had stood at ground level at the middle of the site where the pyramid would be built and kept the mountain to their left, they would have faced sunrise on 11 February and 29 October, and faced away from sunset on 30 April and 13 August – the latter being the date on which the Maya believed the world began. The interval between the recurring sunrises (and sunsets) is 120 days, a period of great significance to the sacred *tzolk'in* calendar (see page 107). These important alignments would have governed the positioning of the sides of the pyramid.

After the structure was built, and the viewing platform at the top came into use, the increase in elevation from ground level would have given a slightly different view of the surrounding horizon – and although the sunrise alignment would have remained

intact, the sunset alignments would have been off by a day (29 April and 14 August). The result appears to have been the modification of the observation platform and eventually the entire pyramid, with its sides skewed slightly so that the setting sun again aligned with the original dates.

Key sunsets The Pyramid of the Sun may have been altered to restore its alignments to sunset on 30 April and 13 August – the latter date considered the day of the world's beginning.

In such mountainous terrain, finding a site where the horizon provided a single alignment to this set of sunrise and sunset dates (and that was also perpendicular to the local sacred mountain) would have been enormously difficult, indicating the value of the alignments to the city's founders. The importance of the alignment to Cerro Gordo is shown by its adoption by other key buildings at the site, including the impressive Avenue of the Dead and its terminus, the Pyramid of the Moon.

OUT OF DARKNESS, INTO THE LIGHT

A cave directly beneath the Pyramid of the Sun may also have influenced its architects. A long subterranean passageway runs westward leading to a four-lobed cavern under the centre of the pyramid. The four chambers may well have symbolized the four cardinal directions, and it is likely that the natural cave was augmented by human hands to enhance the correspondence for ritual purposes (some people suppose it was entirely man-made).

Caves have been sacred to many peoples throughout time, as portals to another world and as symbolic wombs from which spirits, deities and ancestor humans emerge. The entrance to this cave faces the setting point of the Pleiades, as does the pyramid itself. At Teotihuacán, the first appearance of the Pleiades star cluster in the eastern sky before dawn (its heliacal rising) coincided with the day of the sun's zenith, when the sun passed directly overhead – the time when the sun god most closely approached his people. These stellar alignments may have been only supplementary to the main reason for the site being chosen, but they could at least have provided powerful corroboration for the decision.

Cave

ELEVATION OF PYRAMID AND CAVE

PLAN OF CAVE

Modified passage

ALTAVISTA MEXICO

At the Tropic of Cancer, the sun reaches its zenith on just one day of the year, the summer solstice, after which it sinks inexorably down the sky once more (a phenomenon mirrored in the southern hemisphere, half a year later, at the Tropic of Capricorn). At noon on this day the sun is directly overhead and floods the landscape with hard bright light in which upright objects cast no shadows. To many Mesoamericans, believing themselves to be descendants of the sun (and for whom the sun was the principal god), this would have been momentous.

Altavista (or Alta Vista), in the Mexican state of Zacatecas, is also known as Chalchihuites, named after the town 4 miles (6.5km) to the east. Construction appears to have begun in around 315 CE by the same culture that built Teotihuacán. But by c. 1050, Altavista was deserted. It sits defenceless on an arid plain more than 1¼ miles (2km) from the nearest river, and is very hot in summer and cold in winter. The site's potential for astronomical alignments, coupled with its position on the Tropic of Cancer, offer the best explanations for why a settlement grew in an inhospitable location.

From Altavista, the sharp peak of Picacho Montoso, around 7 miles (11km) to the east, marks the equinoctial sunrise, and the shoulders of the same mountainous horizon are flanked on each side by the rising sun on the solstices. This was also the water-source peak, making its direction doubly sacred.

Several of the buildings at the site are aligned to the equinox, unusually in Mesoamerica, including the Hall of Columns, which may have been the first structure to be built here. It contains a series of pillared corridors oriented to the pinnacle of Picacho Montoso, so that as the equinoctial sun rises over the peak, the shadow thrown by the front pillars falls directly on to the pillars behind. The main temple at the site is the Sun Temple, also oriented to the equinoxes through its eastern and western corners, with a ceremonial walkway along the same alignment.

Solar crosses

On a plateau on El Chapin, a hill around 4 miles (7km) almost due south of Altavista, is a ceremonial observation point. Carved in the rock are two "pecked crosses" about 4ft (1.2m) in diameter, each composed of two circles containing a cross with one arm pointing to the pinnacle of Picacho Montoso, over which the midsummer sun can be seen to rise. The complex thus allows for a variety of solar observations, and no doubt other alignments are waiting to be discovered.

Chasing away night At equinoctial sunrise, a dramatic play of light and shadow took place in the Hall of Columns (visible in the background of this photograph).

XOCHICALCO MEXICO

The Maya ceremonial and ritual centre of Xochicalco dates from around 800 CE, and is a World Heritage site. It lies some 45 miles (70km) south of Mexico City. The site includes a natural cave enlarged to a length of almost 65ft and width of 40ft (20–12m). From this cave a vertical tube 16ft long and 16in wide (5 x 0.4m) was excavated so that on those dates when the sun passed directly overhead at noon, a brilliant shaft of light would penetrate the darkness.

In the Tropics, the noon sun passes directly overhead on two days of the year. The dates vary with distance from the equator, where the sun is overhead at the equinoxes. Precisely at the Tropics of Cancer and Capricorn, the zenith coincides with the summer solstice (and occurs just once a year). Zenith tubes are so-called because they are aligned vertically upward, aiming at the highest, "zenith" point of the sky. They also point to the zenith during the night, and may have been used for observing stars or even the moon.

As we have seen, the *tzolk'in* (see page 107) consisted of 260 days – a good approximation to the length of human gestation. At Xochicalco, the sun

Hilltop city The city of Xochicalco, which may once have housed 20,000 people, was destroyed in around 900 CE.

passes directly overhead at noon on 15 May, and again on 29 July. When it does so it shines into the cave as a full circle of light. For some days either side of those dates, some sunlight reaches into the cave. The top of this zenith tube is ringed with stones giving the orifice a distinctive heptagonal shape, and these stones could have been moved to fine-tune the amount of light entering the tube. The dates on which sunlight first and last entered the cave were 52 days either side of the June solstice, so the cave – like the human foetus – was sealed from the light of day for 260 days.

MONTE ALBÁN

The Observatory at Monte Albán (see page 205) is oriented so that a line extended from its pointed tip, through the middle of its opposite wall, will arrive at the steps of Building P and pass over the top of a zenith tube there. This line continued toward the heliacal rising of the star Capella, marking the date of the sun's zenith passage.

The mouth of the zenith tube is located about halfway up the steps of Building P, from where the tube plunges 5ft (1.5m) into an enclosed compartment. This small room would have been flooded with a circular shaft of light on the two dates at which the sun passed directly overhead. Unlike the zenith tube at Xochicalco, however, direct sunlight light would enter this chamber fully 65 days before and after the June solstice. The significance of this time span, if any, has yet to be satisfactorily determined, although 65 contains precisely five cycles of 13 days, one complete cycle more than the four cycles at Xochicalco.

Zenith tube Sunlight is funnelled to an underground chamber at Xochicalco, fully illuminating it on just two days of the year.

PALENQUE MEXICO

The ruins of the Maya city of Palenque are located some 80 miles (130km) south of the modern city of Ciudad del Carmen. Poised between the forested foothills of the Tumbalá mountains to the south and the coastal plain to the north, this World Heritage site seems almost to hover between two worlds – the wild realm of the jaguar in the lush jungle, and the tamed plain whose fertile agriculture allowed the settlement to thrive.

Archaeological evidence suggests that the area has been occupied since *c.* 300 BCE, with most buildings constructed between 700 and 1000 CE. Unlike many Maya sites, Palenque was served by numerous water sources, including the Otulum stream that flows through the centre of the city. As collection and storage of water were not a priority here, the inhabitants had more time for cultural pursuits.

Cuckoo in the nest

The steeply stepped pyramidal Temple of the Inscriptions is named for the wealth of informative and intricate carvings it contains. Deep within, at its base, is the tomb of a famous Maya king – K'inich Janahb Pakal. He reigned for 68 years, a period in which learning flourished and many of the city's most important buildings were constructed. Construction of his tomb began around 675 CE.

The sarcophagus cover has been one of the Maya culture's best-known artefacts since it featured in Erich von Däniken's book, *Chariots of the Gods*. In his book, published in 1968, von Däniken declared the central figure of the intricate stone sculpture to be a depiction of a space traveller. In the years of the moon landings, people became used to imagining astronauts huddled in the nose cone of a vertical rocket, and the

Spiritual journey (*Opposite*) The central, seated figure on the cover of Pakal's tomb is thought to be voyaging to take his place in the afterlife.

Solar orientation (*Right*) A range of solar alignments have been found in the central area of Palenque, and more probably remain to be discovered.

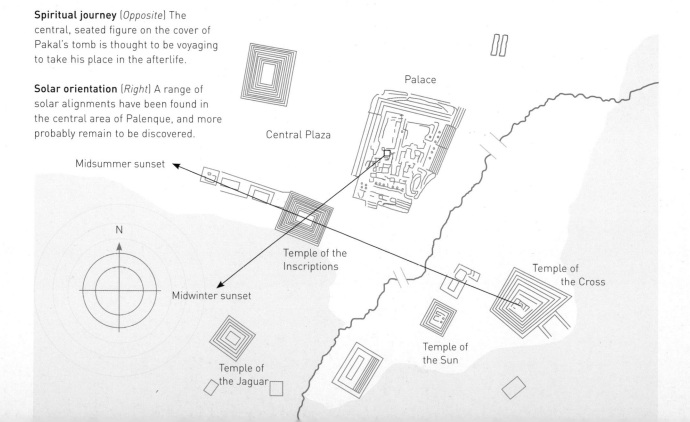

Midsummer sunset

Central Plaza

Palace

N

Midwinter sunset

Temple of the Inscriptions

Temple of the Cross

Temple of the Sun

Temple of the Jaguar

similarity with the stone image caught the public imagination. The tomb's cover became an important (if not infamous) exhibit in the debate about whether Earth had been visited, and perhaps even colonized, by extraterrestrials.

Rocket ships from outer space are still the stuff of science fiction, but Däniken was probably right about the idea that Pakal was making a voyage to another world. This iconic image most likely represents the king journeying into the underworld to unite with his deified ancestors and become a god himself.

Like many of the great ancient cultures, the Mesoamericans perceived the world as having an axis around which the universe revolved. This world axis – *axis mundi* – was seen in the Far East as a sacred mountain, such as Mount Meru; in Teutonic Europe it was a world tree called Yggdrasil. In Mesoamerica, a world tree, sometimes called Yaxché, was literally central to their cosmology. Yaxché had three parts: the upper realm, where the gods dwelt and where the stars and planets held their course; the middle realm, where humans lived; and the lower realm, where spirits went after the death of the body (and from where, very often, they were born anew). It is a highly stylized version of this world tree that we see bearing Lord Pakal to his destiny in the afterlife.

Solar alignments at Palenque

Various structures at Palenque have been shown to be aligned with solar events. Unusually, it appears that there are even alignments *inside* some of the buildings at Palenque: their internal walls may have been positioned to allow the interplay of illumination and shadow on highly significant dates. This seems to be particularly true of the large building known as the Palace, which contains a variety of dwelling quarters, interior patios, subterranean passages and even a four-storey tower.

Temple of the Sun The entrance hall of this temple is penetrated to varying degrees by the rising sun at its zenith, at the equinoxes and at the solstices, creating an accurate solar calendar.

Much of the play of light and shadow may have been intended to offer convenient demarcations of the 365-day year, dividing it into a 105-day agricultural cycle and the 260-day sacred cycle of the *tzolk'in* (see pages 106–7).

A calendar of light and shade

Anthropologist and Latin American art historian Susan Milbraith noted a T-shaped window on the west side of the tower at the Palace, through which a beam of sunlight is cast onto an oblique wall from 30 April to 12 August. This illumination lasts for precisely 105 days, with the light reaching its maximum width on the summer solstice. For the other 260 days of the year, this wall is in darkness.

A 2008 paper by Chance Coughenour (then a student at the University of North Carolina) reports that scholar Alonso Mendez discovered that the western walls of the Palace's prosaically named Houses C and D face sunset on the dates of the sun's zenith (9 May and 2 August at this latitude).

Centre of Maya culture Palenque, while modest in size, has some of the finest examples of Maya stone craftsmanship. Among its grand buildings is a wealth of hieroglyphic inscriptions telling the story of this important site.

An observer on the top of the Palace tower (or, perhaps more properly, from the house designated E inside the Palace, where Pakal was crowned) would have seen the winter solstice sun set over the centre of the Temple of Inscriptions – at the entrance to the underground chamber leading to the tomb of King Pakal himself. The sun also sets over the Temple of the Inscriptions at midsummer, when viewed from the top of the Temple of the Cross, which was built by Pakal's son, Chan B'ahlaml. The "cross" in its name is an explorer's reference to the shape of the world tree depicted in a carved panel at the top of the temple.

Temple of the Sun

Palenque's Temple of the Sun is aligned so that the rising sun at the winter solstice shines into the entrance, but only reaches halfway to the rear wall.

At sunrise on the days when the sun is at the zenith, light again penetrates the entrance way, but this time its path is blocked by the corner of an internal wall. At the equinox and summer solstice, however, sunlight fills the entrance all the way to the rear wall, where it forms a narrow shaft. Such solar alignments can track the course of the year with precision.

Alonso Mendez also noted that the diagonal axis of the Temple of the Sun is aligned to the rising and setting major lunar standstill (see pages 134–5). Only the central part of Palenque has been investigated; it has been speculated that the entire site extends for about 5 square miles (13 square km), so there is still much to discover.

SOLAR DEITIES AND MYTHOLOGY

The sun's annual progress from spring to summer, through autumn to winter, can be seen as a natural mirror of the human "seasons" of youth, maturity, middle age and old age. In this analogy, the sun's adventure ended in death on the winter solstice. But that date was actually the turning point of the year, and immediately afterwards the sun began its new journey back to vigour – reborn. In much the same way that the New Year's celebration in the West marks both the end of one year and the beginning of the next, all that the sun possessed at its death at midwinter is given to the new sun at its birth the next morning.

The birthday of Sol Invictus ("the unconquered sun") was celebrated on 25 December in the Roman Empire in 354 CE, and possibly much earlier. That day was the traditional date of the winter solstice, which had been established in 46 BCE when the Roman dictator Julius Caesar reformed the calendar. Although the Julian calendar had already begun to slip out of synchronization with the solstices, the date

Rayed halo Sol Invictus, shown here (*top*) in a 3rd-century BCE Roman marble relief, is adorned with a halo similar to that of the sun god Shamash in a Mesopotamian sculpture from around the 2nd–3rd centuries CE (*bottom*).

remained associated with the solstice in the Roman religious calendar.

The cult of Sol, the sun god, had been raised to one of the most powerful of all the Roman official cults by the emperor Aurelian in 274 CE, and remained so until Christianity ousted the entire pagan pantheon. However, Christian theologians apparently recognized the powerful symbolism of the solar cult, and adopted 25 December as the date of the miraculous nativity of their own dying Lord, whose advent was hailed as ushering mankind from spiritual darkness into a new dawn of undying life. The Church fathers even dubbed Christ as Sol Iustitiae – "sun of justice". The gift giving that is such a noted feature of the festival of Christmas recalls the dying sun's legacy of the world itself, bequeathed in trust to his young successor.

The Roman sun god Sol was often portrayed as riding across the heavens in a chariot drawn by four horses (see page 49), and the chariot-borne sun god is a theme common to many Indo-European mythologies, including the stories of Helios, the Greek antecedent of Sol and the brother of Selene, the moon goddess. Many of the attributes of Helios were taken over by Apollo in the 5th century BCE, including his chariot and rayed halo.

Race of sun and moon In this *c.* 1612 painting by Guido Reni, Hippomenes (the sun) throws an apple to distract Atalante (the moon), allowing him to win the race and her hand in marriage.

The unmistakable power of the sun has ensured that it features in mythology the world over. The following handful of examples illustrate some diverse ideas about this natural wonder, especially those that seek to explain its behaviour (eclipse myths are described in the lunar chapter, on pages 150–51).

Atalante and Hippomenes

The lovely Atalante was raised in the mountains by a she-bear, and she grew up wild and free, a virgin huntress. She vowed that no man would win her unless he first beat her in a running race, and that any suitor who lost the race would also lose his life. Many men tried, and died.

The goddess of love, Aphrodite, saw that for love to be consummated, her intervention was required. She helped Atalante's next would-be lover, Hippomenes (Melanion in other versions), by giving him three gold apples. Over the course of the race, whenever Atalante threatened to outdistance him, Hippomenes threw down one of the apples. When Atalante stooped to collect it, Hippomenes surged ahead. And so, although the race was perilously close, she did not beat him.

Some modern scholars see this myth as a means of synchronizing the cycles of sun and moon. After eight solar years, the moon's phases will have passed through 99 complete cycles. During this period there are 12 full moons in each year, except for three years when there are 13 – these extra three full moons are symbolized by the three apples.

At the end of the race, the moon's phase recurs on the same calendar date as it did when the race began (almost: the moon lags behind by 1.5 days, representing Atalante's narrow defeat). It is this reunion that, according to some scholars, is celebrated in the marriage of Atalante and Hippomenes.

Amun-Re

In the ancient Egyptian city of Thebes, Amun was the supreme creator god, and all other deities were mere manifestations of his power (a position of divine authority that borders on monotheism). Amun stood aloof and hidden: he was not even revealed in his creation, but actively veiled by it.

Elsewhere in Egypt, many of his powers were attributed to the sun god, Re, and after the Theban rulers invaded the north of the realm and established the New Kingdom in *c.* 1540 BCE, the two deities merged into the figure of Amun-Re, combining the sun's dual aspects of the hidden and the revealed – night and day.

In his hidden role, which began once the sun disappeared below the horizon, the sun god travelled through the underworld, which was populated with all manner of nightmare creatures. As he passed through the watery underworld – the Duat – on board a ship, he was assisted by powerful allies including the 12 "Ladies of the Boat" who guided him through the perils of the 12 hours of the night. Eventually, the sun god approached the eastern horizon where, at the dawn of a new day, he was reborn from between the thighs of the sky goddess, Nut.

This everyday miracle of the sun's apparent annihilation, suffering and resurrection sheds a timeless light on religions based on the promise of life after death.

Shamash

In the middle of the 3rd millennium BCE, the Mesopotamian god of the sun, of justice and of revealing the future was Shamash ("sun"), son of the moon god, Sin. This family relationship made the sun subordinate to the moon, which is unusual and may be a legacy from earlier, nomadic times as it was only with the advent of agriculture that the sun became vitally important, primarily for the growing and ripening of crops. During the night, Shamash drove through the underworld in his chariot, returning to his rising place in preparation for the day ahead.

Surya

The idea of a solar chariot is an enduring motif, and is memorably reiterated in the magnificent temple of Hindu sun god Surya, at Konark in Odisha, India. Constructed to resemble the god's chariot, this 13th-century temple has 24 wheels, each with eight spokes, and is drawn by seven sculpted horses. The temple

The falcon-headed god The sun god Re, in his bird-headed manifestation Re-Horakhty ("Re who is Horus of the two horizons"), emits rays in the form of lily wreaths in this Egyptian painting from the 22nd Dynasty (*c.* 945–715 BCE).

Apollo's Chariot This work by Odilon Redon (*c*.1908) depicts the Greek sun god borne across the sky in his chariot.

is aligned to the east so the rays of the equinoctial sunrise enter it through its main entrance.

Sunna (Sól)

Sunna (Sól in Old Norse), the German sun goddess, was the sister of Mani, the moon. She too drove a chariot across the sky and was described in the *Poetic Edda* as "lovely wheel" and "everglow". The *Poetic Edda* was written in Iceland in the 13th century CE, as was the *Prose Edda*, and both drew on a body of bardic verse already hundreds of years old – the repertoire of Scandinavian minstrels. In the *Prose Edda* both Sunna and her brother Mani are described as moving so fast because they are forever chased by two wolves that will eventually catch and devour them at the ending of the world – Ragnarök.

Suns of the five ages

The Aztecs had five sun deities corresponding to the five ages of the world: the first was Tezcatlipoca ("smoking mirror"), the second Quetzalcoatl ("feathered serpent"), the third Tlaloc ("of the earth") and the fourth was a goddess – Chalchiuhtlicue ("lady of the jade skirts").

The sun god of the present age was chosen from two contestants who had to sacrifice themselves in a fire. One was Tecciztecatl, who was wealthy and powerful, and the other was Nanauatl, who was modest and humble. Nanauatl leapt straight into the fire, but Tecciztecatl was fearful and drew back. Eventually, though, Tecciztecatl followed his rival into the flames – but the world could not survive with two suns, so the other gods threw a rabbit into Tecciztecatl's face, blocking the heat. He became the moon, with the rabbit still visible in the markings on its face. This saved the current age – Nahui Ollin ("earthquakes") – from being destroyed too early.

All these Aztec deities required sacrifice – human and otherwise – to keep the sun running on course and to maintain the stability of the universe.

THE MOON – MIRROR TO OUR SOUL

The moon governs the tides and it is said to have power over female fertility, yet as the bright orb wanes it seems to become weaker and weaker. But at the very moment it appears most irrelevant, the moon can eclipse the sun, plunging day into night. There is wonder, raw beauty and romance in its changing phases. The moon reigns supreme over our world of dreams.

MAPPING THE MOON

The moon has inspired many captivating myths and dreams, and it is even said to be powerful enough to induce lunacy – a word derived from *luna*, Latin for moon. Despite some anecdotal evidence, proof of madness caused by lunar phases is elusive – as intangible as moonbeams themselves. But we all experience life's roller-coaster of changing moods and fortunes that the ever-shifting phases of the moon represent.

The moon can act as a mirror, reflecting what is in our minds. Just as the famous inkblot or Rorschach test is used by psychologists to reveal what is in our thoughts, the full moon, with all its bright scars of meteorite craters and dark, frozen seas of volcanic lava, has always conjured images in our mind's eye. Our brains are hard-wired to recognize patterns, especially the shape of the human face, and we can see them almost anywhere, including on the surface of the moon – a phenomenon known as pareidolia. As these moon images exist only in the mind of the observer, when the imagination gets to work there is a vast array of pictures that can be revealed. Here are a few of the better-known ones.

Man in the moon

The whole disc of the full moon is often seen as a face, with two large dark eyes separated by a splodge (although some people see this splodge as one of the two eyes) and a dark open mouth below. There is the suggestion of a nose in the middle. This is perhaps the most basic, and therefore possibly the oldest, of the lunar images.

Woman in the moon

In Maori legend, a young woman called Rona was one night abducted by the moon while she was walking to fetch water in a gourd. As the moon lifted her from the ground she grabbed a tree, but to no avail. Rona can be seen on the moon still clinging to the tree, with the fallen gourd at her feet.

First quarter

Full moon

New moon

Last quarter

Phases of the moon As the Moon orbits the Earth in a monthly cycle, the shadow cast upon it by the curve of the Earth changes shape, to create the lunar phases from new to full moon and back again. The red lines indicate the Earth-facing hemispheres at each point in the cycle.

Origin of myth The moon's markings have always inspired us to create stories about our nearest neighbour in the solar system.

The same lunar contours, edged with shadow, had a different interpretation in Europe, where they were said to represent an old woman (or old man) carrying a great bundle of twigs, accompanied by a dog.

A relatively recent addition to the lunar gallery is the Western image of a woman's head seen in profile, gazing to the left. Her pale skin contrasts with her dark hair neatly arranged on top of her head.

Hare of immortality

Ancient Chinese folklore tells of a hare in the moon that grinds herbs for an elixir of immortality. This long-eared figure can be seen sitting on the left of the moon, hunched over a mortar.

YIN YANG SYMBOL

Not all lunar images are best viewed when the moon is full. The resemblance to the yin yang or *taijitu* ("supreme ultimate symbol") is most clearly seen some three or four days after full moon. Although this Chinese symbol is medieval, the idea that it can be seen in the moon seems to have been put forward only in recent years. Whether this was a genuinely new perception or a rediscovery of an old tradition is a matter for debate, but the moon is renowned for unendingly waxing and waning in light and darkness – characteristics that reflect the ever-changing interplay of yin and yang.

NEWGRANGE, KNOWTH AND DOWTH IRELAND

The three Neolithic passage graves clustering in the bend of a river about 26 miles (42km) north of Dublin include Newgrange, which is internationally famous for its solar alignment to the winter solstice sunrise (see pages 74–7). However, these tombs, known collectively as Brú na Bóinne and dating to around 3200 BCE, appear also to have lunar significance.

From the circular mound of Newgrange, the similarly shaped mounds of Dowth and Knowth lie to the northeast and northwest respectively, and author Martin Brennan has proposed that they are aligned with the rising and setting moon respectively at the time of its minor standstill (see pages 134–5). As these tombs are all situated on natural hills, some regard any alignment between them as necessarily accidental, but in view of the known solar alignments that have been found at these sites, it would be imprudent to dismiss out of hand this pair of alignments to such important lunar events.

Unlike at Carnac, where the sheer number of monuments and the size and topography of the area makes any correlation problematic, at Brú na Bóinne the three great mounds of Newgrange, Knowth and Dowth are within sight of each other, and it is entirely plausible that the site as a whole may have been developed in a way that was designed to create complex astronomical interrelationships.

Knowth

The kerbstones that surround the Knowth mound are richly carved (see page 78), and one to the south-southwest of the mound (known as Kerbstone 52) depicts a number of crescents and circles that Brennan and other researchers have described as a lunar calendar.

The markings form a rough but continuous loop, with seven circles arcing along the top of the

Lunar calendar The crescents and circles on Knowth's Kerbstone 52 may depict the moon's changing phases.

Newgrange by moonlight A full moon shines over Newgrange, the ghostly glow making the mound visible for many miles around. The white quartz is a controversial modern reconstruction of the tomb's original facing.

stone and 22 crescents cascading down each side and forming an orderly line across the middle. Unfortunately, whereas the points of the crescent of the real moon are oriented toward both east (when the moon is waxing) and west (when it is waning), the kerbstone crescents all point the same way. However, there are a total of 29 of these circles and crescents which, supporters of the theory claim, indicate the 29 whole days in a lunar month (from any phase to its recurrence).

Philip Stooke, a researcher into extraterrestrial cartography at the University of Western Ontario, Canada, has suggested that one stone inside Knowth (Orthostat 47) is engraved with a map of the face of the moon. Situated at the end of the cruciform,

eastern passage, the stone is engraved with a variety of arcs and dots. One section of the markings consists of three nested crescents, a short curving line and dots in positions that mimic the dark markings known as maria on the moon's surface.

The correlation between the rock art and the celestial orb is not precise, and some sceptics regard such theories as a product of pareidolia, the brain's pattern-recognition capability responsible for the idea of the man in the moon (see pages 124–5). Given the sheer quantity of art on the stones at Knowth, it would not be surprising to find one with a passing resemblance to some other thing. However, if Stooke is correct in his identification, this stone is likely to be the oldest lunar map yet discovered.

INTRODUCING ECLIPSES

Anyone who has experienced a total eclipse of the sun will understand the power of the event. Everyday life is put on hold and all our attention is caught up in the moment as day is plunged into a darkness as deep as the night. We may comfort ourselves with the science: an eclipse is simply caused by the movement of the ball of rock we call the moon, its orbit determined by the constant fight between the moon's centrifugal force and Earth's gravity. But somewhere, deep in the mind, lingers an uneasiness that somehow, *this time*, the darkness may not end.

Such irrational fears seem to be an intrinsic element of human nature. Our brain contains two lobes that process information in different ways. In the left lobe the brain is principally engaged with words and reason – this is the part most active while reading about the geometry of archaeoastronomical alignments. The other half of the brain is about empathy and intuition – helping us to share the vision of the people who wove the myths and built temples to the gods of the sky. Astrologers symbolize these contrasting yet complementary components of our self as the sun and the moon respectively.

Solar and lunar eclipses

Eclipses can only take place at new moon (solar eclipse) or at full moon (lunar eclipse). For an eclipse to occur, the moon must be either at the same declination as the sun (solar eclipse) or at the opposite declination (lunar eclipse) – declination is the coordinate used to plot the position of heavenly bodies either north or south of the celestial equator. When the sun is obscured by the moon as viewed from Earth, a solar eclipse takes place. When the moon moves behind the Earth, so the sun's rays cannot reach it, a lunar eclipse occurs.

A total solar eclipse is one of the world's most dramatic natural events, although an annular eclipse (when the moon is too distant from the Earth to completely cover the sun, leaving a thin ring of sunlight) is also a thing of great beauty. Some partial eclipses pass unnoticed as they cause only minor

Why eclipses happen Twice each orbit, the moon is on the same plane as the sun (the ecliptic) and an eclipse becomes possible, depending on lunar phase. A solar eclipse will be visible in a smaller geographical area than a lunar eclipse, as the moon's shadow cast on the Earth is relatively small. Lunar eclipses are visible from a greater area and for longer, as the Earth's shadow cast on the moon is much larger.

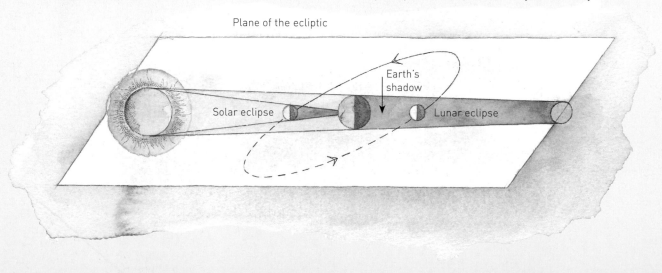

Plane of the ecliptic

Solar eclipse

Earth's shadow

Lunar eclipse

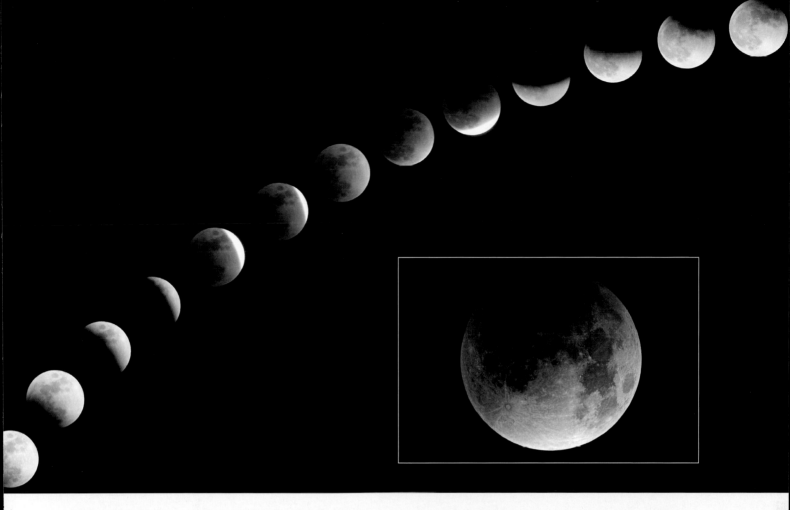

Disappearing act A series of time-lapse photographs illustrates the changing face of a full moon during a lunar eclipse. The inset photograph shows a close-up of the shadow cast by the Earth over part of a full moon.

dimming, while others devour all but a thin crescent of the sun before the moon passes and daylight returns.

A total solar eclipse is only possible because of the remarkable coincidence that the sun and moon appear to be the same size in the sky. The sun is actually vastly larger, at 400 times the diameter of the moon, but they look the same to us because the sun is also 400 times further away from us than the moon.

Our perception of the equality of these opposites of day and night, of the sun and the moon, has inspired astrologers to try to look at every situation from both sides – using both parts of our brain. Inevitably, perhaps, the sun and moon are often viewed as corresponding to the sexes. In the West the sun is viewed as male and the moon as female (ideas derived from classical Greece), but earlier cultures mostly saw

the pair the other way around. In Norse mythology, the sun is represented by the goddess Sol and the moon by the god Mani – who may be responsible for the notion of the man in the moon. Relatively few cultures have viewed the sun and moon as being the same sex; one example was in Sumeria where the son of the moon god, Nanna, was Utu, the sun.

Many cultures regarded solar eclipses as unfortunate events. In China, the sun's disappearance was popularly blamed on an attack by a celestial dog (the people were instructed to make loud noises to frighten the dog away – invariably successfully). But if we are looking for a metaphor to unite the two lobes of our brain in a creative fusion, perhaps we need look no further than the next page, which describes the myths of the indigenous people of Australia.

AUSTRALIAN ECLIPSE

In almost all Indigenous Australian legends, the spirit of the sun is regarded as female and the moon as male. In Arnhem Land, the Yolngu culture know the sun-woman as Walu and the moon-man as Ngalindi. Each morning Walu creates the glow of dawn when she lights a small fire, and colours the sunrise clouds with the red ochre powder she uses to paint her body. The blazing sun is a torch she carries as she journeys across the sky. At dusk she extinguishes the torch and travels under the Earth, back to her camp in the east.

Solar eclipses are caused by moon-man covering the body of sun-woman when they meet and make love. Such stories may have inspired a striking image in the Basin Track collection of the Sydney Rock Engravings in the Ku-ring-gai Chase National Park, New South Wales. Like other such art, the image is difficult to date directly. The area was inhabited at least 3,500 years ago and the rock art may be at least this old, or as recent as the 17th century CE.

Union of opposites At Basin Track, sun-woman and moon-man are shown united in a solar eclipse.

The image, about 6½ft (2m) tall, shows a woman and a man with their arms raised up to a crescent. The position of the crescent, with points hanging down, makes it unlikely to be an image of the moon. Archaeoastronomers have speculated that it is in fact a representation of a solar eclipse, particularly as the arms and legs of the two figures are shown overlapping, which is very unusual in such carefully delineated engravings.

Lunar petroglyphs at Ngaut Ngaut

LUNAR ART AT NGAUT NGAUT

Archaeoastronomy is in its infancy in Australia, not least because of the long history of systematic suppression of native culture. Crescent-shaped petroglyphs have often been interpreted as boomerangs, but at Ngaut Ngaut, on the banks of the Murray river near Greenway Landing, some 60 miles (100km) northeast of Adelaide, the juxtaposition of crescents with circles drawn with short lines radiating like beams of sunlight make an astronomical interpretation likely.

A series of lines and dots resembling tally marks appears near one particular combination of the crescent and radiant circle at Ngaut Ngaut, and these images are known in the oral tradition of the local Nganguraku people as the "cycles of the moon". Work is underway to try to establish whether these markings are indeed a lunar calendar. Although no date has been advanced for the engravings, archaeological excavation of nearby campfires has revealed that the site has been in use for at least 8,000 years.

ECLIPSE COMMEMORATION PAVILION INDIA

The cluster of sacred monuments at Mahabalipuram on the Bay of Bengal in Tamil Nadu, India, is a World Heritage site, celebrated for its superb sculpture. Most monuments were built in the Pallava period of the 6th–8th centuries CE, when Mahabalipuram was a thriving port, but the Eclipse Commemoration Pavilion is thought to be later, dating to the 13th century.

This *mandapa* or pavilion is made of granite and consists of a rectangular flat roof supported by 24 pillars arranged in a 4 x 6 grid. Particularly ornate pillars mark the entrance on the short, south side. The ceiling has an impressive array of carved bas-reliefs that includes a variety of mythological motifs. The first of these, in the central aisle just inside the entrance, is a picture of the holy hunter Kannappa, gouging out his eyes with an arrow as a service to the god Shiva. Other images include a scorpion with a human face, fish, monkeys, a whale, a two-headed bird and stylized lotus flowers.

Eclipse imagery Representations of both solar and lunar eclipses have been found at the 13th-century Eclipse Commemoration Pavilion at Mahabalipuram.

Devouring the sun

The late Raja Deekshithar, spiritual teacher and researcher, who visited the site in 2009, believed some of the reliefs to be depictions of eclipses. For example, at exactly the opposite end of the pavilion to the Kannappa image is a *naga* (mythic serpent) slithering toward a disc as if to devour it. This, he interpreted as an image of a solar eclipse.

In the southeast corner of the pavilion are two further sets of the serpent/disc combination. One is essentially the same as the example above, but the other may represent a lunar eclipse, which is caused by the moon moving into the path of the Earth's shadow, an event that can only occur at full moon. A large crescent is carved into the middle of the disc and the hollow part of the crescent is positioned toward the serpent, as if the disc has been partially consumed already. However, this crescent could also be interpreted as the shining crescent of sun seen during a solar eclipse.

In the mid-point of the pavilion's eastern aisle is a fourth eclipse picture. This is certainly lunar because the disc is carved with the rabbit traditionally seen in patterns on the moon's surface – an association celebrated in early Buddhist scriptures of *c.* 400 BCE.

The story of the hunter Kannappa can also be interpreted in eclipse terminology, the loss of his eyes symbolizing the disappearance of a celestial orb.

Raja Deekshithar found similar carvings, one of a *naga* and disc, and another of a *naga* paired with a disc and crescent, at the 12th-century Sangameshvara temple at Bhavani, Tamil Nadu.

ANGKOR WAT CAMBODIA

Most famous for its solar and stellar alignments (see pages 209–13), this vast temple also has an important lunar significance. For example, staircases in the lowest gallery are separated from each other by 112 cubits – or 4 x 28 cubits. (Here this unit was 17.144in/43.545cm – see page 213.) The number 28 is the maximum number of days on which the moon is visible (when not hidden by the sun's glare at new moon). It has been suggested that these staircases, which seem to go nowhere, actually led to viewing points from which markers set around the horizon aligned with the major lunar standstills (see pages 134–5). The jungle that surrounds Angkor Wat today would have engulfed any such markers, and certainly

Moon watching Markers outside Angkor Wat may have once indicated lunar alignments seen from internal viewing points.

none have so far been found. However, if they existed, they could have been used to help chart eclipses. Such events would have been important to the king who built Angkor Wat, Suryavarman II, whose patron was the sun – a solar eclipse may have signified danger not only to the sun, but to the king and the whole kingdom. But such lunar alignments are controversial as they lack the convincing symmetry of the solar alignments over the entrances (see page 210) and are more likely to be coincidental.

The number 28 and its multiples are found in abundance throughout Angkor Wat; for example, in numbers of windows, columns and steps. The middle of the three galleries is particularly rich in lunar measurements, with the combined length of the east and west sides totalling just a fraction more than 533 cubits, or 19 x 28 cubits, while the combined length

Treasure house This library, like the others at Angkor Wat, was probably a repository not only of sacred manuscripts but also of ritual implements and offerings for use in the "dark" or "light" half of the month.

of the north and south sides total 622 cubits, or 21 x 29.53 cubits. This is the number of days from one lunar phase to its recurrence – the synodic month.

The libraries and the month

There are three pairs of libraries at Angkor Wat, each pair positioned symmetrically along the main axis of the temple running west to east. Khmer inscriptions indicate that the people who served at the temple were categorized in two groups: one to work from new moon to full (the "light half" of the month, dedicated to the gods) and the other to serve from full moon back to new (the "dark half", dedicated to the ancestors). It is likely that the paired libraries corresponded to the light and dark halves of the lunar month, with ritual

objects stored there for use in the appropriate half – but there is also a more intriguing possibility.

The moon does not orbit the Earth's equator – its orbit is tilted with a declination of about 5.1° – so for roughly half the month it is to the north of the celestial equator (the Earth's equator projected into space), and for the other half it is to the south. This movement of the moon in the sky may also be reflected in the pairing of the libraries in mirrored positions to the north and south of the temple's equinoctial west–east axis. A particular significance of this lunar movement is that it is a key factor in determining eclipses, which occur only when the moon and sun are either at the same or precisely opposite declination (solar eclipse and lunar eclipse, respectively).

INTRODUCING THE LUNAR STANDSTILLS

A lunar standstill is the moon's equivalent of a solstice. Each month the moon's rising point moves across the eastern horizon, toward the north and then back toward the south, in an endless repeating cycle. To an observer, the standstills occur at the point where the moon's progress along the horizon reaches its maximum extent before turning back: there will be a northern standstill and a southern standstill (and a corresponding pair at moonset). Our dutiful observer may set up markers aligned to these two moonrise (or moonset) points. Changes in rising (and setting) points

The lunar cycle This artwork shows how high the moon rises in the sky during its 18.6-year cycle when seen from the latitude of Stonehenge (51°N). The northern major standstill takes place at midwinter and the southern major standstill at midsummer (six months later). The northern and southern minor standstills occur 9.3 years later.

would have been important in ancient times because they affect how high the moon rises in the sky. To an observer in the northern hemisphere, a moon rising in the northeast would rise much higher than a moon rising in the southeast (the opposite holds for the southern hemisphere) – and long moonlit nights are useful for travelling and hunting.

Astronomers measure the moon's height relative to the Earth's equator, which they extend into the heavens and call the "celestial equator". Distance above or below the celestial equator is the angle of declination, a coordinate expressed in degrees, minutes and seconds, which will be a positive number for anything north of the celestial equator, and a negative number for anything to the south. If our observer is in the northern hemisphere, then moonrise to the north of east would have a positive

Phases of the moon This time-lapse image shows how the moon is seen from Earth during a lunar (synodic) month. A full moon is at centre, surrounded by pairs of gibbous, quarter and new (crescent) moons.

declination, while moonrise to the south of east would have a negative declination. Alexander Thom is credited with coining the word "standstill", which signifies the moment when the declination of the moon stops increasing or decreasing and stands still before reversing direction.

The standstills move

Returning to our observer: for a few months the moon would keep a regular rendezvous, rising with the standstill markers as expected. But over the course of a few years the monthly standstills would move away from their original, marked positions, requiring a new pair of markers for the northern and southern standstills. In 18.6 years a complete cycle would have been charted. The markers would show the full range of standstills, revealing the positions where the moon rose and set furthest to the north and south – the major standstills that take place every 18.6 years.

This movement of the standstills is caused by the moon's orbit being tilted by about 5.1° from the plane of the Earth's orbit (the ecliptic, to which the Earth itself is tilted by 23.4°). So, at the time of a major lunar standstill, when the moon's greatest tilt occurs at the same time as the Earth's greatest tilt, the two angles are added together, allowing our observer in the northern hemisphere to see the moon soar into

the sky as its declination achieves 28.5°: the northern major standstill. But a fortnight later it reaches its lowest point: -28.5°, the southern major standstill (the views are reversed in the southern hemisphere). In fact, other factors mean the extreme north and south positions are not exactly a fortnight, but about six months apart. However, the scale of the fortnightly swing remains impressive throughout this period. Around nine years later, the moon's declination extremes will have reduced to 18.3° and -18.3° (the northern and southern minor standstills).

Taking the long view

A cycle some 18 years long was more than half a lifetime when life expectancy was short. This cycle also shed light on the eclipse cycle, which is based on the same rhythm, enabling early astronomers to predict times of risk when an eclipse was possible (when the moon and sun were at the same or opposite declination – a solar or lunar eclipse, respectively) and times of safety (when the declinations were far apart). Such cycles inspired ancient people to wonder about even greater cycles – such as the Maya Long Count of 5,125 years and the 26,000-year precession of the equinoxes. By giving perspective to the human lifespan, these long cycles inspire contemplation of our place in the universe.

CALLANISH SCOTLAND

Known as the Sleeping Beauty, the lunar lady of
Callanish lies supine across the landscape of the Isle
of Lewis in the Outer Hebrides. Every 18 years or so
she is brought to life in a spectacular fashion when
the full moon skims her body. In Gaelic she is known
as the Old Woman of the Moors, but Margaret Curtis
(who, along with her then husband, Gerald Ponting,
first drew public attention to this lunar phenomenon)
refers to the suggestively feminine horizon contours
as Mother Earth Hills.

Several local prehistoric sites appear to have
alignments to the Sleeping Beauty, but one in
particular has become famous: a complex stone
circle known as Callanish I (the related sites were
distinguished using Roman numerals, but as we
shall focus on this site alone, we'll drop the suffix).
Callanish overlooks East Loch Roag, a seawater inlet
that penetrates some 6 miles (10km) inland. It is
across these waters that Sleeping Beauty lies.

Natural theatre

Callanish stone circle dates to at least 2200 BCE. Four
rows of standing stones radiate from the 43ft (13m)
circle, approximately toward the cardinal points, giving
it a cruciform shape reminiscent of a Celtic cross.
The northern arm, known as the Avenue, is actually a
double row of stones. Because this arm's alignment is
skewed slightly to the east, it is from its northern end
that the best astronomical observations are said to
be made of the moon's special movements here. The
phenomenon occurs every 18.6 years (most recently in
2006), at the moon's most southerly declination at its
major standstill (see pages 134–5).

Stone giants One myth relates that the Callanish menhirs are
giants turned to stone for their refusal to accept Christianity.

At the time of the lunar display, an observer at the north end of the Avenue sees the full moon rise above the landscape figure as if reborn from her womb, often with a ruddy hue as of a newly delivered babe. The moon arcs low above Sleeping Beauty's naked silhouette, bathing her in silver light, then sets behind her head, which appears to rest on a pillow. Then, in a moment of great drama, the moon briefly reappears to the west of the pillow, where it sets in the centre of Callanish stone circle itself.

In prehistoric times, the stones, the hills and the moon may all have formed the backdrop for a piece of sacred theatre – myth brought vividly to life. For an audience at the northern end of the Avenue, anyone rising up from the ground south of the circle would be spectacularly silhouetted against the shining white disc of the moon. When the moon disappeared the standing figure would remain, perhaps revealed and sanctified as the new priestess. That is, of course, conjecture – but there is an ancient tradition of a Shining One who walked along the Avenue at the

Sleeping Beauty In the hills across East Loch Roag lies a figure on her back, with her knees to the left of the horizon; on the right her head, with its small nose, rests on a pillow.

June solstice, the favoured month for viewing this special conjunction of full moon and Earth. The next recurrence is in 2024.

The riddle of Diodorus
Writing in the 1st century BCE, the Greek historian Diodorus Siculus described an island as large as Sicily, unusually fertile, where the moon appeared close to the Earth. This isle lay far to the north, beyond the lands of the Celts, and a spherical temple there was lavishly decked with votive offerings to Apollo, god of harmony and reason. Every 19 years Apollo visited this temple to dance and play music each night from the spring equinox until the rising of the Pleiades cluster. The hereditary priests were devoted to Apollo because this was the birth place of the god's mother, Leto. Many scholars have supposed the circular temple of Stonehenge could answer this riddle, but Aubrey Burl and others have recently identified Callanish as a convincing candidate for the site.

Decrypting the legend
Diodorus explained the 19-year period between Apollo's visits with reference to the "year of Meton". Meton, a Greek astronomer of the 5th century BCE,

Path of moon at southern major standstill

Sleeping Beauty hills

Ancient theatre Every 18.6 years, at the southern major standstill, the moon appears to climb from the womb of Sleeping Beauty, sailing above her prone figure to set behind her head. The moment when the moon reappears in the very heart of Callanish stone circle is a dramatic one – and may, perhaps, have once been used in rites to sanctify a new priestess or ruler.

determined that the annual cycle of the sun synchronized with the monthly cycle of the moon after 6,940 days, which is (almost exactly) both 19 solar years and 235 lunar months. This Metonic cycle has no special link with Callanish except for the near coincidence of the 18.6-year cycle celebrated there, when the moon, as in the myth, comes close to the horizon – the moon near the horizon seems larger than it does in the open sky.

Leto was one of the many loves of the supreme god Zeus and she bore him two children: the twins Artemis and Apollo. By the time of Diodorus, Apollo had assimilated enough solar attributes to be known as the sun god. It is this solar symbolism that made Stonehenge, with its sun alignments, an attractive candidate for the temple – but the riddle says the priests honoured Apollo out of love for his mother, Leto. She was the daughter of Phoebe and Coeus. Phoebe was associated with the moon (her name means "Shining One", a name familiar to students of Callanish lore), while Coeus appears to have been the embodiment of the fixed polar axis around which the heavens rotate.

Phoebe and Coeus were sister and brother, two of the 12 original Titans who were the children of Gaia (the Earth) and Uranus (the heavens). Most Greek gods are descendants of this primordial couple – Mother Earth and Father Sky. The legend of Leto's maternal

ancestry seems perfectly brought to life by the event in which Mother Earth Hills gives birth to the moon.

There are still more pieces of this tantalizing jigsaw that seem to fit Callanish. The southern stone row, for example, is aligned with the Earth's polar axis, which resonates with Leto's father, Coeus. The western stone row is aligned with the setting sun on the equinoxes, which is when Apollo was said to begin his festivities.

The Isle of Lewis is not as big as Sicily, but if the Hebrides as a whole were intended, the length would be about the same (although the Hebrides are still not as wide as Sicily). It makes more sense to match Sicily to Lewis than to the mainland of Britain, which an identification with Stonehenge would require.

Other geographical details seem to fit: Callanish would certainly have been further north than the territories of the Celts known to Diodorus. The mythic isle's fertility could refer to the relatively mild climate of Callanish despite its northern latitude, brought by the warm Gulf Stream in the Atlantic.

Diodorus cites Hecataeus as a source for his information, the earliest-known Greek historian who lived around the late 4th century BCE. Hecataeus may have heard of Callanish from the famous Greek traveller Pytheas, who visited islands in the North Atlantic around 320 BCE (he gave us the first known mention of the name Britain).

STONEHENGE ENGLAND

Stonehenge is best known for its solar alignments (see pages 24–7), but there is evidence that the site also has important lunar connections. Around 7500 BCE, in the Middle Stone Age, four large wooden posts were erected some 820ft (250m) northwest of where the stone circle would rise. The posts may have been the equivalent of totem poles, with lunar symbolism. At this time, before the flooding of the English Channel, people were hunter-gatherers used to seasonal migration. Lacking permanent homes and without need of the sun for agriculture, such wanderers focused on the moon for their sense of order.

Much later, around 2900 BCE, more than 50 timber posts were positioned in six short parallel rows at the main entrance or causeway across the circular ditch and bank that separated the enclosed space of Stonehenge from the world outside. Looking out from

Complex site Stonehenge is famous for its solar alignments but there is also evidence of important lunar connections.

the centre of this space, archaeologist Aubrey Burl, among others, suggests that the posts were markers set up each midwinter to chart the rising moon through its 18.6-year cycle. The northern edge of the causeway was aligned with moonrise at its northern major standstill (see pages 134–5), a permanent alignment that could have been fixed as soon as observations determined the lunar cycle's extreme limit. However, others suggest that the posts simply supported fences.

Eclipse theory

Lying just inside the ditch and bank is a circle of 56 holes, known as the Aubrey Holes. These probably held large timber posts, but in 1965 astronomer Gerald Hawkins proposed that they worked as an eclipse forecaster. His book *Stonehenge Decoded* explained how objects could have been placed in some of the holes and then moved from hole to hole over the years in a set pattern. This idea of an eclipse

calculator at Stonehenge now seems unlikely. Inner rings of holes found at other ditch and bank circles do not seem to fall into a pattern that supports the ingenious eclipse calculator suggested by Hawkins. Of six examples within 50 miles (80km) of Stonehenge, all but one site have hole rings with only 8 to 14 holes (at Maumbury Rings there are about 45 holes). It is likely that the Aubrey Holes and these other hole rings had a similar purpose, but one as yet unknown.

The coming of the stones

Before the sarsen stones were put up, an initial circle of bluestones was erected around 2550 BCE. These stones seem to have been transported to the site from the Preseli Hills in Wales, either by people or by earlier glacial activity. With the coming of the bluestones, the site's axis was shifted by about 4°, away from the lunar toward the solar. Probably also at this time, four stones were set up just inside the ditch and bank to form a near perfect rectangle – the Station Stones (see plan, page 27). The short sides of this rectangle marked the new alignment to midsummer sunrise (and, in the opposite direction,

Long history (*Above*) When the trilithons were first raised, c. 2450 BCE, Stonehenge was already many centuries old.

Mysteries of the past (*Overleaf*) Even a site as thoroughly investigated as Stonehenge still holds many secrets.

to midwinter sunset). But the rectangle's long sides pointed toward moonrise at the southern major standstill (and, in the opposite direction, to moonset on the northern major standstill, see pages 134–5). At this latitude such a rectangle would automatically incorporate the lunar alignment, even if only the solar alignment had been intended – Stonehenge lies only around 40 miles (65km) north of the latitude where these two solar and lunar lines would intersect at an angle of precisely 90°. However, the diagonal between the most easterly and westerly Station Stones also aligns with moonrise at the southern minor standstill (and moonset at the northern minor standstill). Such a web of lunar alignments may indicate a deliberate homage to the site's earlier lunar axis.

RECUMBENT STONE CIRCLES SCOTLAND

Around a hundred recumbent stone circles dating to the 3rd millennium BCE cluster in the Grampian region of northeast Scotland, unlike stone circles anywhere else. They are personal, even intimate in scale, often having fewer than 10 upright stones standing in a circle around 40–60ft (12–18m) in diameter. Each recumbent stone circle includes its defining feature – a large stone (usually the largest) that was deliberately laid on its side.

This recumbent stone commonly weighs around 20 tons (20.3 tonnes) – although the one at Old Keig weighs some 50 tons (50.8 tonnes) – and is flanked closely by a pair of upright stones. The recumbent

stone is always low enough to not interrupt the view of the horizon, while the flanking stones almost invariably rise high enough to neatly frame a section of skyline.

A survey of the circles

The recumbent stone is always within a 90° arc of the horizon centred on south-southwest, which inspired archaeoastronomer Clive Ruggles to begin a field survey of the 64 circles available for study in 1981.

He found that the recumbent stones had often been carefully levelled to provide a horizontal upper surface. Whereas the stones of the circle are usually local, the recumbent stone is often sourced from some distance away (some, such as at Auchmaliddie and North Strone, are quartz). The stones in the circle are often taller the closer they are to the recumbent,

Daviot stone circle At this hilltop site in Aberdeenshire, as at other similar sites, the recumbent stone lies in the south-southwest of the circle.

Midmar Kirk stone circle Fang-like stones 8ft (2.5m) tall flank the recumbent in this Aberdeenshire cemetery.

with the flanking stones being the tallest of all. Pieces of quartz crystal are often found, as at Berrybrae, scattered near the recumbent stone.

Ruggles measured the height and distance of the horizon at each site, and found the view over the top of the recumbent stone to be always to a distant horizon. No horizon is closer than 0.6 mile (1km), and two-thirds are more than 2 miles (3km) away. Where the horizon is more than 3 miles (5km) away, the recumbent stone is aligned to a prominent hilltop.

Ruggles calculated that the odds of all the circles coincidentally having a recumbent stone aligned in such a tight arc of the horizon as less than one in a quadrillion (10^{24}). He found the great majority of the sites to have alignments to the horizon clustered in a range of declinations (see page 134) between -28° and -33°. This range includes the setting of the moon at its southern major standstill and extends beyond it, so although some sites would see this maximum-declination moon set behind the recumbent stone, others would see the moon passing low over the horizon framed by the flanking stones.

The final clue

The case for the orientation of the recumbent circles with the moon is clinched by the evidence of cup marks. These man-made hollows in the rock are found at only a dozen sites, eight of which were available to Ruggles to investigate. He found that most of the cup marks are on the recumbent stones themselves, and these invariably mark (to an accuracy of within 2°) the position of moonset at either the southern or northern major standstill, as seen from the centre of the circle.

It seems the sites may have been set up during any midsummer full moon, not just the one that occurs at the climax of the 18.6-year lunar cycle. Then, over the years as people witnessed the changes in the moon's position, they noticed the standstills and began to commemorate the events by marking the stones.

In the absence of archaeological excavation, we can barely begin to guess at what ceremonies may have accompanied the annual observances that took place at these sites.

LE GRAND MENHIR BRISÉ FRANCE

Just 6 miles (10km) east of the megalithic centre of Carnac, Brittany, is the small port of Locmariaquer, which boasts the remains of what would have been the tallest standing stone in Europe, Le Grand Menhir Brisé – "the great broken standing stone".

This colossal stone originally measured 67$\frac{1}{2}$ft (20.6m) in height and weighed around 275 tons (280 tonnes). It was brought to this site from an outcrop of rock at least 2$\frac{1}{2}$ miles (4km) away – a colossal undertaking by the people of the time. The stone now lies flat, broken into four pieces.

Because this monument would have been so prominent in the surrounding landscape, archaeoastronomer Alexander Thom claimed it was used as a sort of universal marker for all four of the moon's standstills (see pages 134–5). He proposed

Fallen giant The broken megalith of Le Grand Menhir Brisé would once have been visible for many miles around.

that this standing stone would have been encircled by observation posts that were aligned to mark all the standstills, both rising and setting. An examination of the area provided candidates for most if not all of these eight predicted sites.

However, the claimed observation sites include a wide variety of different monuments – some sites may not even be old enough to have existed when the great stone was still standing. And given the enormous number of megalithic sites in the area, it would be unlikely if at least a few of them didn't align with the great standing stone by pure chance.

It has also been discovered that Le Grand Menhir Brisé was just one in a row of 19 stones that are no longer in position. The holes in which they once stood have been excavated and marked on the ground for the benefit of visitors, but no astronomical alignments are known for this vanished stone row that may once have contained an even larger monolith.

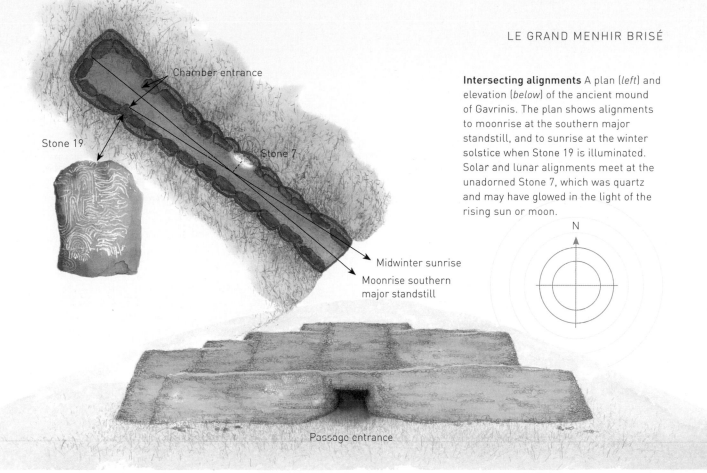

Chamber entrance

Stone 19

Stone 7

Midwinter sunrise

Moonrise southern
major standstill

N

Passage entrance

Intersecting alignments A plan (*left*) and elevation (*below*) of the ancient mound of Gavrinis. The plan shows alignments to moonrise at the southern major standstill, and to sunrise at the winter solstice when Stone 19 is illuminated. Solar and lunar alignments meet at the unadorned Stone 7, which was quartz and may have glowed in the light of the rising sun or moon.

THE GAVRINIS LUNAR ALIGNMENT

The small, granite island of Gavrinis in the Gulf of Morbihan lies about 1¼ miles (2km) east of Le Grand Menhir Brisé. On this island is a passage tomb with a single chamber, dating to about 3300 BCE. The monument is some 165ft in diameter and 30ft high (50 x 9m), with a straight passage some 40ft (12m) long and aligned so that it is illuminated by the light of the rising moon at its southern major standstill.

This passage is lined with 29 slabs, 23 of which are adorned with carvings. Many feature linear swirls resembling the looping arches of fingerprints, reminiscent of the visions of psychedelic drug users. One of the passage stones is of quartz, which

shimmers ghost-like in the gloom. The link between the moon and the imagery of a dream-like, drug-induced trance state resonates with many of the people who visit this site surrounded by seawater – the moon's own element. But we need to remember that not only was the water level lower when the tomb was built, so that the site was actually part of the mainland, but that the lunar alignment is also consistent with the winter solstice sun climbing into the morning sky – an alignment that falls within the range of the well-known solar orientation of this sort of tomb.

While it is impossible to disprove a lunar interpretation of the tomb, Gavrinis shows how it may be a mistake for visitors to simply accept their first impressions about a site.

Swirling carvings at Gavrinis

SHORT STONE ROWS SCOTLAND

Recent developments in landscape archaeology, which looks at the environment surrounding a site of interest, proved particularly valuable in a study of Bronze Age stone rows in the north of the Isle of Mull, off the west coast of Scotland. There are seven of these short stone rows, with up to six stones standing in a line less than 82ft (25m) long (one of the sites is a double row).

All seven sites were analyzed in the 1980s and 1990s as part of a project led by professor Clive Ruggles. He found that the rows all pointed roughly toward the east-southeast, within an arc of horizon about 12° across, but didn't appear to point toward anything special – except the row at Glengorm, which pointed toward the rising of the full moon on its southern major standstill (see pages 134–5).

Ben More, the highest mountain on Mull, lay in exactly the same direction, 15½ miles (25km) away, but the researchers weren't sure if it would have been visible at the time the row was constructed (a plantation blocks the view today). If it had been visible, it would have been partially obscured by a closer hill. And this curious feature – Ben More being only just visible – was found to apply to four other sites. Often, just 10 paces to either side of the row would either bring the mountain into full view, or hide it completely. In each case the summit of the mountain is within a couple of degrees of the rising moon at its southern major standstill. The chances of such positioning occurring by chance are tiny.

A hidden horizon Now surrounded by trees, this row of five stones at Dervaig on the Isle of Mull, Scotland, once pointed to Ben More and the rising midsummer moon.

Insight into the past Comparing similar sites reveals the shared design of rows such as this one at Baliscate on the Isle of Mull, Scotland.

solstice, the sun is seen to set into the distinctive peak of Hecla on South Uist, 60 miles (97km) across the sea to the northwest. From some of the other sites, distant peaks also mark the summer solstice sunset (and sometimes also the sunrise).

In general, the seven sites appear to have been selected to avoid panoramic views, with restricted visibility focusing attention toward a distant horizon between south-southeast and west-southwest, where the full moon of midsummer arcs low across the land. The stone rows themselves, however, do not always point directly at the mountain (the Glengorm row is unique in this), but could be oriented up to 18° away. Merely studying the alignment of the rows themselves would miss the bigger picture in which these monuments mark a special place in the landscape from which to observe the midsummer moon.

Cluster research

Studying clusters such as the stone rows of northern Mull offers us vivid insights into a local tradition, and shows the painstaking detail with which sites need to be investigated. The lunar orientation of these short stone rows, of Scotland's recumbent stone circles and of the complex of Callanish may also form a wider area of interest in the moon.

Other short stone rows in southwest Ireland also demonstrate clear lunar alignments. In the years to come, many more lunar sites may be identified around the world as these investigative techniques pioneered in Scotland are applied in other nations.

From the two sites that are out of sight of Ben More, only one prominent, distant hilltop is visible, and it marks the same moonrise as the others. One of these two sites – Ardnacross (which, uniquely, has a pair of rows) – has been excavated. It dates to between 1250 and 900 BCE, and the standing stones had been sprinkled with hundreds of fragments of white and transparent quartz crystals.

The site at Quinish not only witnesses the moonrise over Ben More, but is also positioned so that, in the hours before moonrise on the summer

LUNAR DEITIES AND MYTHOLOGY

Like most natural planetary satellites, our moon is in synchronous orbit, which means it rotates around its axis in the same time it takes to orbit the Earth, and always turns the same face to us. Seeing always a mysterious disc instead of a sphere must have helped our silver companion in the sky to accumulate magical rather than practical explanations for its origins, markings, behaviour and meaning. Its phases, for example, have widely found interpretation as the cycle of life, from birth to adulthood to old age to death – and back to birth again.

Origin of the moon

In Aztec myth, Coyolxauhqui and her 400 brothers were the children of the mother goddess Coatlicue. When their mother became impregnated by a ball of feathers, Coyolxauhqui was disgusted and persuaded her brothers to kill their pregnant mother. However, their attempt was thwarted when Coatlicue's womb disgorged a god – fully grown and armed. This new god was Huitzilopochtli, god of the sun and war. He killed his 400 brothers and beheaded his sister Coyolxauhqui, tossing her head into the sky where it became the moon.

Eclipses

In India, Rahu and Ketu are two of the nine planets of Vedic astrology (the others being the five planets visible to the naked eye, plus the sun and moon), and they are the mythic embodiments of the two points at which the moon's orbit crosses the ecliptic each month. These are the only times when eclipses can occur, a fact commemorated in the word "ecliptic".

Rahu and Ketu were formerly the head and body of a single *asura* or demon. Once, this *asura* seized the *amrita* – the drink that bestows immortality – as it was being passed between the gods of the sun and moon, and drank some of the divine liquor. One of the other gods instantly cut him in half but the elixir had already worked and the demon couldn't be killed. Some stories say the sundered body grew the head of a snake – a *naga* – and was called Ketu, while the severed head grew a *naga*'s body and was called Rahu. Others say Rahu remains as a decapitated head and

Coyolxauhqui This Aztec engraving shows the goddess's slain body and decapitated head – which was thrown into the sky to become the moon.

soars through the heavens in a chariot pulled by eight black horses. When he catches up with either the sun or moon he swallows it, causing it to disappear, but it soon escapes through his severed neck.

In Japanese Shinto myth, the brother of the sun goddess Amaterasu is the moon god Tsukuyomi-no-mikoto. Disgusted by the way the food goddess Uke-Mochi produced foodstuffs from the different orifices of her body, his rage grows until he kills her. Unable to bear looking at Tsukuyomi-no-mikoto, the distraught Amaterasu sends him to the other side of the sky. He tries to approach her, but is always rebuffed. When he draws too close, the sun goddess closes her eyes and makes herself invisible until the moon god withdraws again – a poetic description of the solar eclipse.

Phases of the moon

Among the Indigenous Australian legends in Arnham Land is one that tells how the moon waxes because Ngalindi – the moon-man – is putting on weight. He persists in his increasingly indolent lifestyle until he is positively rotund (full moon). Far from happy at his selfish ways, his wives attack him with axes. He is too lazy and corpulent to protect himself, and they slice away at him until he is so thin that he dies (new moon), but after three days he returns to life.

Hindu myth records a similar fate for the god of the moon and fertility, the handsome Chandra. The moon is his chariot drawn by 10 white horses, which he rides across the sky. He was married to the 27 *nakshatras* (the asterisms in the sectors of the ecliptic in Hindu astrology), but favoured and gave preference to Rohini

Thoth This sculpture found at Luxor and dating to *c.* 600 BCE depicts the ibis-headed moon god, one of the most powerful of Egypt's many deities.

(Aldebaran, in Taurus), much to the despair of the others. For this insult, their father, Daksha, cursed him to die a slow death – but as Chandra weakened, so did everything alive on Earth. Daksha relented, reducing the curse to a never-ending monthly cycle of waxing and waning.

Lunar gods and goddesses

The ibis became associated with the moon in ancient Egypt, not least because of the bird's long, almost crescent-shaped beak. In the Old Kingdom (during the 3rd millennium BCE), the moon god Thoth, who had the head of an ibis, was tasked with keeping track of time. The moon was used to note the passage of time as its regular phases were visible throughout the kingdom. Thoth became a powerful god, invoked for his wisdom and knowledge of powerful mysteries. He was said to have created writing, and to direct the motions of the celestial bodies (a substantial promotion from his early role as lunar timekeeper). But the moon remained important in its own right, and Thoth's role as moon god was eventually taken over by Khonsu whose name – "traveller" – referred to the moon's swift passage around the heavens.

The Greek goddess Artemis was an eternal virgin and the twin sister of Apollo the sun god. She was originally the goddess of the hunt, wild animals and the wilderness, but people also invoked her aid in matters of female fertility and childbirth. She was often identified with Selene, the earlier Greek moon goddess, particularly in the phase of the waxing moon, which may have been mirrored in the curve of her bow. Artemis was full of contradictions, for example as goddess of virginity as well as childbirth, and her complex character mirrored the ever-changing moon.

The Greek goddess Hecate was associated with the waning and dark phases of the moon, and had occult insight and special knowledge of the natural processes of decay and death. She presided over women's secrets and the profound choices women make, which meant men often viewed her with keen suspicion. To women, though, she was a powerful ally in coping with the darker side of life.

Divine succession The Greek lunar goddess Selene (*far left*) was a Titan, shown here in a 1st-century CE fresco from the House of Ara Maxima at Pompeii. She yielded to the Olympian Athena, who became Diana (*left*) in Roman times, here depicted in a 2nd-century CE mosaic from Tunisia. The drawn hunting bow of Athena/Diana echoes the shape of the crescent moon.

153

3 THE STARS AND PLANETS – IMMORTAL HEAVENS

Above our cities the night sky looks deserted, all but the brightest stars drowned in artificial light, but elsewhere the skies still blaze with jewels. We may recognize planets and trace patterns among the stars, taming the fear of gazing up at countless alien worlds. There is both majesty and order in the heavens, and each year in due season the constellations return like friends.

INTRODUCING THE PLANETS

The relative position of the stars does not appear to us to change, but there are other bodies that seem to journey across this stellar backdrop. Shooting stars or meteors – fragments of stone or metal that are caught by Earth's gravity and fall into its atmosphere where most are incinerated – move rapidly, and those that survive the journey to the surface of our planet have often been regarded with religious awe (see pages 166–7). But it is those moving bodies that remain aloft for all to see, the planets, that have most captivated the human imagination. The word planet means "wanderer" and aptly describes the shining lights that seem to move among our fixed stars so serenely. In the West at least, it is the planets that have been incorporated into our most basic understanding of our world – the measurement of time.

No one knows exactly why days were formed into groups of seven to make a week, although the moon is a favoured explanation because each of the four lunar phases lasts 7.38 days. Nor do we know when each day became linked with one of the seven astrological planets. But a little detective work reveals the ancient design that gives us the sequence of days in a week.

The seven astrological planets comprise those slow-moving heavenly bodies that are visible to the naked eye. In antiquity, this category was said to include the sun and moon, although today we know that neither of these is a planet. Although the planet Uranus is visible to the naked eye, it is very faint and was simply overlooked as a planet by the early Mesopotamian and Mediterranean astronomers.

It may seem strange to put the sun and moon into the same class as tiny specks of light like Mercury and Saturn, but they all appear unfailingly to follow the same route around the sky (the ecliptic), which clearly binds them all together. As these "planets"

are defined by the fact that they move in relation to the "fixed stars", it is a simple task to sort them into a sequence according to the speed of their movements – from the slowest to the swiftest: Saturn, Jupiter, Mars, Sun, Venus, Mercury, Moon.

That sequence, thought to have been established in the 1st century BCE, is not widely known outside the ranks of astrologers or students of medieval magic, but it is the source of the order of days in the week and it incorporates the idea of the 24-hour day. In astrology, each of a day's 24 hours is ruled by one of these planets. Working through the list of planets in order from Saturn to Moon and allocating a name to each hour of a day will give, after 24 hours, the planet associated with the next day (see box, opposite).

In English three days reflect Roman deity/"planet" names, while the remainder refer to Norse deities that are equivalent to the Roman deities. Romance languages such as French reflect the Latin origins more closely (although *samedi* and *dimanche* refer to the Christian Sabbath and the Lord's Day respectively).

Deity/"planet"	Latin	French	English
Luna/moon	*dies Lunae*	*Lundi*	Monday
Mars (Tiw)	*dies Martis*	*Mardi*	Tuesday
Mercury (Woden)	*dies Mercurii*	*Mercredi*	Wednesday
Jove/Jupiter (Thor)	*dies Iovis*	*Jeudi*	Thursday
Venus (Freya)	*dies Veneris*	*Vendredi*	Friday
Saturn	*dies Saturnis*	*Samedi*	Saturday
Sol/sun	*dies Solis*	*Dimanche*	Sunday

Whenever we see the names of the days in a calendar or newspaper, we are witnessing the living legacy of ancient astronomical theories about the nature of time and the sacred cycles of the cosmos.

NAMING OF DAYS

Astrology allocates a planetary ruler to each of a day's 24 hours, and their sequence gives us the names of the days of the week. To understand this, we may work through the example of a single day, say Sunday. The moment of dawn on the day of the sun sees the sun born anew, so this first hour is sacred to the sun itself. The second hour is ruled by the next planet in our list (working from slowest to fastest, from Saturn to the moon) – Venus. The third hour is ruled by the next planet – Mercury; and so on.

When we've worked through all 24 hours of the day of the sun, we find that the next hour – the first hour of the next day – is ruled by the moon. Again, the first hour of the day is devoted to the deity that rules it, making this the day of the moon – Monday. The next hour is ruled by Saturn, the next by Jupiter and so on. Having worked through this 24-hour cycle, we find that the first hour of the next day is ruled by Mars – Tuesday (Tiw being the Germanic god equated with Mars). In this way we can work through the list to name the days of the week, the process being exactly the same for every day.

Sun
Venus
Mercury
Moon
Saturn
Jupiter
Mars

Gods of the week (*Left*) Mars, depicted here in a fresco in the Casa de Venere, Pompeii, gave his name to the French word *mardi* (Tuesday). (*Above*) Thor and Freya, here shown (with Odin) in an 11th-century Swedish sculpture, are the Norse deities from whom the English words Thursday ("Thor's Day") and Friday ("Freya's Day") are derived.

THE DENDERA ZODIAC EGYPT

This famous stone carving dates to 50 BCE, in the reign of Egypt's last pharaoh, the famous Cleopatra. While the piece is distinctly Egyptian in style, by this time the country had been under the sway of Greek thought for nearly three centuries. The 12 zodiac figures had been standardized in Greece as early as the 4th century BCE and so many of the Dendera Zodiac's constellations are recognizably the same as ours.

Dendera lies beside the Nile about 30 miles (50km) north of Karnak and the old Egyptian capital city of Thebes. But at the time the zodiac was created, Egypt's capital city was more than 370 miles (600km) away, at the Mediterranean port of Alexandria.

The planets

Now in the Louvre, Paris, the zodiac was created for the ceiling of Dendera's Temple of Hathor, goddess of love and motherhood, and was sited in the entrance to a chapel used to celebrate the rites of Osiris. The sandstone bas-relief is 8ft 4½in from top to bottom and 8ft 3½in wide (2.55 x 2.53m), and depicts the five classical planets – Mercury, Venus, Mars, Jupiter and Saturn – among the constellations.

The positions of the planets may depict the heavens around the middle of July 50 BCE, when all the visible planets except Venus were roughly in their astrologically auspicious "exalted" positions. In astrology, the constellations through which the planets pass are the zodiac signs, and some signs suit a visiting planet better than others. The concept of a sign in which a planet is said to be exalted is seldom used in modern astrology, but is of great antiquity, having been adopted by the Greeks from Mesopotamia.

In the Dendera Zodiac the planets are shown among the constellations as human figures, each holding a staff of power. Mercury stands between Leo and Virgo (Mercury is exalted in Virgo). Venus stands between Aquarius and Pisces (Venus is exalted in Pisces). Mars stands between Capricorn and Aquarius (Mars is exalted in Capricorn). Jupiter stands between Cancer and Leo (Jupiter is exalted in Cancer). And Saturn stands between Virgo and Libra (Saturn is exalted in Libra).

The decans

The circle of the sky is supported by four standing women representing the four pillars of the cardinal points – the arms and legs of the sky goddess Nut whose body arches into the heavens. Inside the inner circle are 36 figures representing the decans – stars or asterisms that are approximately evenly spaced around the heavens. Their heliacal risings, when after a period of obscurity they first become visible on the eastern horizon just before dawn, were used as a sort of calendar of the year, with one rising every 10 days (hence the word decan), an Egyptian system that dates back to at least 2300 BCE.

The best-known decan is Sirius, the herald of the Nile's annual inundation (see page 177). Their nocturnal risings were also used to chart the watches of the night, and because twilight rendered some decan stars invisible, leaving only 12 that could be seen and counted in the short nights of midsummer, this eventually evolved into the idea of a 12-hour night complemented by a 12-hour day.

The zodiac

Inside the circle of the sky are figures representing constellations in the northern sky that appear never to set (the circumpolar region), such as the Plough (Big Dipper), which is located in the very centre and

Circle of the sky In the Dendera Zodiac, four women, representing the four pillars of the cardinal points, support the celestial sphere containing the planets and constellations.

depicted as the long, narrow foreleg of a bull (see page 192). Contained in the zodiac constellations (which do set) is the line of the ecliptic along which the sun appears to travel when viewed from Earth, close to which the planets and moon are found.

Aries, the Ram, is at the 3 o'clock position, midway between the centre and the encircling decans. Looking clockwise we find Taurus, the Bull, whose tail points toward Gemini, the Twins. Behind them is Cancer, the Crab. In the 9 o'clock position is Virgo, the Maiden, a female figure holding a stalk of wheat.

Clockwise from Virgo is Libra, the Weighing Scales, followed by Scorpio, the Scorpion, Sagittarius, the Archer and the Fish-tailed Goat, Capricorn. Immediately behind Capricorn's tail is Aquarius, the Water Carrier, pouring water from two jars. Then we find Pisces the Fish in a V-shaped constellation.

The concept of a circular sky expressed in the Dendera Zodiac is thought to be the origin of the cartouche that appears in Egyptian hieroglyphics enclosing royal names, thus indicating the pharaoh's power extending throughout the heavens.

INTRODUCING VENUS

The bright spark of the Evening Star gleaming in deepening dusk is a memorable sight and can be exceedingly romantic when love is in the air. This planet is the brightest heavenly body after the sun and moon so it is no wonder that we call it Venus, after the Roman goddess of love. The classical Greeks knew this goddess as Aphrodite, in the Bible she was Astarte and the Babylonians called her Ishtar, whose priestesses gave their affections freely to the faithful.

Just as the pangs of love may cause heartache as well as delight, Ishtar had two sides to her character, which represent the planet's motion. While the Evening Star (see pages 222–3) expresses the phase of passion and love, it is the Morning Star that we encounter when anxiety breeds insomnia and we wake in the pre-dawn dark. In this phase, Ishtar heralds the inevitability of

Aphrodite

the coming day, and in this guise she was goddess of battle.

Ishtar is often accompanied by a lion that represents the sun, and sometimes the goddess and the lion are connected by a chain. This symbolizes the fact that Venus appears never to stray far from the sun (at most 48° away), which is because her planetary orbit lies closer to the sun than Earth's does.

Ishtar's pentagram

Detailed observations of Ishtar's planet were recorded in the 16th century BCE over a period of 21 years, in cuneiform writing on clay tablets. The original tablets are lost but many copies survive, and they are known as the Venus tablets of Ammisaduqa. These Babylonian records clearly revealed a unique astronomical property of this planet: its eight-year pentagram cycle.

PLOTTING THE PENTAGRAM

This artwork shows a specific moment in Venus's cycle (its greatest eastern elongation, or the point at which its orbit appears furthest from the sun) plotted on the circle of the year (zodiac) over an eight-year period. Lines link the original moment with each recurrence 584 days later. It can be seen that, over an eight-year period, these lines trace the figure of a pentagram. The match isn't quite perfect – the recurrence eight years later is off by a couple of days or so – but it is still impressive.

Night goddess This terracotta relief from *c.* 1750 BCE may show Ishtar/Inanna
or her sister Ereshkigal, queen of the underworld, or a composite.

Venus in Mesopotamia

As well as being associated with the pentagram, Ishtar
was represented by an eight-pointed star – in honour
of the planet's eight-year pentagram cycle. These
stars often feature on the boundary or *kudurru* stones
of the Kassites, who ruled Mesopotamia between the
16th and 12th centuries BCE. The eight-pointed star of
Venus is sometimes shown along with the sun (often
symbolized as a cross within a circle) and the moon
denoted by a crescent. Sometimes other planets
and even constellations of the zodiac are thought to

be depicted, leading some scholars to suppose the
carvings may represent the position of the planets in
the sky on the date at which the boundary was set.

Pythagoras (*c.* 569–*c.* 475 BCE) was among the first
in Western civilization to propose that the Morning
Star and Evening Star were the same planet – known
to the Babylonians since at least the 17th century BCE.
He interpreted the pentagram as the ultimate symbol
of health. Today, a pentagram in a circle is a popular
symbol for Wiccans, who are interested in the "divine
feminine" exemplified by the goddess of this planet.

UXMAL MEXICO

Uxmal, 40 miles (65km) south of Yucatán's capital city Mérida, is an exceptionally well-preserved Maya city dating from around 500 CE. Abandoned in the 10th century, it is now a World Heritage site.

The Governor's Palace is a three-storey building, 320ft (97m) long, set on a raised platform that is dramatically skewed 19° from the axis of surrounding buildings. From the main entrance at the top of the stairs at the front of the palace, a line of sight extends toward the 65ft (20m) pyramid at Cehtzuc, 3 miles (5km) away. This alignment marks the maximum southerly rising of Venus; the reverse view, from the pyramid to Uxmal, marks the most northerly setting point of the same planet.

Venus orbits the sun at a slight inclination (3.4°) that takes it north and south of the ecliptic. This angle can be added to or subtracted from the sun's declination, which means that Venus can range to the north or south of even the solstice extremes of sunrise and sunset. Other factors also affect its apparent position, most notably the geometry that appears to magnify Venus's angular distance from the sun when the planet is physically close to us.

The Governor's Palace is decorated with many glyphs, more than 300 of which represent Venus, and some are combined with the glyph of the rain god Chac, who was particularly revered at this site because there are no nearby rivers. The northernmost extreme of Venus as the Evening Star occurred between 1 and 6 May, which coincides with the start of the rainy season.

Some glyphs also include the number eight. This number probably refers to the number of days on which the Maya reckoned Venus was too close to the sun to be visible (it may also refer to the planet's eight-year cycle – see page 160). The Maya were avid observers of Venus, with five pages of the *Dresden Codex* (the oldest surviving book created in the Americas, from around the 12th century CE) charting the planet's movements over 104 years.

Alignment to Venus (*Left*)
The Governor's Palace was deliberately oriented to the maximum southerly rising of Venus, as is shown by its derivation from the axis of the other buildings. From the entrance at the top of the stairs the alignment extends over a stele and jaguar statue in the courtyard toward the pyramid at Cehtzuc, marker for this celestial event.

Governor's Palace

♀
Southernmost rising point of Venus *c.* 750 CE

N

Governor's Palace (*Below*) On an elevated platform, this ruin towers above the other buildings of the ancient city.

CHICHÉN ITZÁ MEXICO

Some 65 miles (105km) east of Mérida in the Yucatán Peninsula lies the World Heritage site of Chichén Itzá. Founded by the Maya in the 5th century CE, and taken over by militaristic Toltecs in the 10th century, Chichén Itzá has at least two significant astronomically oriented buildings: the pyramid of Kukulcan (see pages 62–3) and the Caracol. The latter, a round structure on top of a lopsided square base, is very unlike other Mesoamerican monuments, with their straight lines and right angles.

Caracol is Spanish for "snail", and this building is named for the spiralling staircase it encloses. The walls contain narrow windows that seem to frame

celestial events occurring at or near the horizon – notably the northernmost and southernmost settings of Venus. Other alignments may include the setting sun at the winter solstice and equinox, sunrise on the summer solstice, the sun's zenith passage, the heliacal rising (first appearance in the eastern sky before dawn) of stars such as Canopus, Castor and Pollux, and the setting of Fomalhaut.

The ruinous state of part of the structure limits our understanding of its use. The Caracol is sometimes also known as the "Observatory", but its visual resemblance to a modern astronomical observatory is purely coincidental. However,

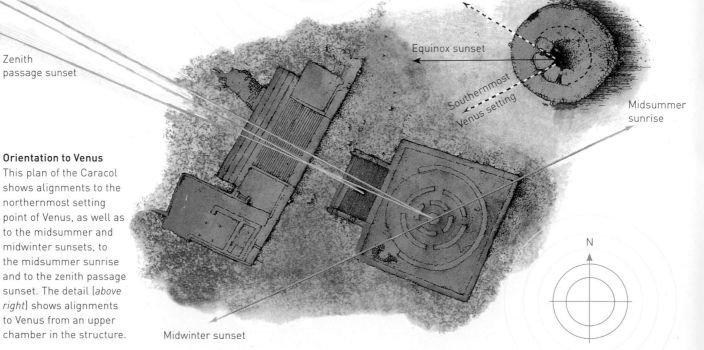

Midsummer sunset and northernmost setting point of Venus

Zenith passage sunset

Northernmost Venus setting

Equinox sunset

Southernmost Venus setting

Midsummer sunrise

Orientation to Venus
This plan of the Caracol shows alignments to the northernmost setting point of Venus, as well as to the midsummer and midwinter sunsets, to the midsummer sunrise and to the zenith passage sunset. The detail (*above right*) shows alignments to Venus from an upper chamber in the structure.

Midwinter sunset

N

Atypical design The rounded structure of the Caracol is unusual in Mesoamerica and no doubt indicates that the building had a special purpose – exciting discoveries may await further archaeoastronomical research.

there must have been a very significant purpose incorporated in the design of such an atypical building.

Waters of life

Castor and Pollux are the two brightest stars in the constellation we know as Gemini. Art historian and anthropologist Susan Milbraith noted that, viewed from the Caracol at Chichén Itzá, these two stars can be seen to rise at the position of the sun at the summer solstice – the time when the all-important rains were at their heaviest, bringing the fertility essential to a successful harvest. In Maya lore, Castor and Pollux were known as the Turtle, an animal that for the Maya represented the Earth itself.

METEORITES

Modern science has discovered that most meteorites are from the asteroid belt, with some even traced back to their parent asteroid (such as 6 Hebe or 4 Vesta), but when lumps of rock or metal fell from the heavens in ancient times, they were often interpreted as a divine message. This tradition has a certain logic to it: if the skies are the abode of the gods, then anything coming from that direction must be coming from the gods. But what were they trying to communicate?

Opening of the Mouth The blade of the ritual tool used in this ancient Egyptian ceremony may have been of iron meteorite.

Opening of the Mouth ceremony

Translating dead languages is a painstaking process, with some words continually being reinterpreted. The word *bija*, which the ancient Egyptian *Pyramid Texts* use for the adze blade employed in the Opening of the Mouth ceremony, is variously translated as "meteorite", "iron" or "copper". This ceremony, in which the mouth of the pharaoh's mummy was cracked open, was also carried out on statues, seemingly as a way of bringing them to life. It is only with an open mouth that the mummy or statue could receive the priest's offerings of sustenance, or give voice to its spirit and allow its spirit to come and go.

Holy relic The Black Stone, which may well contain material of meteoric origin, is venerated by crowds of pilgrims as they circumambulate Islam's sacred Kaaba during the yearly Hajj (pilgrimage to Mecca).

The *bija*'s wooden handle is said to have been shaped like the constellation of the Bull's Foreleg – the Plough or Big Dipper (see page 192). In some rites a sacrificed bull's leg was also used. This link with the circumpolar stars reinforces the idea of communication with the abode of the gods, so a blade of iron meteorite would have been the perfect tool.

The Opening of the Mouth ceremony dates to Egypt's Old Kingdom, a thousand years before the time of Rekhmira (*c.* 1425 BCE), a vizier at Thebes whose tomb-chapel walls contain one of the best surviving examples of the *Pyramid Texts*. The ceremony itself is famously depicted in the tomb of Tutankhamun. The adze also appears in the cartouches of the names of many pharaohs, where it carries the meaning "chosen" (by a patron deity).

Many people believe that the Benben Stone, now lost, was a large cone-shaped metallic meteorite that was enshrined on a pedestal in the Mansion of the Phoenix at Heliopolis, a once magnificent temple complex dedicated to the sun god Re but now obliterated by the city of Cairo.

The Black Stone

The fragmented Black Stone is widely rumoured to be a meteorite. It is located on the outside of the east corner of the Kaaba, the cube-shaped structure that stands in the centre of the Grand Mosque of Mecca, Saudi Arabia, and is the focus of the Hajj pilgrimage in which devotees walk anticlockwise around it seven times. In Islamic tradition the stone was white when it was sent from paradise to show Adam where to build an altar, but became blackened by the sins of humanity. Such a tale was bound to make 19th-century empiricists interpret it as a meteorite, but the actual material of this holy stone is uncertain. But even if it is not itself a meteorite, it may still be of meteoric origin – in 1980 Elsebeth Thomsen suggested that it is a tektite: natural glass fused from terrestrial sand and meteoric debris during impact.

INTRODUCING THE CIRCUMPOLAR STARS

As the name suggests, the circumpolar stars revolve around the north and south celestial poles (the extension of the Earth's north and south poles into the sky). They don't rise or set – in other words, they remain above the horizon at all times. Whether stars are circumpolar or not depends on the observer's latitude. All visible stars are circumpolar at the poles. At the equator, on the other hand, there are no circumpolar stars: for one half of the year the north celestial pole is on the horizon of the night sky, then, as these stars set, the stars close to the southern celestial pole come into view on the horizon.

Never rising or setting, circumpolar stars stand in marked contrast to the sun, whose rising and setting inspired so many myths of death and resurrection. The circumpolar stars inhabit a realm where the undying gods themselves dwell. For the ancient Egyptians this was a supremely important place, to which the pharaohs aspired to ascend, to live with the gods as equals.

Beijing

In ancient China, too, the region of the polar stars was special. When the Chinese saw the fixed stars of the heavens rotating around a single still point, they envisaged the cities of their empire held in place by imperial order – revolving around the person of their emperor.

Under the Zhou dynasty (1100–221 BCE), the ideal plan for a capital city was a nine-sectioned square oriented on the north–south axis, with the royal palace at the centre. Individual buildings were also carefully oriented toward the north, as at the early Zhou site of Zhouyuan, in Qishan county, Shaanxi province. This interest in oriented design may have originated in the Bronze Age during the Shang dynasty (1700–1100 BCE), as cardinally aligned settlements have been found at Zhengzhou and Anyang.

Now a World Heritage site, the imperial palaces at Beijing have been described as the last of the long line of cities enshrining this sacred cosmology. The grid pattern of the Zijinchéng – Purple Forbidden City – remains intact since its foundation in 1406 CE. From

Spinning on its axis Long-exposure photography reveals the rotation of the Earth, showing the circumpolar stars as concentric streaks. Closest to their centre is Polaris, which we call the pole star.

Heaven's vault The Hall of Prayer for Good Harvests, Beijing, unites the square of Earth and the circle of heaven. Rings of pillars represent the four seasons, 12 months and 12 hours of daytime, totalling 28 – the constellations of the celestial equator.

the principal entrance at the southern Meridian Gate, one approached the emperor by moving north – again a reference to the celestial pole. Along the same axis lay the main ceremonial centre of the palace, the Hall of Supreme Harmony, where festivals and other major events took place, including the celebration of the winter solstice. Further north on this axis was the Inner Court, where the emperor himself lived.

Kyoto
Kyoto became the capital of Japan in the late 8th century CE, and remained so until power shifted to Edo (later Tokyo) during the 17th century. The original

city was built on a north–south, east–west grid in accordance with ideas derived from the Chinese tradition. The palace complex was built in the north and faced south, to place the emperor symbolically in the northern celestial pole.

Astronomical observations were conducted in the southwestern part of the city as early as the 10th century. Over the centuries a series of civil wars and invasions gradually destroyed almost all of Kyoto's original architecture and practically nothing remains of these historic sites today. However, the grid of celestial geometry on which the city was built is still visible, particularly in the centre.

GIZA EGYPT

Of more than a hundred pyramids in Egypt, the most famous by far are those of the Giza plateau just outside the capital city of Cairo. A World Heritage site, this pyramid complex includes the Great Pyramid – the last of the Seven Wonders of the Ancient World still standing – as well as temples, tombs, workers' dwellings and the Sphinx. Like many other structures at the site, the pyramids are aligned with extraordinary

Theories of the pyramids Some writers have suggested that the pyramids of the Giza plateau map the constellation of Orion and the Hyades asterism, and even that the Nile mirrors the path of the Milky Way, but such theories are not popular with academics. What is undeniable is the orientation of the pyramids to the cardinal directions.

precision to the cardinal directions, probably because of the religious importance of north as the location of the "imperishable" circumpolar stars – the heartland of cosmic order and the abode of the immortal gods and pharaohs.

However, it is to the east, scene of the sun's daily rebirth, that the Sphinx gazes. This gigantic enigma with a lion's body and a man's head resolutely watches the horizon at which sunrise takes place on the two equinoxes, the two dates at opposite times of the year when day and night are in balance. These two events are months apart yet occur at a single spot on the horizon – a clue perhaps to the riddle of this hybrid creature.

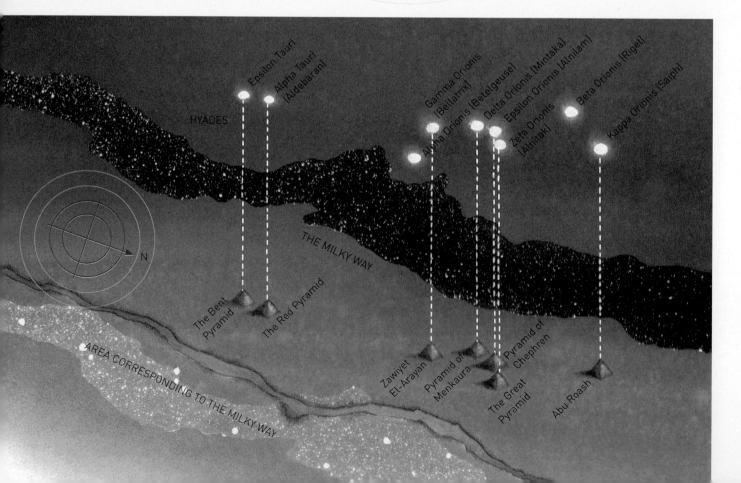

To the Hunter Above the pyramids, Orion's Belt is visible in the night sky. A shaft from the King's Chamber in the Great Pyramid is oriented to Alnitak in this asterism.

The Great Pyramid

The immense Great Pyramid, which is composed of more than two million limestone blocks weighing 2–15 tons (2–15.2 tonnes) each, once rose to a height of more than 480ft (145m). Its sides, which before erosion were around 756ft (230m) long, each face the cardinal points. Associated with Khufu (Cheops, to the Greeks), second ruler of the Fourth Dynasty, the pyramid may have been built *c.* 2528 BCE, although this date has been challenged.

In 2000 Egyptologist Kate Spence published a new theory about how the base of the Great Pyramid came to be aligned to true north with an error of just ³/₆₀th of one degree. Although there was no convenient pole star with which to orient the building, she proposed that circumpolar stars could have provided the solution. Around the time the pyramid was probably built, the celestial pole was positioned precisely between two close, reasonably bright stars: Mizar in Ursa Major (Great Bear), and Kochab in Ursa Minor (Little Bear).

When these two stars aligned vertically, the architects could have used a simple plumb line to bring the alignment with true north down to the ground. An assistant some distance away, presumably armed with a lamp, could have been directed to move from side to side until his light aligned perfectly with the plumb line, the stars and therefore with the celestial north pole.

The other pyramids at Giza are less perfectly aligned. Spence argued that these discrepancies could be explained by subsequent architects using the same alignment method – without realizing that the celestial pole had moved since the construction of the Great Pyramid (due to the precession of the equinoxes, see page 220). Spence calculated that the astronomical survey of the site where the Great Pyramid would be built took place within five years of 2480 BCE.

Another date has been proposed for the Giza pyramids' construction – 10500 BCE. However, this is not taken seriously by academics. Robert Bauval noticed in 1983 that three pyramids resembled the three stars of Orion's Belt. This idea evolved to include another four pyramids as representations of other prominent stars: Bellatrix and Saiph in Orion, and Aldebaran and epsilon Tauri in the Hyades asterism in Taurus, with the River Nile as the Milky Way. The layout of this vast sky map would need the pyramids to be fully 8,000 years older than usually reckoned. As appealing as this grand scheme may sound, the date is simply too remote for conventional scholars to tolerate, and the idea remains a fringe topic.

The star shafts

There are two main rooms within the Great Pyramid. The higher and larger of the two, the King's Chamber, is aligned to the cardinal directions like the pyramid itself, while the Queen's Chamber is horizontally in

the centre of the structure. The names are modern; there is no evidence that the Queen's Chamber ever accommodated a queen, and while the King's Chamber contains a large stone box, which is usually referred to as a sarcophagus, it does not contain a body. However, any treasure the pyramid held was plundered long ago, perhaps including a body.

The Great Pyramid is the only pyramid with star shafts – four small, precisely constructed tunnels through the north and south sides. Only the two leading from the King's Chamber are known to pierce the structure all the way to the outside. The Egyptologist–astronomer team of Professor Alexander Badawy and Dr Virginia Trimble discovered in the 1960s that these star shafts, which extend horizontally for a short distance before bending upward, were aligned to celestial objects.

The northern shaft in the King's Chamber is 7in wide by 5in high (18 x 13cm) and ascends at 31°. It was aligned to the star Thuban (alpha Draconis) which, at the time the pyramid was built, was close to the celestial pole.

Voyage into the afterlife The King's Chamber of the Great Pyramid has two star shafts, one aligned with Thuban (alpha Draconis), and another with Alnitak in Orion's Belt. The Pharaoh was required to visit both these stars to gain immortality before taking his place among the gods.

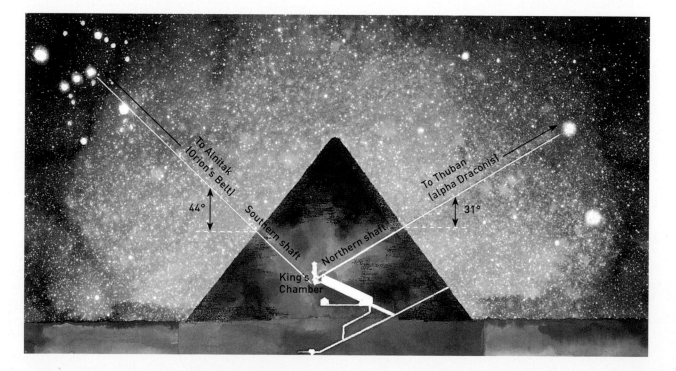

Moon over Giza The pyramids were once faced with white limestone that would have been resplendent in moonlight.

The southern shaft starts more than twice as wide and four times as high, but rapidly narrows to less than half that size. Its ceiling is domed. After about 6ft (1.8m) it bends upward with an angle of 44° and becomes oval in shape, then after a further 8ft (2.5m) the shaft become rectangular and veers very slightly to the west. It points to Alnitak in Orion's Belt, an asterism representing Osiris, the Egyptian god of death and rebirth. The so-called *Pyramid Texts* found in later Old Kingdom royal tombs say the pharaoh had to visit both stars in the afterlife in order to attain immortality and take his place among the gods. The two shafts could have enabled the pharaoh's spirit to leave the pyramid in precisely the direction required.

The shafts in the Queen's Chamber are about 8in (20cm) wide and, as far as is known, were deliberately blocked before reaching the outside air. The southern shaft was aligned to Sirius, the brightest star in the sky after the sun. Sirius is the celestial embodiment of Isis, goddess of fertility and wife to Osiris. This star was particularly important to the early Egyptians because its heliacal rising (first appearance in the eastern sky before dawn) signalled the annual flooding of the Nile – on which the people were entirely dependent for their livelihood.

The northern shaft, it seems, would have been aligned to Polaris – which would not become the pole star until around 1000 CE. The movement of the celestial pole (which only occasionally coincides with a notable star) is due to the gradual shift of the Earth's axis in a 26,000-year cycle known as the precession of the equinoxes (see pages 220–21). Evidence is lacking that the ancient Egyptians understood this cycle (Kate Spence's dating work presumes they were completely ignorant of it), so the reason for this alignment remains one of the pyramid's great mysteries.

VIJAYANAGARA INDIA

The great city of Vijayanagara ("city of victory") was founded around 1336 CE, the centre of the empire that bore its name. It grew from the village of Hampi, which was and remains a religious centre. The ruined city, a World Heritage site, is in southwest India some 220 miles (350km) north of Bangalore and 45 miles (75km) from Bellary in the Karnataka district.

Covering 15 square miles (40 square km), the city was divided into several sectors, including the royal centre with palaces, halls, courts, baths and watchtowers, and the sacred centre of shrines and temples. Much of the city was sacked and destroyed in 1565 in a fierce battle with the Deccan sultanates, the Muslim kingdoms to the north, and most of the city has been deserted ever since. The remains are

Sacred centre Vijayanagara's religious sector (*below, left*) contains many temples, including the Virupaksha. There, a small hole at the sanctuary works like a pinhole camera, projecting an upside-down image of the tower (*below, right*).

extensive, and considerable archaeological research has been carried out here. Although there is much of interest for archaeoastronomers, it is difficult to arrive at firm conclusions about such a complex and long-lived site.

The city's buildings appear to have often been constructed according to astronomical or terrestrial alignments. Many of the structures are cardinally aligned to celestial bodies, but others are oriented toward the surrounding hills. Dr J. McKim Malville, of the University of Colorado at Boulder, notes that temples and shrines to the monkey god Hanuman are aligned to the sunrise at the sun's zenith, while other streets point toward the rising place of Sirius. He and fellow researcher John M. Fritz theorized that the cardinally oriented structures would be favoured by the nobles and priests, while the workers and peasants may have found the geophysical features of the surroundings more relevant.

Virupaksha Temple This magnificent nine-storey gateway or *gopura* marks the entrance of Vijayanagara's largest temple, which is still functioning as a centre of worship today.

Virupaksha Temple

Predating the Vijayanagara Empire is the 7th-century Virupaksha Temple, which contains shrines to the god Shiva and his consort, the local goddess Pampa. At the temple's eastern gateway stands a nine-storey pinnacle of sculpted masonry that soars 160ft (49m) into the sky. A small hole at the sanctuary to the west projects an upside-down image of the tower onto a recess in a dark chamber.

This and other ancient structures at the city's sacred centre, notably the Sri Krishna Temple, which is located some 400ft (120m) directly south of the towering gateway, appear to have been oriented to the cardinal directions.

Centre of the universe

The city's royal centre was divided in two by a ceremonial gateway along a roughly north–south axis, providing separate living areas for the king and queen. This axis cuts across Matanga Hill, 1 mile (1.6km) to the north of the royal centre, on top of which is a temple dedicated to Virabhadra (a fierce warrior deity). An observer standing along the axis to the south would see the pole star shining above the temple. This combination creates a dramatic symbolic representation of the holy mountain Meru, the metaphysical centre of the universe, with Polaris, the centre and pivot of the heavenly sphere, shining brightly above.

INTRODUCING SIRIUS

Sirius is often called the brightest star in the sky, but appearances can be deceptive. While Sirius is 25 times brighter than the sun, there are actually many other stars that shine more brilliantly. For example, Betelgeuse in Orion is 135,000 times brighter than our sun, and star R136a1 in the Tarantula Nebula holds the luminosity record at 8,700,000 times brighter than the sun. Sirius outshines all other stars simply because it is one of our closest stellar neighbours – it is the fifth closest star to us after the sun. Even so, its light takes 8.6 years to reach us.

Egyptian herald of prosperity

The wealth of ancient Egypt was founded on a single natural phenomenon: the flooding of the Nile that deposited nutrient-rich black silt over all the low-lying ground along the river valley. Each year the floods brought fertility to the deserts and the entire year's work revolved around this event: controlling the waters through complex drainage ditches and irrigation canals, nurturing the crops and then storing and distributing the harvest.

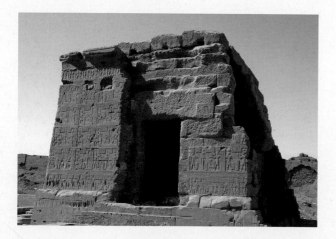

Although the ancient Egyptians knew nothing of the process by which rainfall washed sediment from the Ethiopian Highlands down into the Nile, they discovered the river's behaviour was reasonably predictable. Each year the floods arrived after the heliacal rising of the brightest star – the first sighting of Sirius in the eastern, pre-dawn sky. This astronomical event, which coincided with the summer solstice, was so important that it was celebrated as the start of a new year – the Sothic year (as distinct from either the lunar or solar calendars, which were also in use).

Sothis

The ancient Egyptians called this star Sepdet, but in the Hellenistic period that began in 332 BCE with the arrival of Alexander the Great, it became known as Sothis. The Dendera Zodiac (see pages 158–9) from the Temple of Hathor depicts Sothis as a cow lying on a boat, with a star between its horns (it is located on the zodiac near the constellation of Leo).

Immediately east of Hathor's temple at Dendera lies a small temple dedicated to the goddess Isis. She is closely associated with Sirius because in myth she is the sister and spouse of Osiris, who is seen in the night sky as the adjacent constellation of Orion. The processional way, which connects this temple of Isis with a gateway in the wall that surrounds the entire complex, points toward the heliacal rising of Sirius in around 50 BCE, when this alignment appears to have been established.

Temple of Isis A processional avenue leading from this small temple at Dendera is oriented to the heliacal rising of Sirius in *c.* 50 BCE. The star was associated in Egyptian myth with Isis, whose brother-husband Osiris was linked to nearby Orion.

Panoply of power This ceiling painting from the tomb of Seti I, who ruled Egypt *c.* 1290–1279 BCE, depicts stars and constellations including Sirius (star of Isis, who is elegantly crowned on the far left) and Orion (star of Osiris, who gazes back at his wife).

Alignments at Thoth Hill and Elephantine

Another alignment claimed for Sirius is from the temple of Horus at Thoth Hill, the highest peak west of the Nile at Luxor. The first temple at this site dates to around 3200 BCE, when the heliacal rising of Sirius lay at almost the same position as the rising winter solstice sun. Opinion is divided over whether the star, the sun or both were the intended object of alignment. The same controversy exists over the temple of Satet at Elephantine, which dates to the same period.

Greek herald of misfortune

With Sirius the brightest star in the heavens, we might expect it to feature prominently in ancient sky myths. We know that around 700 BCE the Greek poet Hesiod wrote this following advice in his *Works and Days*, addressed to his brother Perses: "When Orion and Sirius reach midheaven, and rosy-fingered Dawn sees Arcturus, then cut all the grapes, Perses, and bring them home." The prescribed date for this harvest in the agricultural calendar, which saw Sirius high in the south at the heliacal rising of Arcturus, was around the middle of September.

The ancient Greeks and Romans regarded Sirius with dread. The name Sirius means "scorcher" and its heliacal rising in July ushered in the hot, dry season – weeks or months of baking heat known as the Dog Days after the constellation Canis Major (Great Dog) of which this star is part.

Turtle power

The Minton Turtle geoglyph (an effigy delineated on the ground by boulders) in Saskatchewan, Canada, has an almost circular body, four short legs, a pointed tail and a head with two bulging eyes. An alignment straight through its body from the tip of its tail shows it is oriented to the heliacal rising of Sirius in around 2300 BCE, which coincided with the summer solstice. However, archaeological evidence that could date its construction has yet to be found, so the astronomical significance is speculative. The First Nations people respected the turtle as representing life and wisdom.

177

Flickering fox tails

Stars are renowned for twinkling, and being the brightest of all stars, Sirius twinkles in a class of its own. However, it is only after the light has completed its 8.6-year journey through interstellar space that it develops its sparkle. The Earth's atmosphere is full of natural turbulence and many slight fluctuations in the density of our air cause the light to be refracted in random directions, producing the prismatic lightshow.

Some Inuit traditions regard stars as holes in the sky and see the scintillating Sirius as two foxes, one white and one red, vying to be the first into a single foxhole. The Inuit homelands lie in the extreme north, with some communities inside the Arctic Circle, so because Sirius has a declination of -17° below the celestial equator it is only ever seen low down in the southern sky during the winter months. This may account for the redness of the fox: starlight is affected by the same process that gives the rising or setting sun its red hue (light is refracted toward the red end of the spectrum as it slants through the Earth's atmosphere). This may also explain why the Egyptian astronomer Claudius Ptolemy in *c.* 150 CE grouped Sirius, a white star, with red stars such as Betelgeuse.

Brightest star Sirius shines above the Atacama desert (top left of the image); Canopus (on the right) is next brightest.

TWINKLE, TWINKLE LITTLE STAR

Earth's atmosphere bends starlight – the more atmosphere, the more refraction. When starlight travels on a slanting path through the atmosphere, it is bent (and twinkles) more.

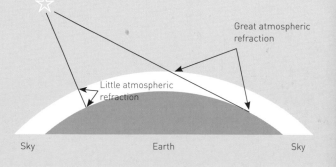

Great atmospheric refraction

Little atmospheric refraction

Sky   Earth   Sky

INTRODUCING THE PLEIADES

This family in the constellation of Taurus is actually a cluster containing more than a thousand stars. It shines with the blue light of hot, young stars a mere 20 million years old. Although most of us find it difficult to count even seven individual Pleiades stars with the naked eye, some people can see more than a dozen. This attractive asterism (a group of stars forming just part of a constellation) is relatively close to Earth, and is one of the most distinctive sights in the sky, celebrated in ancient records and myths from Europe to Australia, and America to China.

Early observations

The earliest documented record of the Pleiades is in the Chinese *Canon of Yao*, which includes observations of the Pleiades made *c.* 2357 BCE. Unfortunately, the oldest surviving copy only dates to the time of the philosopher Kong Fuzi (Confucius) who died in 479 BCE.

The oldest picture of the Pleiades (if we discount the Lascaux claim, see page 200) is the famous Nebra Sky Disc (see page 36), dating to around 1600 BCE. Made of bronze, this famous artefact is inlaid with gold images resembling the crescent moon and solar disc, along with dozens of small gold spots that are clearly stars. Seven of these golden dots are assembled in a cluster and these are generally accepted as representing the Pleiades.

A traditional image of the Sky Father from the Navaho Nation also depicts symbols of the sun, moon and stars including the Pleiades. And the Black Point Ceremonial Pathway of the Yuma Nation in Arizona also contains representations of those elements, as

Devil's Tower This rock in Wyoming is said to have been raised to protect a group of girls from a marauding bear; the young women were then placed in the sky as the Pleiades.

well as the Milky Way. The ancestors of the Yuma are traditionally said to have come from the Pleiades.

Stories of young women

The story goes that the Devil's Tower, Wyoming, was raised up from the ground to protect seven young women from a bear – the creature's claws gouged the distinctive vertical stripes on the rock. The Great Spirit then protected the women from all earthly harm by transforming them into the Pleiades. This extraterrestrial tale is said to have influenced Steven Spielberg in selecting the site as the setting for his 1977 film *Close Encounters of the Third Kind*. Although the formation of arriving UFOs in the film appears to represent the Plough (Big Dipper), the brightest stars in the Pleiades make a remarkably similar pattern.

A legend from southeast Australia tells of a group of girls who were about to perform the initiation ceremony into womanhood, but wished to undertake the more challenging boys' initiation instead. The young women successfully endured the male initiation and were rewarded with transportation into the heavens as the stars of the Pleiades.

AGRICULTURAL CALENDARS

In the 8th century BCE, the Greek writer Hesiod wrote that it was time to plough in readiness for sowing winter wheat when this asterism leaves the skies – that is, when the Pleiades set as the sun rose in October (their cosmical setting). It was time to harvest this winter crop when the Pleiades were first seen in the east, emerging from the dawn glow in April or May (their heliacal rising).

Japanese rice farmers noted how the Pleiades, which they called Subaru, set a little earlier each day. When this asterism set at sunset (its acronychal setting), the farmers knew that they must plant the rice seeds; the Pleiades were said to resemble grains of rice.

THE *HEIAU* HAWAII

Like many Polynesian cultures, the indigenous people of Hawaii made extensive use of temple enclosures or platforms. Called *heiau*, these sacred sites had many functions, such as acting as meeting places for kinship groups or particular ranks in the social hierarchy. They could also be devoted to specific purposes ranging from medicine to warfare and were dedicated to the appropriate deities. Some were small cleared spaces with a stone or wooden perimeter wall surrounding a solitary hut, while others were enormous terraced temples. Some were the scene of human sacrifice.

Archaeologists seeking astronomical alignments amid the many different forms of *heiau* face a daunting and perhaps impossible task. It took a lot of research

to discover that, for example, *heiau* dedicated to fishing shared a common alignment at all, so apparently random were their axes. It turned out they were simply aligned to the sea, in much the same way as temples of the ancient Egyptians were principally oriented to their great life-bringer – the Nile.

The *heiau* of Maui

A rare opportunity to study a group of well-preserved *heiau* in a relatively undisturbed archaeological landscape exists on the island of Maui. In the Kahikinui region of southern Maui, and south of the volcano Haleakala, nearly 30 *heiau* have been found, all dating to around 1600 CE.

A recent survey of this cluster of structures suggests they were divided among the four principal Hawaiian deities, with some being aligned to the sea, some to the north, some to the east and some to a point between north and east at around 70° (roughly east–northeast). This latter group were geographically associated with agriculture and are thought to have been dedicated to the god Lono, who was petitioned by his priests for rain to make agricultural land fertile.

In the winter festival of Makahiki the priests praised Lono, and one of their chants included the observation that he positions the stars in the heavens. Significantly, the stars themselves determined the date of this festival, which usually began in November. It commenced on the evening of the first new moon

Ancient and modern Dedicated to the rain god Lono (*above*), among other deities, the Maui *heiau* are grouped south of the Haleakala volcano (*left*), where the first of the Pan-STARRS telescopes now warns of approaching asteroids and comets.

Pi'ilanihale Heiau This impressive temple platform, in the Kahanu Gardens on the northeast of Maui island, is the largest *heiau* in Hawaii and was built to serve a royal family. It dates back to the early 14th century but was rebuilt and rededicated *c.* 1600.

following the sunset when, in the deepening twilight of dusk, the Pleiades were last seen to rise over the eastern horizon (their acronychal rising). The start of summer was also determined by the Pleiades, and usually fell in May when the star cluster was first seen in the east before sunrise (their heliacal rising).

Apart from being the name of the winter festival, Makahiki also means "year" and is believed to be an abbreviated form of *makali'i-hiki* – which translates as the "rising of the Pleiades". On the north of the neighbouring island of Molokai is the peninsula of Kalaupapa, and here is another *heiau* that is oriented to the same direction. The promontory on

which it stands is called Makali'i – a name which translates as "Pleiades".

Defending our planet

The indigenous people of Hawaii used astronomy to determine the ritual and agricultural year for their convenience and well-being. Today, the University of Hawaii is working with other institutions around the world to use the volcanic mountain of Haleakala for a similar purpose. In 2010 the first of four Pan-STARRS telescopes went live in the high, clear air. The primary purpose of this complex is to warn of asteroids and comets that are on course to collide with our planet.

THE *MOAI* RAPA NUI

The tiny island of Rapa Nui (known to Westerners as Easter Island due to its discovery on Easter Sunday, 1722) is one of the most isolated places on Earth: the nearest inhabited land is Pitcairn Island more than 1,200 miles (2,000km) away. Rapa Nui was formed by three extinct volcanoes and is only around 15 miles long by 7½ miles wide (24 x 12km).

When the original inhabitants, who probably came from the Marquesas Islands in what is now French Polynesia, reached the island some time between 500 and 1200 CE, the fertile land of Rapa Nui was largely covered with subtropical broadleaf forest. By the time the first Europeans arrived in the 18th century, the island was essentially treeless and mostly barren – an ecological disaster had occurred.

The deforestation of the island, which seems to have started around 1200 CE, was partly due to a culture of carving and erecting *moai*. The moving of these famous stone statues doubtless involved many tree trunks. The *moai* have hugely exaggerated heads and are thought to have represented deified ancestors. There are nearly 900 of them, although around half still lie only partially formed in the quarry where they were being carved from hardened volcanic ash. On average, these monoliths are 14½ft (4.4m) tall and weigh some 14 tons (14.2 tonnes).

Orientation of the *moai*

Most *moai* are found at the coast, with the statues forming a perimeter guard all around the island. Given the sheer number of statues ringing the island, anyone seeking astronomical alignments is bound

Gazing at the stars Originally thought to be facing away from the summer solstice, the *moai* of Ahu Tongariki are now believed to be oriented toward the setting of the Pleiades.

to find them. *Moai* are positioned with their backs to the sea; although some also seem to be aligned to astronomical events, alignments are usually regarded as false positives – merely accidental by-products of their intended placement with respect to the ocean.

In the 1960s, archaeologist William Mulloy noted alignments that he suggested related to the solstice sun. His work was built upon in the late 1980s by astronomer William Liller, whose survey of the island found notable astronomical alignments to the sun at the solstices and equinoxes among the *moai* that were inland or not oriented topographically to the sea.

Around 125 *moai* were originally placed on their own *ahu*, a ceremonial and sacred platform that served as a dais for the statues. Ahu Tongariki on the southeast coast near Poike is the largest on the island, with 15 *moai* – including one huge statue weighing some 85 tons (86 tonnes). The long, narrow *ahu* struck researchers because a perpendicular line extended from it would head directly across the sea toward sunrise at the summer solstice (which, as Rapa Nui lies south of the equator, is in December).

However, this site presented a challenge for archaeoastronomers because, like the solitary coastal

moai, these figures are positioned with their backs to the sea. It may be that this particular site provided a perhaps unique combination of solar orientation and traditional coastal positioning.

In fact, Ahu Tongariki, like all the other *ahu* with supposed solstice and equinox alignments, posed another profound problem. Why were the Easter Islanders, alone among all their Polynesian kin, favouring solar alignments at all?

Looking to the Pleiades

In the 1910s, ethnographer Katherine Routledge recorded the traditional astronomical lore of the island's elders. Tragically, her best efforts could only collect a tiny fraction of the once vast knowledge of the indigenous people. Before the arrival of Europeans, the Rapanui had been isolated for many centuries and had acquired a great understanding of the heavens, which was essential for their survival. Priests used astronomy to regulate the seasonal cycles of agriculture, hunting and fishing, and these were celebrated in annual festivals.

First contact with Europeans in 1722 heralded a time of great upheaval for the Rapanui. In the mid-19th century many were taken as slaves; introduced diseases took their toll on the remaining population; and the arrival of evangelical Roman Catholicism not only replaced the ancient calendar of festivals with the Christian feasts of the saints, but also denounced the ancient wisdom as paganism and suppressed it vigorously. Even the secrets of the indigenous writing system known as Rongorongo were lost. Although many researchers believe one example of Rongorongo contains details of a lunar calendar, it remains, like all the other texts, yet to be deciphered.

However, the scraps of astronomical knowledge that Routledge preserved have been invaluable in assessing the *moai* and other monuments. Recent

Mystery of the *moai* Archaeoastronomical interpretations for some of the carved monoliths erected by the Rapanui have evolved from solar to stellar, but most *moai* seem to have been positioned simply in relation to the coast.

Ahu Akivi Once given a solar interpretation, the seven *moai* of Ahu Akivi are now thought to be positioned to face the setting of the asterism that forms the three stars in Orion's Belt.

and ongoing research, by Juan Belmonte, Edmundo Edwards and his daughter Alexandra Edwards, has revealed that the key marker for annual festivals was not the sun but Matariki – the Pleiades. The 15 *moai* of Ahu Tongariki were not turning their backs on the solstice sunrise, but were facing the setting of the Pleiades over the nearby hill of Rano Raraku.

Ahu Akivi, built around 1500 CE, supports seven *moai* gazing toward the ocean from the southwestern slope of Terevaka, the largest of the island's three volcanoes. These *moai* were originally interpreted as staring at the equinoctial sunset, but now are regarded as watching the setting asterism of Tautori – the three stars of Orion's Belt.

The rock for seeing the stars
Routledge had been told of a site called Papa ui hetu'u ("rock for seeing the stars"). This was a seemingly clear reference to a stellar observatory, identified as a basalt outcrop on the northeastern flank of the extinct volcano Poike. It is perhaps the best place on the

island for observing the Pleiades as the asterism both rises from and sets into the sea.

A basalt boulder at the site bears numerous petroglyphs of the traditional stone fish hooks used for deep sea fishing. The astronomical marker that announced the start of the important deep sea fishing season was the first sighting of the rising Pleiades seen through the twilight of sunset (the acronychal rising) on 16 November. Another boulder near by is renowned as a star map, with cupules (small, hemispherical indentations) carved into it in a pattern closely resembling the stars of the Pleiades.

Edmundo and Alexandra Edwards are also undertaking an investigation into the low, stone towers known as *tupa* which, according to ethnographical evidence, were observatories used by priests to determine important calendrical dates. Of the 18 *tupa* surveyed in 2010, 17 demonstrated alignments to important seasonal stars or asterisms, or were oriented to the cardinal points. Clearly, Rapa Nui has many secrets yet to be revealed.

INTRODUCING THE MILKY WAY

The Milky Way galaxy is a spinning disc of stars, dust and gas from whose central hub flow either two or four main spiral arms composed of stars. Our sun is situated on the inner edge of a minor arm named Orion-Cygnus, about halfway out from the centre of the galaxy. When we gaze at the Milky Way we are looking along the plane of the galactic disc – full of stars. In and around July we can gaze into the galaxy's heart, home to the greatest concentration of stars and a supermassive black hole (the largest type of black hole), around 26,000 light years away.

In folklore, the Milky Way is generally deemed a river or road, ethereal and distant, travelled only by spirits of the dead or a variety of deities. But there are some notable exceptions. Near the Elvina Track in the Ku-ring-gai Chase National Park near Sydney, Australia, is an elegant engraving of an emu. Although

it is only an outline, it carefully re-creates the details of the bird's physiognomy, yet the legs are drawn at an angle that means they would be unable to support the body. This apparent defect has been interpreted as the hallmark of an accurate astronomical observation.

One legend, widespread in southern and parts of central Australia, tells of a gigantic primal emu called Tchingal who was fearless and fierce. Eventually, the other creatures combined their forces and succeeded in slaying the ravenous predator. The bird of this legend is unforgettable because the bird is there for all to see in the night sky, not in constellations joined by imaginary lines as in Western myths, but silhouetted by the glowing star fields of the Milky Way. The head of this vast emu is the Coalsack Nebula and the asterism of the Southern Cross (part of the constellation Crux). The bird's long, sinuous neck, oval body and extended legs trail through the sky toward the southern constellation of Scorpius, the Scorpion.

The emu is of great cultural and spiritual significance to Indigenous Australians and not always viewed as a malevolent or destructive character. It is regarded as a totem animal for the male Aboriginal elders, because it is the male emu that incubates and nurtures the eggs, just as the male elders nurture and initiate the young men. The bird's eggs, meat and feathers all play a part in Aboriginal livelihood. Emus lay their eggs in May and June, and the engraved emu at Ku-ring-gai is oriented on the stone so that when viewers raise their eyes from the rock and see the emu in the sky soaring in parallel, directly above it, the time is ripe for egg gathering.

Emu in the sky (*Far left*) The Milky Way is visible above the emu engraving at Elvina Track. (*Left*) Here, the shape of the bird is highlighted in the sky and on the ground.

TEMPLE OF THE FOX PERU

Buena Vista is an ancient settlement in the Rio Chillón Valley in the Andes north of Lima. It was discovered in 1987 by Frederic Engel, and detailed archaeological investigation into the site has been led by Robert Benfer since 2002. The site, on a barren, rocky hillside, overlooks a fertile valley that is the source of the site's name – Buena Vista ("good view"). The fertility of this valley stems from its river, whose tributaries reach high into the mountains. Each year, as the spring sun thaws the ice, the river rises in spate and covers the valley floor with fresh, rich soil.

Temple alignments

At the rear of one temple, a large sculpture depicts a menacing, circular face flanked by two unidentified animals. The face gazes straight through two doorways toward sunset on the winter (June) solstice.

Adjacent stands a temple pyramid some 33ft (10m) high, which was built over an earlier building nearly 55ft (17m) long. Benfer called this older structure the Temple of the Fox in honour of the remarkable image inside, which appears to depict a fox-like creature curled like a foetus in the womb of a llama.

Standing inside this temple and looking through a small window behind the altar, Benfer noticed what seemed to be the profile of a human head framed by a natural notch in the hillside around 200ft (60m) away. He found that the head was carved on an 8ft (2.5m) rock situated on an alignment running from the temple to the rising sun at midsummer (December).

The construction of this temple has been reliably dated to around 2200 BCE, making it older than any other astronomically aligned building previously discovered in South America. At that time, the Andean dark cloud constellation of the Fox (a shape consisting of interstellar dust that blots out the stars behind it)

Menacing disc This sculpture of an angry face at the Temple of the Fox stares through two doorways at the midwinter sunset.

would have been visible before dawn on the summer solstice, rising from the same hillside as the sun. This was the time of the river's annual flood, a pivotal event that announced the season of sowing. The fox is revered in the Andes for having taught people the secrets of irrigation and agriculture.

The shape of the fox in the temple is a remarkable match to the sinuous shape of the dark constellation of the Fox, while the body of the "llama" that contains it appears to represent the fuzzy white haze of the Milky Way. The dark constellation of the Fox straddles the modern constellations of Sagittarius and Scorpio, while its tail extends into Ophiuchus.

Spookily, on the day Benfer's team started their excavation, a fox arrived at the site and settled down to watch – and stayed until the work was complete.

MISMINAY PERU

Midway between the ancient Inca capital of Cuzco and the citadel of Machu Picchu lies the isolated village of Misminay. Here, some 12,500ft (3,800m) up in the Peruvian Andes, the Quechuan inhabitants live in much the same way as their ancient Inca ancestors. Corn, potatoes and quinoa are grown as staple crops in hand-tilled or oxen-ploughed fields, llama and alpaca hair is woven into clothing, and knowledge of the cycle of the seasons is vital to survival.

The beliefs of the people in this settlement were investigated in the 1970s by Gary Urton, who had a particular interest in ethnoastronomy. His endeavours revealed a wealth of detail about calendar lore still in use in the modern era. For instance, the times for planting and harvesting are determined by the sun and moon rising or setting at specific locations in the mountains. The Pleiades and the tail of Scorpio (which are opposite each other in the sky) are referred to as the "celestial storehouses". But the most significant heavenly object for the people of Misminay is the Milky Way, resulting in a unique interplay of sky and village.

The cross in the circle

At this latitude (14° south of the equator) the galactic plane that we call the Milky Way, and which local people call the "river of the sky", has a distinct and fascinating cycle. The stars are exceptionally clear and bright in the mountain air, and our galaxy arches overhead across the evening sky in June and July. The Milky Way divides the sky, stretching from the northeast horizon to the southwest. As the Earth rotates, this luminous band seems to slide down to the horizon, where the answering half of the Milky Way has been rising to meet it – the observer is briefly encircled in its majestic glow.

This shifting of the starry heavens continues, but is made invisible by the returning light of day. However, six months later the heavens that were obscured by sunshine are now revealed at night. In December and January the sky after dusk is again bisected by the Milky Way – this time from northwest to southeast.

These two lines have become superimposed on the minds of the villagers and are replicated in the design of the village – as above, so below. Two pathways are aligned to the intercardinal points marked by the Milky Way. Beside each path flows an irrigation channel, again reflecting the two positions of the river of stars. At the crossroads in the centre of this terrestrial design, and at the heart of the village, stands a small chapel aptly called Crucero – "cross".

The intercardinal directions of the paths also align roughly with the positions of the rising and setting sun at the solstices, further tying the celestial sphere to the cycles of the Earth below. Misminay is thus a reflection of the sky above, and in harmony with the whole cosmos.

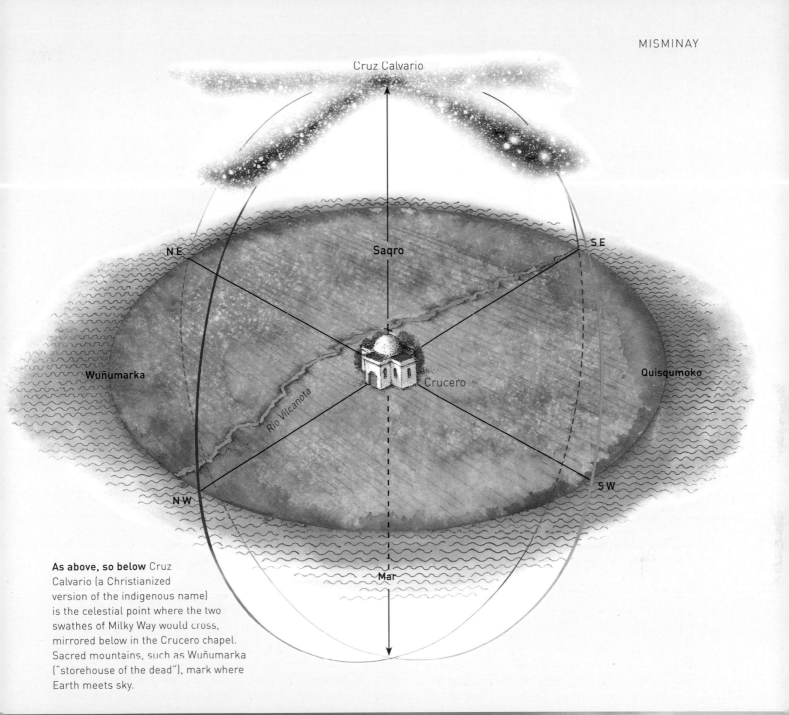

Cruz Calvario

N E

Saqro

S E

Wuñumarka

Río Vilcanota

Crucero

Quisqumoko

N W

S W

Mar

As above, so below Cruz Calvario (a Christianized version of the indigenous name) is the celestial point where the two swathes of Milky Way would cross, mirrored below in the Crucero chapel. Sacred mountains, such as Wuñumarka ("storehouse of the dead"), mark where Earth meets sky.

INTRODUCING THE GREAT BEAR

The seven brightest stars of Ursa Major (Great Bear) are popularly known as the Plough or Big Dipper. This asterism is very familiar in the northern hemisphere because of its traditional value as a navigation aid, with two prominently positioned stars pointing toward the north celestial pole, marked by the star Polaris. However, this relatively modern alignment has only been notable in the last thousand years or so, caused by the gradual shift of the pole in the 26,000-year cycle of precession (see pages 220–21).

The Bull's Foreleg

In ancient Egypt, Ursa Major was pictured as the foreleg of a bull and was instrumental in determining some temple alignments. An inscription on the wall of the Temple of Hathor, Dendera, describes a ceremony called the Stretching of the Cord during which the pharaoh noted the course of the stars rising into the heavens. It was said that when he found the *ak* of the constellation of the Bull's Foreleg (Meskhet), he could establish the orientation and layout of the temple. The word *ak* is variously translated as "middle", "spirit" or "brilliant", but in this context it is likely to have a specific, technical meaning that awaits rediscovery.

Founded in the mid-1st century BCE, the temple is aligned 18° east of north. There may be a clue to the meaning of *ak* in the fact that at this site the Bull's Foreleg is not entirely circumpolar because the star at the "hoof", Alkaid, sets – and, at the time the temple was built, this star rose again 18° to the east of north.

The Stretching of the Cord ritual has astronomical associations dating to the raising of the Giza pyramids, 3,500 years before the temple at Dendera. The Temple of Horus at Edfu, built early in the 3rd century BCE, bears a similar inscription to that at Dendera. The pharaoh is described taking a pole and mallet, fixing

Stretching of the Cord A relief at the Red Chapel of Hatshepsut, Karnak, depicts this ritual, linked to the Plough.

his attention on the Bull's Foreleg and awaiting the right moment to determine the temple's position.

This ceremony was sometimes undertaken in the presence of the goddess Seshat, as depicted at the Red Chapel of Hatshepsut, Karnak. Here, the pharaoh and the goddess each have a mallet poised to strike the poles into the ground, to establish a line for the temple's foundation. An early symbol of Seshat was the crescent moon, the celestial timekeeper, but she is also associated with a seven-rayed star that may relate to the seven bright stars of the Plough.

The Bull's Foreleg also features in the important Opening of the Mouth ceremony (see pages 166–7).

Celestial signpost The asterism known as the Plough or Big Dipper is possibly the most readily recognized in the night sky, perhaps because of its traditional role as a marker pointing to the north celestial pole.

Encounters with bears

Many people claim to have found representations of Ursa Major in rock art. In 2008 Jiacai Wu recognized the shape of the constellation among the 19 cup marks he found on an elongated oval stone some 10ft (3m) long on Baimiaozi mountain in Inner Mongolia. The carvings are thought to be Hongshan, a Stone Age culture that inhabited the area around 4000 BCE.

Another example is a large standing stone with 56 cup marks at Dalby, Denmark, identified in 1920 as showing Ursa Major and the zodiac constellations Gemini, Cancer, Leo and Virgo. Other sites with cup-marked stones supposedly featuring Ursa Major

have been found in England, France, Germany and Switzerland. Claims in South Korea not only include Bronze Age dolmens (stone burial chambers) with markings that resemble Ursa Major, but also a cluster of dolmens arranged in the shape of the constellation's principal seven stars. A stone found in 1978 beside a dolmen at Adeugi, Chungbuk province, was hailed as a star chart depicting Ursa Major, Ursa Minor and Draco – whose star Thuban was the pole star at the time the dolmens were built, c. 1500 BCE.

While undoubtedly sincere, such claims are treated with scepticism by many people. Although some may actually depict these stars, so many stones have cup marks that some are bound to show patterns similar to constellations, simply by chance.

Myths of Glastonbury

Often dismissed as coincidence, a theory published in 1990 by John Michell suggests that the seven prominent stars of Ursa Major were mapped onto seven sacred islands at Glastonbury, England. These were identified as being at Nyland, Marchey, Panborough, Godney, Meare, Beckery and the Isle of Avalon (around the site of Glastonbury Abbey), matching the Ursa Major stars from Alkaid to Dubhe. Michell's work builds on the Glastonbury Zodiac envisaged by Katherine Maltwood in the 1920s. She believed that the streams, roads and fields and other physical boundaries around Glastonbury traced gigantic figures in the landscape that, she said, were crafted in ancient times to mirror the celestial zodiac.

The sky bear

Archaeoastronomy still has many puzzles that hint at ideas as yet unwelcome in the canon of mainstream thinking. Why, for example, were the stars of Ursa Major named for a bear? The constellation doesn't resemble the animal and some old star charts give the creature a long tail (accounting for Alkaid, Mizar and Alioth) that is absent in real bears. Yet the idea of a sky bear, the ancestor of the human race, is compellingly widespread – occurring from Alaska in the far west to Siberia in the east. Roslyn Frank has suggested that these traditions may be the remnants of a cultural belief dating to the Upper Palaeolithic period (40000–10000 BCE). Some weight is given to the theory by stories of the sky bear prevalent in the Basque Country which, as its people are the last in western Europe to speak the pre-Indo-European language that is over 6,000 years old, is thought to retain a relatively pure legacy from that period of the Stone Age.

Glastonbury star map The Glastonbury area is believed by some to have contained in ancient times seven sacred islands standing for the seven brightest stars of Ursa Major.

OTHER STARS AND CONSTELLATIONS

The human imagination has conjured up many stories and theories about the stars. In ancient times, people must have used the stars to organize their lives in various ways, noting the way the visible constellations changed with the seasons – certain constellations presided over warm summer evenings, for example, while others twinkled above winter frost. The heliacal rising of particular stars or constellations (their first appearance on the eastern horizon before dawn) at certain times of year could provide reliable cues for a wide range of natural events and farming activities, and the stars could even act a summons for people to start the journey to an important secular gathering or religious celebration.

Consulting the oracle at Delphi

One of the 48 original constellations listed by the Greek astronomer Ptolemy around 150 CE, the small but distinctive constellation of Delphinus, the Dolphin, is very ancient. Legend tells that a dolphin acted as an ambassador of Poseidon, god of the sea, who had fallen in love with the beautiful but chaste nymph Amphitrite. His suit being successful, the grateful god raised the dolphin to immortality in the sky. With a little imagination it is easy to see the five stars as a dolphin joyously leaping in the heavens.

An example of stars being employed to determine when to make a pilgrimage may have occurred at Delphi, the famous oracular centre in ancient Greece. The heliacal rising of the constellation Delphinus could have indicated when pilgrims should begin the journey to Delphi in order to arrive in time to question the priestess of the sacred oracle.

Delphi was considered to be the centre of the ancient world and, even before its oracle became famous, the location was sacred to the Earth Mother, Gaia. The names of both the place and the mammal come from the same Greek root meaning "womb", Delphi being the womb of the Earth Mother, while the dolphin was known as the fish with a womb.

In later times, worship of Apollo displaced the other deities – Themis, Poseidon and Gaia herself – who were once associated with Delphi, and the site grew to include a temple, gymnasium and stadium. Pilgrims made their way to Delphi to ask questions of the oracle, an opportunity that some researchers believe occurred on only one day each year. As a timely arrival was imperative, paying attention to the behaviour of Delphinus would have been all the more important.

Delphi's omphalos (*Left*) The omphalos ("navel"), indicating the centre of the world, was probably sited near the oracle and was said to be itself a channel of divine communication.

Centre of pilgrimage (*Right*) The Sanctuary of Athena at Delphi. Little evidence remains today of oracular rites at Delphi, as the Temple of Apollo was razed by Christians in the 4th century CE.

THORNBOROUGH ENGLAND

On a plateau about half a mile (just under 1km) west of the English village of Thornborough, North Yorkshire, is one of the most intriguing structures of the prehistoric world: the Thornborough henges.

Dating to the 3rd millennium BCE, these three henges are aligned northwest–southeast in an almost straight row about 1 mile (1.6km) long. They are very similar in size, shape and distance from each other. Each henge is around 790ft (240m) across, with a flat central area, an encircling ditch and a high enclosing bank featuring two opposing entrances oriented to the overall alignment. The soil excavated from the ditch was heaped up as a bank outside the ditch (the opposite way round to a conventional fortification).

There are many other Neolithic remains in the area, as well as subsequent Bronze Age monuments. Close to the southernmost henge is a double row of pits, which were probably dug to accommodate large wooden posts. These rows are aligned north-northeast–south-southwest, and near the terminus of each row is a round barrow (burial mound).

As is often the case with Neolithic sites, the henges appear to form part of a wider sacred landscape in which monuments are subtly connected. Ritual sites were integrated with agricultural and living spaces, forming a harmonious whole.

The cursus

Thornborough has long been a focus for controversy because of commercial pressure to expand nearby aggregate quarrying, which has already encroached on the west and north of the area and destroyed the western terminus of the cursus. This cursus is a narrow enclosure at least 3,600ft (1,100m) long and just 144ft (44m) wide, which was constructed around 3500 BCE. This sort of monument, which is demarcated by banked ditches, is one of the mysteries of the Neolithic period. Although cursus are presumed to have served a ritual purpose, there is no telling precisely what form or purpose they had. The destruction is not exclusively modern: the central henge actually overlays part of the cursus, supplanting it in the landscape.

This cursus is aligned roughly northeast–southwest and a study by Dr Jan Harding of Newcastle University found it to be aligned to the rising sun on the summer solstice. He also determined that, in the opposite direction, the axis pointed toward the setting of three stars in the constellation of Orion, an asterism known as Orion's Belt.

The henge alignment

Although the southernmost henge is in very poor condition, the northerly one has survived remarkably well, perhaps because it has been protected inside a patch of woodland. Archaeological investigation of the central henge suggests that the high, circular banks were covered with gypsum, a glistening white crystalline mineral found in the locality. The general consensus of opinion is that this was an important ritual or ceremonial centre – a pilgrimage site that attracted people from a wide catchment area.

Positioned on a plateau, the Thornborough henges were each surrounded by an embankment so high that, from within, the distant horizon would have been invisible. These henges were places deliberately set apart from the outside world, where attention could be focused upward toward the sky.

Time for pilgrimage

If Thornborough was a centre of seasonal pilgrimage, and if its henges superseded the earlier midsummer

Integrated landscape The three similarly sized henges are each enclosed by a ditch and bank, their entrances oriented to the overall alignment. The central henge's southern edge overlays the cursus, which is perpendicular to the henge axis.

sunrise event commemorated by the cursus, could they have been constructed during a period of increased interest in Orion's Belt? If so, the heliacal rise of this asterism in late summer may have been a trigger for pilgrims to prepare for the journey to the ceremonial centre.

A few weeks after the belt first appears in the pre-dawn sky comes the heliacal rise of Sirius, the brightest star in the sky. A feature of the three stars of Orion's Belt is that they possess a natural alignment toward Sirius. At the first sight of Sirius, the three stars of the belt would already be bright and clearly visible above the southern entrance of each henge.

It has also been suggested that the three henges were constructed to mirror the shape and alignment of Orion's Belt. Without further proof, this theory remains speculative. However, the rising and setting positions of stars change due to the precession of the equinoxes (see pages 220–21), and the position of Orion's Belt in relation to the alignment of the henges happens to match for the very period when the henges are thought to have been constructed. If further dating evidence confirms this appealing and plausible but academically tentative conjecture, the possible association of henges with a Neolithic star cult could have major implications for the reinterpretation of many other sites of this age. Such proof would also catapult the Thornborough henges into the company of the most important archaeoastronomical sites in Europe.

LASCAUX FRANCE

The magnificent paintings of the Lascaux cave system were discovered near Montignac in the Dordogne, southwest France, in 1940 when a group of four teenagers and their dog found a hole in the ground left by a fallen tree.

Eight years later, tourists were allowed in and the damage to the irreplaceable artwork began. Water vapour, carbon dioxide and heat given off by what eventually amounted to around a thousand visitors a day encouraged the growth of fungi and algae that ate away at the fragile pigments. Inappropriate and misguided attempts to fix the problem only made it worse and in 1963 the cave had to be closed to the public. Visitors were placated with Lascaux 2, a replica built a short distance away from the original. The problem still persists and access to the cave is now extremely limited, even for the scientific community. Lascaux is a World Heritage site.

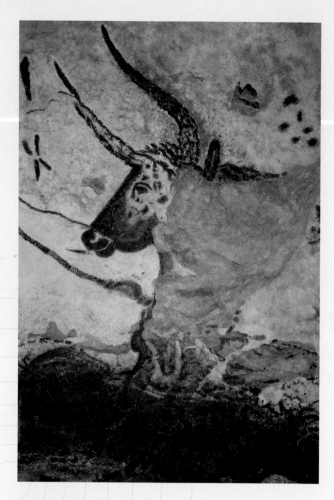

Star symbolism (*Above*) The six dots above this aurochs' shoulder may represent the Pleiades; the dots on its face may stand for the Hyades (also part of Taurus).
Protected art (*Opposite*) Visitors today may only view replicas of the stunning prehistoric images at Lascaux.

The Hall of Bulls

Most likely created over many generations, the Lascaux paintings represent some of the finest and oldest prehistoric art in the world. The site's most famous feature is the Hall of Bulls, a chamber roughly 60ft long and 21ft wide (18 x 6.5m). As might be expected, this cave contains many images of bulls – or rather aurochs, an extinct species of giant cattle that roamed the plains when these paintings were created, around 15000 BCE.

The most prominent aurochs, some 18ft (5.5m) long, has several intriguing features that have led several researchers to believe it represents part of the constellation of Taurus, the Bull. In the early 1990s Luz Antequera Congregado noted a cluster of six dots above the aurochs' shoulder that, she thought, closely resembled the Pleiades. She also suggested that the dots on the animal's face may represent the Hyades, whose V-shaped asterism forms the most familiar part of the constellation Taurus. But even where an identification looks positive, it may still be discounted if other similar patterns do not support it. Elsewhere in the Hall of Bulls other aurochs have similar painted speckles around their eyes, but these are not V-shaped. Further analysis is required before the Pleiades can safely be said to be depicted in the Hall of Bulls.

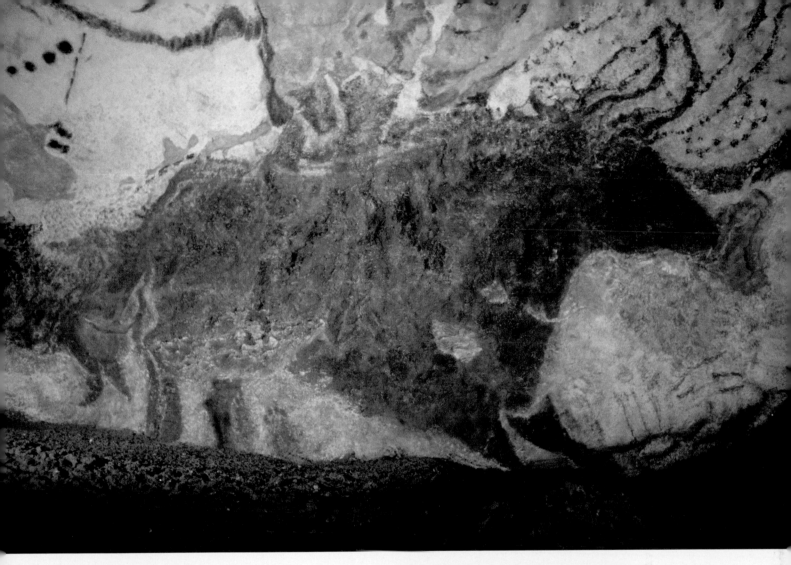

THE BULL – A POWERFUL SYMBOL

Throughout the ages the bull has been seen as a symbol of physical strength and mental determination, from Nandi, the white bull ridden by the Indian god Shiva, to the bull whose form the Greek chief god Zeus took in his pursuit of the princess Europa. Around 1200 BCE the first letter of the Phoenician alphabet – from which we derive our letter A – was named in honour of the ox (this letter is like a sideways A, or a bull's head with two horns). As noted on page 194, some researchers have speculated about a Palaeolithic origin for the widespread tradition of the celestial bear (Ursa Major) – perhaps the celestial bull has a similarly long pedigree.

The same aurochs (known prosaically as number 18) seems to be looking toward a row of four dots, and these have been interpreted as the distinctive stars in the belt of the constellation Orion. But the belt actually consists of a row of three stars, not four, a discrepancy that is difficult to explain.

Aurochs by moonlight

The Hall of Bulls is sometimes called the Rotunda owing to the arched roofspace above a broad swathe of white calcite that runs like a ribbon around the lower part of the chamber's ceiling. The American astronomer Frank Edge has suggested that the frieze of paintings on the crystalline canvas represents an arc of the night sky containing stars along more than half the ecliptic, including the constellations of Canis Minor, Libra, Scorpius and Sagittarius.

Of the 11 aurochs depicted in the cave, only two face each other head to head and these stand on the wall opposite the Taurus bull. Edge linked the pair of head-to-head aurochs with the constellations of Leo and Orion/Gemini, and has argued that when they were painted, the space between the aurochs' horns would have contained the position of the full moon at the summer solstice. At that time of year, he explained, this pair of constellations would be low down in the sky after sunset, appearing as if they were standing on the horizon.

The Lascaux cave complex contains more than 2,000 painted and engraved images, so sceptics point out that chance alone could create a juxtaposition of elements that resemble a prehistoric star map.

Paired constellations In an unusual head-to-head stance, these aurochs in Lascaux's Hall of Bulls have been linked with the constellations of Leo and Orion/Gemini.

The Summer Triangle

Mystery surrounds the meaning of a group of three paintings in a side passage known as the Shaft. This group contains the only human figure painted in the caves. He is not in a natural pose but appears to be lying rigid as if he has fallen with his arms out to his sides. In front of him is an aurochs with its head lowered as if charging him, and behind him is a curious depiction of a bird perched on a vertical stick.

All are depicted in profile, presenting three visible eyes. These, according to German scholar Dr Michael Rappenglueck, may correspond to the three stars of the asterism we know as the Summer Triangle, which are among the 20 brightest stars in the entire sky. In this scenario, the eye of the man is Deneb (in Cygnus, the Swan), the eye of the aurochs is Vega (in Lyra, the Lyre) and eye of the bird is Altair (in Aquila, the Eagle). Around the time of the painting, the closest bright star to the celestial pole was Delta Cygni, a star on the Swan's wing. This would have been situated almost midway between Deneb and Vega, and the Summer Triangle (along with the entire heavens) would have appeared to revolve around it each day.

The man's head is not drawn in a realistic way but is remarkably similar to the bird's head, which has led some commentators to suggest that he is a shaman whose totem creature was the bird (the stick on which the bird stands may have been a sort of wizard's wand or staff). Perhaps the man is not dead, as many modern visitors assume, but actually lying in a trance while his spirit takes flight into the vault of the heavens.

Bright stars The three visible eyes of the human figure, aurochs and bird in the Shaft are said to represent the three bright stars of the Summer Triangle asterism.

STAR CHARTS OF MALTA

The carved limestone slab found at the Tal Qadi temple in the north of Malta's main island underlines the importance of astronomy to the people who built this Mediterranean island's famous temples (see pages 32–5). Around 11½ x 9in in area and 2in thick (29 x 24 x 5cm), the stone is incised with radiating lines that divide the surface into five segments. Carved between these lines are numerous star symbols. One segment contains only a wide crescent like the moon when it is nearly at (or just past) its half-moon phase.

Many people suppose this rough-edged slab was originally part of a disc – a sky map – that would have been divided by carved lines into around 16 segments. This number is consistent with the idea of the year being divided into four seasons by the solstices and equinoxes, and then being subdivided further.

Although it is not possible to date the stone itself, pottery and other items found at the Tal Qadi temple have been dated to between 3000 and 2500 BCE.

Counting the days

The interest of the early inhabitants of Malta in the stars also appears to be confirmed by curious markings on two stone pillars at the northern temple at Mnajdra (see pages 32–5). This temple is the oldest of the three in the complex, dating to 3500–3000 BCE. Each pillar is marked with uneven rows of small holes. The numbers of holes in each row do not match exactly, but after a few rows or so the cumulative total of holes on each pillar does match remarkably closely. And a few rows later the totals match again, and so on. This unexpected consistency was identified in 1993 by Frank Ventura, Giorgia Fodera Serio and Michael Hoskin, who interpreted the dots as a sort of tally, counting off the days between the first sightings of significant stars or asterisms.

Mapping the night sky Stars are represented on the Tal Qadi stone by criss-crossing lines; the moon by a wide crescent.

The heliacal rising of the Pleiades was taken as the starting point. This event coincided with the spring equinox *c.* 3000 BCE and the passage of the complex's southern temple is aligned precisely in this direction. The dots on the pillars were found to correspond to intervals between the heliacal risings of: Aldebaran in Taurus; the Hyades in Taurus; Betelgeuse in Orion; Bellatrix in Orion; Rigel in Orion; Sirius in Canis Major; Mirzam in Canis Major; Arcturus in Boötes; gamma Crucis in Crux; and Hadar in Centaurus.

Comparisons with other early star lists such as the decans of ancient Egypt (see page 158) have been suggested, but as those are perhaps a thousand years younger than the list at the Mnajdra temple, it would be difficult to trace any spread of ideas.

MONTE ALBÁN MEXICO

Monte Albán, the ancient capital of the Zapotec people, lies immediately to the west of Oaxaca City, Mexico. Founded around 500 BCE, the city was built nearly 1¼ miles (2km) above sea level, on an artificially levelled ridge. The citadel lacks conventional dwellings and is believed to have been a purely ceremonial centre, occupying an area roughly 1,500 x 2,600ft (450 x 800m). This site was abandoned around 750 CE.

The buildings of Monte Albán are usually aligned between 4° and 8° east of north, and are square or rectangular in plan, but there is a single dramatic exception – the structure designated Building J, better known as the Observatory. This curious building is roughly the shape of a pentagonal shield – the shape has also been described as a triangle with two corners cut away.

Damon E. Peeler and Marcus Winter suggested in 1995 that if the structure's three main sides are extended to form a triangle, the resulting measurements offer evidence that the Observatory enshrined calendrical significance. If the two sides that form the pointed tip are extended to meet a line projected from the longer, third side (to the northeast), then this third side of the triangle would measure 253ft (77m). The lengths of the shorter sides are not quite equal, being 158ft on the southern side and 181ft on the western side (48 and 55m). However, the ratio of the northeastern side to the western side is 1:4 – the ratio between the solar year of 365 days and the sacred Maya cycle of 260 days (see page 107).

Furthermore, a line drawn from the Observatory's pointed tip through the middle of the side opposite indicates the heliacal rising of the bright star Capella at around 1 CE, when the structure is thought to have been built. This heliacal rising heralds the date when the sun reaches its zenith. This alignment also

Herald of the zenith The Observatory is aligned with the heliacal rising of Capella, which signalled the sun's zenith.

coincides with a zenith tube in the nearby Building P (see page 113), which is only illuminated to the bottom when the sun is directly overhead.

The shape of the Observatory at Monte Albán is unusual for the Americas, but there is a similar building about 30 miles (50km) away, at Caballito Blanco, which appears to be oriented to the setting of Sirius. Sirius and Capella lie either side of the Milky Way, to the south and north respectively, at one of the two points where the bright band of stars is crossed by the ecliptic. The Milky Way had a particular importance for the ancient cultures of Central and South America – both as an element of their mythology (see page 189) and their calendar (see pages 190–91). Whether the intersection of the ecliptic and Milky Way at this point, flanked by Capella and Sirius, held a special significance is uncertain.

MEDICINE WHEELS NORTH AMERICA

Medicine wheels, also known as medicine hoops, are a North American phenomenon and can be of great antiquity. More than 130 have been discovered and, as their name suggests, they mainly consist of a circle or oval of stones, with spokes radiating from a central cairn (mound of stones). Other cairns are often found dotted around the site. Their size can vary from 33ft to over 330ft (10–100m) in diameter and most are found in the southwest of Canada and northwest of the USA, usually on high ground with panoramic views.

At least 15 medicine wheels have been shown to be oriented to true north. It may be significant that in Plains Indian tradition the central pole of the Sun Dance lodge was regarded as World Pole, the axis of the sky around which the heavens revolve and which for a thousand years has been associated with Polaris, the pole star.

Majorville medicine wheel

It may also be that the 28 rafters of the Sun Dance lodge are reflected in the 28 spokes of the Majorville wheel in southern Alberta, Canada (only 26 spokes are visible today). This division may relate to the siderial month, which is the time taken for the moon to return to any particular position among the stars – 27.32 days. It is, of course, pure coincidence that this hoop has a diameter of some 27m (90ft).

The central cairn at Majorville has been dated to around 3200 BCE and the site remained in almost constant use until the 19th century CE. Damage to the structure makes archaeoastronomical analysis difficult, but various alignments have been proposed, including to the summer solstice sunrise and to the heliacal rising of Sirius, Rigel and Aldebaran.

Majorville medicine wheel The 28 original spokes of this site may represent the 28 rafters of the Sun Dance lodge, or the number of days in a siderial month.

Big Horn medicine wheel At this site, the 28 spokes may also refer to the number of days that separate the heliacal risings of Fomalhaut and Rigel from the summer solstice, and the heliacal rising of Sirius from that of Rigel. Alignments to all these events are commemorated in the wheel.

BIG HORN MEDICINE WHEEL

Another medicine wheel with 28 spokes is the Big Horn wheel in Wyoming, USA, which was built between 1200 and 1700 CE and has a diameter of 80ft (24m). Here, another explanation for the significance of the number 28 has been proposed. This site not only has a central cairn but also six others arranged around the wheel – five just outside and one just inside, the latter located to the northwest. If we call this northwest mound Cairn 1 and count clockwise, we may note a range of claimed alignments:

Cairn 1 to Cairn 2: heliacal rising of Aldebaran (Taurus)
Cairn 1 to Cairn 3: heliacal rising of Rigel (Orion)
Cairn 1 to centre: heliacal rising of Sirius (Canis Major)
Cairn 1 to Cairn 5: heliacal rising of Fomalhaut (Piscis Australis)

The Fomalhaut event would have taken place 28 days before the summer solstice, Aldebaran two days before the solstice, Rigel 28 days after the solstice and Sirius 28 days later again.

The summer solstice sunrise itself is commemorated in an alignment from Cairn 6 to centre, and the summer solstice sunset from Cairn 4 to centre. To assist the precision of these alignments, a pole may have been set in the central cairn.

Alignments with the summer solstice sunrise and the heliacal risings of Aldebaran, Rigel and Sirius have also been claimed for Moose Mountain medicine wheel, created around 500 BCE in southern Saskatchewan, Canada.

The Big Horn wheel is unusual not only in its excellent state of preservation, but also because all its major constituents have been allocated an astronomically significant event. Most wheels that have been investigated have features that defy identification with astronomical events, inviting more research in this field.

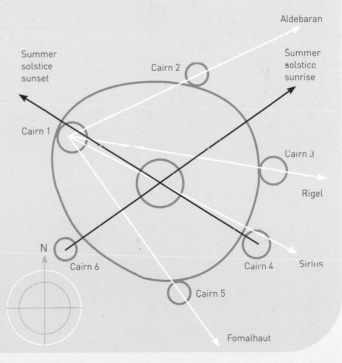

INTRODUCING TEMPLES OF THE COSMOS

In the 11th century, the Indian architect Ramachandra Mahapatra Kaula Bhattaraka described what was involved in building a truly sacred temple. He said that the architect must consciously model himself on Visvarkarman, the highest of the cosmic architects and creator of the universe. Only then can the temple be a perfect collaboration between a creative human mind and the divine creator's will.

The temple, he explained, is a microcosm, a miniature version of the universe, and must be created in harmony with the macrocosm of which it is part. To achieve this, the architect must ensure that the temple reflects the harmonious relationship between the Earth and the sun, the moon and the planets. In particular, it must also be designed to incorporate, in its linear measurements, the cyclical measurements of the heavenly bodies.

Union of all opposites

A World Heritage site, the Khajuraho temples of central India were built by Hindu kings in the 9th–12th centuries CE, and it seems likely that their main entrances were aligned to sunrise on the date of their consecration. For example, the Temple of Lakshmana, built in the first half of the 10th century, was oriented toward sunrise at the spring festival of Holi, held at full-moon day in the lunar month Phalguna (February–March).

The often erotic carvings on these temples celebrate the spiritual union of all opposites, symbolized here by male and female figures (placing the Hinduism of that era in marked contrast to religions where sexuality is taboo). The supreme expression in anthropomorphic terms of the indivisible unity of opposites is a sculpture known as the Shiva *lingam*, which is a stylized representation of the male generative organ (frequently coupled with the female *yoni*). In the heart of the Temple of Kandariya, the Shiva *lingam* is housed in a dark sanctuary that is only illuminated on a few days each year when the sun's dawning rays penetrate the temple to bathe the stone sculpture in light, perhaps as the climax of seasonal ritual of revivification.

This theme of unification is also enshrined in the idea of a temple as a miniature version of the cosmos – a microcosm.

Dark and light The sanctuary containing the Shiva *lingam* in Kandariya temple is flooded with sunlight on just a few days each year, signifying the endless cycle of death and rebirth.

ANGKOR WAT CAMBODIA

The construction of Angkor Wat seems to have been guided by a desire to enshrine cosmic truths in a temple structure, with traditional Khmer principles of sacred numbers and proportions incorporated throughout the architecture of the temple.

The Angkor region of northern Cambodia is extraordinarily rich in ancient monuments set like jewels in the lush tropical jungle. The massive and intricate structure of the temple of Angkor Wat was built early in the 12th century CE. Covering an area some 4,900 x 4,250ft (1,500 x 1,300m), it took around

Sunrise over Angkor The temple has alignments to sunrise at the summer and winter solstices, and at both equinoxes.

30 years to construct. It is surrounded by a moat 620ft (190m) wide that has helped to keep the jungle at bay. The Angkor area is a World Heritage site.

Compared to similar temples, Angkor Wat is unusual in facing west instead of east. East is the direction of the rising sun and life; west the direction of the setting sun and death – so Angkor Wat may have been intended as a funerary temple for its builder King Suryavarman II (his name derives from Surya, the sun deity, and may be translated as "protected by the sun"). However, the temple appears to have been dedicated to the god Vishnu the Preserver, who is associated with the west. These explanations are not mutually exclusive.

The sacred mountain

Inside the moat is a long rectangular gallery, part of which contains bas-reliefs showing earthly events from King Suryavarman's life, and from Indian tradition. A second gallery within the first, also at ground level, forms a square and is devoted to Brahma and the gods (*devas*). Inside this is a staircase to the third and final gallery of Vishnu. The stairs rise at an angle of around 85°, representing the extreme difficulty of aspiring to ascend closer to the gods. This third gallery has a tower at each corner, and in the very centre is the large tower representing the sacred mountain – Mount Meru.

Dedicated to Vishnu (*Opposite*) Offerings lie in front of a statue of Vishnu, associated with the cardinal direction of west and the deity to whom west-facing Angkor Wat is dedicated.

World in miniature (*Below*) Angkor Wat provides a model of Hindu cosmology, its multi-tiered structure rising from the realm of mortal kings up to the abode of the gods.

With its tiered structure, Angkor Wat is a sculpted stone representation of Hindu and Buddhist cosmology, with Mount Meru at its heart. This mountain is the abode of the gods, and is revered as the supremely spiritual place and metaphysical centre of our universe and of all the other universes that are, were or shall ever be.

Solar meaning

The entrance to the sacred domain of Angkor Wat has an awe-inspiring triple solar alignment. Viewed from the western end of the bridge over the moat, the sun is seen to rise at the winter solstice over the right-hand ceremonial entryway (located at the southern end of the temple's outer perimeter wall). The summer solstice sun rises over the matching northern ceremonial entry. At the equinoxes, the sun rises above the central tower at the heart of the complex, the pinnacle of the symbolic Mount Meru, abode of the gods.

Some of the measurements of walls, galleries and other features within the complex tally with numbers associated with the lunar cycles (see pages 132–3), and there are also many solar correspondences.

Solar numbers are particularly apparent in the uppermost gallery, devoted to the solar deity Vishnu. Each of the entrances has 12 windows and 12 pillars, and the distance between sets of steps in this topmost gallery is 12 cubits, the number 12 symbolizing the months of the solar year. A ritual path around this part of the monument, which the pilgrim follows to move steadily from the mundane to the spiritual life, is 365 cubits long, the number of days in a year. And the axes of the central tower add up to 365.37 cubits, a close approximation to the 365.25 days of the solar year.

Sun and stars

The first gallery contains a carving 161ft (49m) long that portrays the central theme of the legend of the Churning of the Sea of Milk, said to explain the creation of the Milky Way. There are several versions of this legend, which appears in a number of ancient texts including the *Mahabharata*, one of the major Indian epics, which reached its final form around 400 CE.

The *devas*, the legend says, had fallen victim to a curse. Having been deprived of much of their strength along with their immortality, they were losing battles to the *asuras* (demons). A truce was arranged, and both sides agreed to share the elixir of immortality that was hidden in the sea of milk. Using a mountain as a churning pivot and the king of snakes as a rope wrapped around the mountain, the *devas* and *asuras* took hold of the snake and, alternately pulling to and fro, churned up the sea of milk.

Eventually, the elixir surfaced. When the *asuras* discovered the *devas* had no intention of sharing it, a dramatic fight broke out. Finally, Vishnu assisted the *devas*, retrieved the elixir and removed it from anyone's reach (or, in other versions, shared it with the *devas*, thus restoring their immortality and strength).

The remarkable bas-relief symbolizes both renewal and rejuvenation, and it does so with reference to the revolving seasons of the year and the tension between the two halves of the year symbolized by the *devas* and *asuras*. Sunlight streaming into the temple illuminates key figures along the bas-relief on significant dates. Bali, king of the *asuras*, is highlighted at the summer solstice; Sugriva, king of the *devas*, is highlighted at the winter solstice; and the solar deity Vishnu at the central pivot of the carving is lit by the equinoctial sun.

Deciphering the temple

Eleanor Mannikka, an American professor of art history, began studying the temple in the early 1970s, and has spent decades unravelling its mysteries.

Churning of the Sea of Milk This sculpture represents the opposition of the year's two halves. The king of the *asuras* is lit up by the sun at midsummer; the king of the *devas* at midwinter.

***Naga* balustrade** Seven-headed serpents guard the entrances to temples at Angkor, escorting visitors from the profane world to the realm of the sacred.

Her conclusions, while not accepted in full by all academics, are certainly intriguing and in tune with the ancient architectural traditions noted above.

The path to perfection

The Khmer used the cubit as a basic linear measurement. Known as the *hat*, this was the distance between the elbow and the tip of the middle finger. Naturally, this length varies, but Mannikka's study of Angkor Wat refined it to a unit of 17.144in (43.545cm).

When different parts of the temple were measured using this unit, Mannikka discovered that distances corresponded to precisely defined spans of time. The overall plan of the temple refers to a cycle composed of four ages, each called a *yuga*. These *yugas* grow progressively shorter and less sophisticated, and correspond to the ages of classical Mediterranean myth – gold, silver, bronze and iron. We are currently

in the age of iron, the Kali Yuga, the harshest and shortest age of all.

These time spans form a sort of countdown, and are multiples of the numerical progression 4, 3, 2, 1 (in which the golden age lasted four times as long as the current iron age is destined to endure, and the iron age is just one 10th of the whole). The numbers of years in each *yuga* are represented in distances incorporated in the temple's layout, allowing a pilgrim who enters Angkor Wat to travel from the bleak present day at the bridge back through time to the golden age at the heart of the temple. (It is interesting to reflect why so many people, regardless of time or place, tend to look *back* to an earthly perfect age, instead of forward.)

The combined length of the two spans of the bridge across the moat is 432 cubits, representing the 432,000 years of the Kali Yuga (each cubit measuring 1,000 years). The next *yuga*, Dvapara, is represented by the 864 cubits (864,000 years) from the main entrance in the perimeter wall (just inside the moat), along the raised causeway to the balustrade of the broad Naga Terrace. The distance from the pier in the middle of the bridge, through the Naga Terrace to the doorway of the first gallery equates to the Treta Yuga (1,292 cubits or 1,292,000 years). Finally, the mythical golden age of the Krita Yuga (1,728 cubits or 1,728,000 years) is symbolized by the distance from the start of the bridge at the outer edge of the complex through to the inner face of the middle gallery. Here, the pilgrim is rewarded with the sight of the third gallery – at the heart of which soars the central tower, the symbolic Mount Meru, home of the gods and the metaphysical space beyond terrestrial time.

Until the end of time

The four *yugas* together make up a cycle known as a *mahayuga* (great *yuga*) – 4,320,000 years. 1,000 of these equal one day of Brahma – a *kalpa*. 720 *kalpas* are one year of Brahma, and 100 years of Brahma equal the time between the creation and destruction of the universe (analogous to the Big Bang and the Big Crunch).

BOROBUDUR INDONESIA

In the heart of Java, about 26 miles (42km) northwest of the city of Yogyakarta and bracketed by two pairs of twin volcanoes, rises the magnificent and serene step-pyramid of Borobudur, a World Heritage site. It was erected between 750 and 842 CE to honour the Buddha – and the Buddhist king who ordered its construction – and was shaped in the form of a mandala.

A mandala is a geometric design representing the universe, and combines the circle of the heavens with a square denoting the Earth and its four cardinal directions. The tiered circles of Borobudur rise above a platform of stepped squares, and pilgrims climb from level to level, learning from the Buddha's life and teachings depicted in bas-relief carvings on the walls as they spiral clockwise around the galleries. The physical act of climbing is intended to be accompanied by awakening to higher levels of spiritual enlightenment. At the very centre of Borobudur, the highest point, is a pinnacle symbolic of Mount Meru (or Sumeru), holy mountain of the gods.

Spiritual liberation

Any mandala can be used as a focus for meditating on the cycle of creation and destruction, and on our relationship with the infinite, and to walk around inside a three-dimensional mandala is a quantum leap for anyone used to meditating sitting down. The temple of Borobudur offers a taste of true spiritual freedom and makes an extremely powerful culmination to a pilgrimage away from the carnality of human desires.

The temple was built around a natural hill, but one that may have been augmented into the correct shape

Model of the cosmos
The plan of Borobudur contains both the square, representing Earth, and the circle, representing the heavens. Three realms are symbolized: the realm of desire, the realm of form and the realm of formlessness.

Three-dimensional mandala Walking Borobudur's galleries, pilgrims ascend from the earthly plane to the realm of spirit.

with soil and stone chippings. This additional material may have been unstable, requiring a supporting foundation to be added to the base of the temple. Excavation of this foundation has revealed what may be the original base, which hosts 160 carvings illustrating the law of cause and effect – karma.

The foundation is 387ft (118m) long on each side and from it rise the five square galleries. The main entrance is on the temple's western side, and the upper part of the building has an entrance in the middle of each side, forming a cross when viewed from above. The sides of the square galleries are precisely parallel to the cardinal directions. Above the square galleries are three circular galleries, each with

stupas (shrines) that each contain a single statue of Buddha. The apex of the temple is occupied by a large stupa representing the axis of the world and the realm of the spirit – Mount Meru. This stupa is empty and it is not known whether it has ever held a statue – or if it has always been empty save for the spirit of Buddha.

With the exception of its orientation to the cardinal points, and some carvings of the sun, moon, planets and stars, no obviously astronomical features have been persuasively cited for this temple, yet the entire structure is a model of the cosmos. Borobudur not only reveals humanity's place within the universe, but is a book written in stone, guiding its visitors on the means of escaping corporality – a way of climbing to the stars.

Spirit of the Buddha
(*Above*) The many *stupas* at Borobudur each contain a single Buddha statue – all except the large *stupa* at the very peak of the temple, which remains empty.

Ancient wonder (*Right*) For more than a thousand years, the statues of the Buddha on the temple's eastern terraces have gazed serenely at the sun's return each morning.

QIN SHI HUANG MAUSOLEUM CHINA

Anyone ambitious enough to head an empire may eventually set their sights higher and strive to rule not only the world but also the cosmos. A man famous for uniting the warring tribes that had fought each other for centuries, and infamous for his cruelty and wholesale burning of all books not relevant to his reign, Qin Shi Huang (259–210 BCE) is now best known in the West as the originator of the Terracotta Army, a massive collection of over 8,000 statues, which was discovered guarding his tomb in 1974. Qin also has the distinction of giving his name to a country – China.

The mausoleum is 19 miles (30km) northeast of Xian, capital of Shaanxi province, at the foot of Lishan Mountain. Some believe the land around is shaped like a dragon, with the mausoleum as its eye. The earth mound is now 155ft high, 1,690ft from south to north and 1,590ft from east to west (47 x 515 x 485m), but two millennia of weather erosion have reduced it to perhaps half its original height. A conservative estimate reckons it would have taken 16,000 men two years to build. The sides of the nearly square mound are aligned to the cardinal points, attesting to Qin Shi Huang's importance by referring to the symbolism of

Terracotta Army These lifelike and life-size sculptures of soldiers, officials, musicians, horses and chariots were buried along with Qin Shi Huang to guard his huge mausoleum.

the celestial pole, abode of the celestial emperor (see pages 168–9). Although no other archaeoastronomical alignments have been determined, the interior of the tomb has not been examined (although it is believed to be intact), and wondrous surprises may lie in store.

A legend has grown from the few details recorded by Sima Qian (c. 140–86 BCE) in the *Shiji – Records of the Grand Historian*. Many believe that the central tomb contains a replica of Qin Shi Huang's empire, its rivers and seas filled with mercury (a toxic substance Chinese alchemists thought could produce an elixir of eternal life). Above, the vault of the sky is believed to arc, with constellations and other celestial bodies marked out in precious metals and jewels. It is said the architects and labourers were put to death to preserve the secrets of the tomb, and that it is booby-trapped to prevent anyone from plundering the site. The modern authorities are rightly reluctant to allow exploration of the mausoleum until the preservation of any ancient treasures can be guaranteed. Perhaps an investigation by camera, as was carried out at the Kitora Kofun in Japan (see opposite), might soon become possible.

Non-intrusive investigations near the mound have provided some tantalizing evidence for the veracity of the ancient legend: the local soil does contain unnaturally high levels of the liquid metal mercury.

TOMB PAINTINGS OF JAPAN

Beautiful paintings in Japanese tombs dating to around the start of the 8th century CE were discovered in the 1970s, and are considered a national treasure. One of the tombs, the Takamatsu Zuka Kofun, is an earth mound some 52ft in diameter and 16ft high (16 x 5m), located near the village of Asuka, some 18 miles (29km) southeast of Osaka. This area was a significant centre of political power in the 6th and 7th centuries CE. Today, the mix of urban dwellings and ancient tombs and temples is striking.

Inside the mound is a small, stone-lined tomb, measuring just 39 x 106in (1 x 2.7m) and about 43in (1.1m) high. It is aligned to the cardinal directions. On the eastern wall is the sun, painted in gold leaf; facing the sun on the western wall is a silver moon. Each of the four walls portrayed one of the Chinese emblems for the cardinal directions: the azure dragon of the east, the white tiger of the west, the black tortoise of the north and the red bird of the south (the latter destroyed during an early break-in). Each of these four guardians is linked to a sequence of seven of the 28 mansions of the moon (traditional Chinese asterisms). Also on the walls are male and female servants (or consorts), presumably to comfort the deceased.

On the ceiling is a stylized sky, with stars marked by circles of gold leaf about $1/2$in (1cm) in diameter, with lines painted in red connecting the stars in each asterism. The north star, Polaris, is in the centre to signify the Celestial Emperor, who bestowed his mandate on China's supreme ruler. The surrounding space, which contains the circumpolar stars including the stars of Ursa Minor, was his Purple Forbidden Enclosure in which dwelt the spirits of China's past emperors. Two further parts of the northern sky, the Supreme Palace Enclosure and the Supreme Market Enclosure, were respectively the domain

Takamatsu Zuka Kofun Its name means "tall pine ancient burial mound", but today the *kofun* is covered with bamboo.

of the Celestial Emperor's immediate family and closest courtiers, and that of the magnates of trade and commerce. Beyond these lay the stars of the 28 mansions of the moon, through which the moon, sun and planets passed on their journey around the heavens. But unlike the Western zodiac, which features constellations along the ecliptic, the mansions of the moon are ranged along the celestial equator, which rises directly due east and sets directly due west.

Just $2/3$ mile (1km) to the south is the Kitora Kofun. This has been explored using cameras, first in 1983 and more recently in 2001. The four cardinal guardian animals are still in beautiful condition, painted in a less formal style than in the Takamatsu Zuka Kofun. The ceiling stars are, again, represented by discs of gold leaf, and show a more natural image of the sky, although many stars are neither to scale nor in quite their correct positions.

MYSTERIES OF MITHRAS ITALY

The mystery cult of Mithraism was one of the most important religions of the Roman Empire, but because its teachings were never written down, and its initiates were sworn to secrecy, we know little about this early competitor to Christianity. Archaeological remains of the cult's temples are scattered across the empire. However, attempts to interpret the enigmatic and elaborate stone sculpture often found in the subterranean vaults of these temples have led to a dramatic insight into the formation of religion itself.

Ancient science, ancient religion

In the 1980s David Ulansey traced the foundation of the cult of Mithraism to a scientific breakthrough that occurred in or just after 128 BCE, when the Greek astronomer Hipparchus discovered the precession of the equinoxes. Hipparchus had noticed that his observations of the positions of stars differed from the records left by earlier astronomers. Although a few discrepancies could simply have been errors, these appeared to be consistent – and Hipparchus concluded that it was the sky itself that had moved.

Hipparchus published his discovery, which initially made no impact on day-to-day life as the change he calculated was just 1° in 100 years (we now know it is closer to 1° in 72 years). At that time the gods were considered to control the forces of nature on earth, such as fertility, weather and volcanoes; and they also governed the sun, moon, planets and stars in the heavens. The philosopher Aristotle had proclaimed in his work *On the Heavens* (350 BCE) that the greatest god was the one who controlled the rotation of the fixed stars, because that axis was both the grandest and most stable thing known.

The group of philosophers called Stoics realized a new god had been discovered, a god who moved the very axis of the heavens. This god – surely the greatest of all – came to be known as Mithras.

Slaying the bull

When Hipparchus made his discovery, the spring equinox occurred while the zodiac constellation of Aries was behind the sun. Precession moves backward through the zodiac, taking nearly 2,200 years to travel

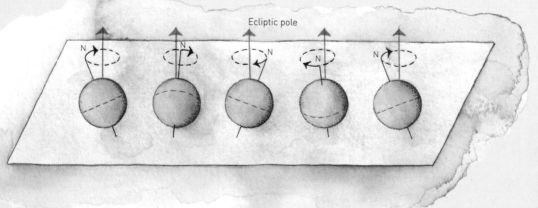

Ecliptic pole

Precession of the equinoxes
Over 26,000 years the pull exerted by sun and moon on the Earth's equator causes our planet to "wobble" out of alignment with the ecliptic pole. The variations during this astrological Great Year explain why zodiac signs appear to be moving backward when viewed on the same date each year.

Rites of Mithras This 2nd-century CE mural in the Mithraeum of Marino, Italy, shows Mithras slaying the bull at the change of the spring equinox from Taurus to Aries. Above are the sun and moon, and to the sides are torch-bearers, and scenes from the myth.

through each of the 12 signs. Before the equinox began occurring in Aries, the Ram, it had taken place in Taurus, the Bull. In the Mithraic mysteries, this transition was symbolized by Mithras slaying the bull of Taurus. The scene of Mithras standing over the dying bull is depicted in many of the stone tablets found in the cult's sanctuaries (the scene is also reminiscent of the constellation Perseus, which stands above Taurus).

This dramatic tableau is sometimes flanked by a pair of trees, one of which is in full leaf while the other bears fruit – symbolizing spring and autumn. And beside these trees may be found a bull's head and a scorpion respectively, emblems of the signs of the

zodiac that stood at the spring and autumn equinox – Taurus, the Bull, and Scorpio, the Scorpion. More frequently, however, these positions are occupied by torch-bearers; the one in the position of the spring equinox holds his torch with the flame downward, while the other holds his torch aloft. The two torch-bearers signify, respectively, the sun's descent below the celestial equator at the autumn equinox, and its re-ascension in the spring.

A small sun and moon are often seen shining at the top of the scene, emphasizing that both are dominated by Mithras, who holds the central and literally pivotal role in the heavens as mover of the axis of the sky.

221

PLANETARY AND STELLAR DEITIES AND MYTHOLOGY

When people gazed at the planets without knowing what they were, it was perhaps natural for them to assume they had a supernatural meaning. Ancient constellations depict mythological scenes; for example, all the characters in the story of the rescue of Andromeda, daughter of Cassiopeia, by Perseus on the winged horse Pegasus, have stars named after them, in adjacent positions in the sky. The examples of

Mars and Venus A fresco from the House of Mars and Venus in Pompeii. Astrology lends planets the attributes of deities after which they are named: warlike Mars, for example.

mythic themes below cannot give more than a flavour of the global lore devoted to these heavenly bodies.

Deities of the planet Venus

Venus, voluptuous Roman goddess of love, was roughly modelled on the earlier Greek Aphrodite, goddess of physical passion and also of spiritual love. This powerful deity has a long association with the planet Venus and has been called many names, including Astarte, Ishtar and Inanna.

A legend from the 2nd or 3rd millennium BCE describes a strange journey undertaken by the

Quetzalcoatl The Aztec god of love and war was associated with the dual-natured planet Venus.

beautiful Inanna, Sumerian goddess of the planet Venus. When Inanna began her journey into the underworld, she told the gatekeeper that she was heading east. At each of the seven gateways along her route, she was divested of items of magical or personal power, from tools, such as her measuring rod and line, to jewelry and eventually all her clothes. Then Inanna entered the heart of the realm of the dead, where she remained until she was rescued.

This myth may describe the journey of Venus as the Evening Star, from its first appearance low in the western sky just after sunset. In the weeks that follow, the planet moves further from the sun, each night shining more brightly and appearing higher in the sky a little further east. Then its journey stalls, and night after night it sinks inexorably down through the sky, gradually losing its brilliance until it is completely lost from view and sets beneath the horizon. Dates for this regular event were recorded in the 16th century BCE, in the astronomical tablets of King Ammisaduqa, which observed that there was an average period of seven days during which Inanna was utterly invisible, until she reappears as the Morning Star – in the east.

Quetzalcoatl–Kukulcan

Much like Ishtar, who had a romantic evening aspect and a warlike morning aspect, the Aztec deity associated with the planet Venus was Quetzalcoatl, god of both love and war. Tracking this planet's movements gave essential information for timing military campaigns and battles. The heliacal rising and setting were particularly important, with the rising bringing great danger. Sacrifices (some human) were made when Venus was at its dimmest, and certain rituals had to be performed to avert disasters when Venus and the Pleiades were close in the heavens.

Worship of Quetzalcoatl, the feathered serpent deity, has been traced back to *c.* 5th century BCE. His earlier Maya version – Kukulcan – was a wise creator who organized the cosmos, brought humans into being and embodied wisdom and knowledge. While worship of this deity was widespread throughout Mesoamerican, his attributes vary widely. In one story, he was one of the twin virgin-born sons of the serpent goddess Coatlicue. He invented books and agriculture and was the god of Venus as Morning Star; his twin brother Xolotl, the deity of bad luck and fire, was the god of Venus as Evening Star. In another story, he was seduced while drunk into sleeping with a virgin priestess (possibly his sister), and afterwards was so stricken with remorse that he immolated himself, his heart becoming Venus in the heavens. Eventually, he was seen as a god of death and resurrection, and became the patron god of priests.

Polaris – life's innermost mystery

At the centre of the circumpolar stars in the northern hemisphere is the pole star, Polaris. Although modern mystics cite Polaris as an emblem of the spiritual core within each of us, it would be wise to remember that the precession of the equinoxes only brought Polaris to proximity with the celestial north pole around a thousand years ago. Previously, no bright star had been there since Thuban (alpha Draconis) in the centuries around 2780 BCE (just as today there is no particular pole star in the southern hemisphere). Instead, it was a dark void – and this idea of a central emptiness was celebrated in Daoism, which dates to the 6th century BCE. In archaeoastronomical terms, seeing life's innermost mystery as empty and dark, or active and bright, is merely an accident of timing.

Beacon of hope, constancy and justice

The story of Dhruva is told in the *Vishnu Purana*, an important text of Vaishnava Hinduism.

Dhruva was the eldest son of a king, but the king's younger wife, Suruchi, was ambitious for her own son and had Dhruva and his mother sent away from the palace. One day, while Dhruva was still a child, he met his father and tried to climb onto his lap – but Suruchi told him off. Distraught and humiliated, Dhruva ran to his mother. She told him to fight for what was right, saying that the rigours of penance would make him worthy. Dhruva ran away to the forest, where he was taught by the sage Narada. After he had fasted for half a year, he was visited by the god Vishnu, who restored him to his rightful place as a prince. Following his death, Dhruva was appointed by Vishnu to become the pole star around which all else revolved – making Dhruva a beacon of hope, constancy and justice.

Isis – bringer of abundant blessings

A mother goddess, under one name or another, has been revered since time immemorial. She represents

Morning Star Quetzalcoatl bursts from the Earth as the Morning Star. This pre-Maya stele from Santa Lucia, Guatemala, could have recorded a specific celestial event.

Holy family This pendant from 874–850 BCE depicts Isis (right), Osiris (centre) and their son Horus. The mother goddess Isis was linked to Sirius, while Osiris was associated with Orion.

both Mother Nature – the Earth that sustains life – and the human mother who gives birth to us and nurtures us. The ancient Egyptian mother goddess was Isis, wife of Osiris, the god of death and rebirth. She symbolized fertility, and was often depicted seated with her son Horus on her lap (a pose similar to the Christian icon of the Madonna and child).

Isis was intimately associated with the annual flooding of the Nile, which covered the land with mud and water, bringing agricultural fertility to the desert. The heliacal rising of the brilliant star Sirius happened just before this vital event, and Isis became closely associated with the star that was herald of the Nile's abundant blessings.

Arianrhod

Like most Celtic deities, the goddess Arianrhod – "silver wheel" – was a complex figure. Both a moon and star goddess, she symbolized the full moon and was connected with the tides; she was also associated with the spider as a weaver, especially of human destiny. Some people suppose her name indicates the Milky Way, or even the circle of the ecliptic along which the planets revolve around the sky. Her realm was Caer Arianrhod, which some see as the circumpolar stars, while others know it as the pretty, crescent-shaped constellation of Corona Borealis (Northern Crown), where Arianrhod took the dead to await rebirth.

TAKING ARCHAEOASTRONOMY FURTHER

Encounters with aliens

The 1968 book *Chariots of the Gods* by Erich von Däniken contains photographic evidence of archaeological sites and artefacts supposedly created by or for extraterrestrials. The idea that aliens were responsible for ancient achievements did not begin with von Däniken's international bestseller, but arose gradually from popular science fiction. In 1898, for instance, in a serialized novel, Garrett P. Serviss wrote that the Sphinx and pyramids of Giza were created when Egypt was ruled by Martians.

Such cosmic speculations were simply the latest incarnation of a time-honoured tradition in which dramatic theories have been invented to explain archaeological mysteries. An illustration in a manuscript of the 12th-century historical poem *Roman de Brut*, for example, shows a stone circle being built by a giant – this is the earliest known picture of Stonehenge. In the medieval period it was common for giants or devils to be credited with the erection of megalithic structures whose enormous stones seemed to call for a superhuman creator.

Such stories were often presented as fact, but that didn't lessen their entertainment value, and today we still seem to relish a fizzing cocktail of history and fiction. Many modern movies invoke similar themes. Maya crystal skulls (quartz skulls carved using primitive tools to a seemingly impossible perfection) appear in *Indiana Jones and the Kingdom of the Crystal Skull* (2008). Ancient conspiracies over mysterious

Visitors from the stars The strange figures at Nazca, which are only properly recognizable from the air, have been interpreted as proof of contact with travellers from other planets.

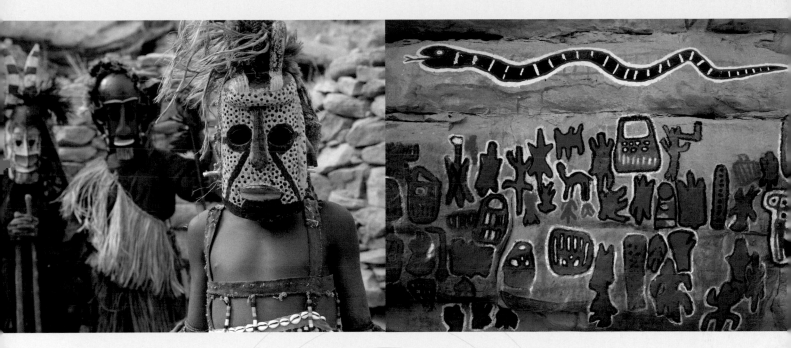

Sirius controversy Apparent knowledge held by the Dogon people (*above, left*) of the Sirius star system is cited by some as proof of alien visitation; Dogon rock art, such as this example at Bandigara (*above, right*), depicts strange alien-like figures.

artefacts and planetary alignments feature in *Lara Croft: Tomb Raider* (2001). And interplanetary travel from the Great Pyramid of Giza is notable in *Stargate* (1994) and the subsequent TV series.

The Dogon mystery

A tribe living in the remote central plateau of the Republic of Mali, West Africa, became internationally famous when author Robert Temple explored the controversial idea that the Dogon people had astronomical knowledge derived from visitors from the Sirius star system.

The Sirius Mystery (1975) describes the amphibious extraterrestrials known to the Dogon as Nommo, whose watery home planet orbits Sirius C, the supposed third star of the Sirius system. The book suggests they may have come to Earth before 3000 BCE, inspiring many ancient legends including that of the fish-tailed god Oannes who brought cultural gifts to the Sumerians. At its heart, the mystery revolves around how certain Dogon elders apparently knew

without the benefit of astronomical technology that Sirius is not a single star, but a multiple star system. This knowledge was recorded by anthropologists who studied tribal myths in the 1930s to 1950s.

Sirius, often called the Dog Star, does indeed have a companion, a star whose size is comparable to that of the Earth but whose mass is similar to that of our sun. This white dwarf, Sirius B (affectionately called the Pup), is invisible to the naked eye, and was first observed through a telescope in 1862. Another companion star, Sirius C, was suggested in the 1920s, but proved to be a misidentification of a background star.

Sceptics of the alien-visitation hypothesis either dismiss the Dogon's detailed knowledge of Sirius, or insist it must have been learned through conventional means – probably casual contact with travellers.

Modern machines, ancient shapes

The concrete domes sprouting high above the clouds on the mountaintops of Hawaii, such as the

Canada-France-Hawaii Telescope on Mauna Kea, provide iconic images of telescopes studying the sky. It was the visual similarity between these modern watchtowers and the domed Caracol building at Chichén Itzá that led to its nickname, the "Observatory". As ancient priests once sought out the high places in order to get as close as possible to the sky and the deities who lived there, so 21st-century astronomers have to rise above the pollution of the lower altitudes.

Today, there are many research sites where the mysteries of the skies are probed. We have noted that

the alignments of some ancient sites are set at right angles, such as the pyramids of Giza that are keyed to the cardinal points of the compass. In Louisiana, at the Laser Interferometer Gravitational-Wave Observatory (LIGO), two concrete arms each $2^1/_2$ miles (4km) long are set at an exact right angle, each housing a steel vacuum tube 4ft (1.2m) in diameter. Light from a single laser is split into two beams, each travelling along one of the paths. At the far end of each tunnel is a mirror that bounces the light back along the tunnel to a detector.

Under normal circumstances the light waves arrive at the detector in perfect synchronization. But LIGO exists to measure disruptions in space-time caused by gravity waves emanating from events such as supernovae explosions. One day it may be possible for

Studying our universe The visitors' centre of the Large Hadron Collider. Scientists here bring protons into head-on collision at extreme speed to investigate the nature of existence.

the scientists there to detect the gravity waves from the Big Bang itself.

Other experiments look at the infinitesimally small to cast a light on the infinity of space. A perfect circle is the fitting shape of one observatory, and its dimensions are impressive – a circumference of 17 miles (27km). The Large Hadron Collider (LHC) is part of the CERN Laboratory (world-famous as the birthplace of the World Wide Web), which straddles the border between France and Switzerland. The LHC was constructed to be the world's most powerful high-energy particle accelerator.

This machine accelerates protons to speeds just a few metres per second slower than the speed of light itself. Two beams of speeding protons, travelling in opposite directions, are brought into convergence by powerful magnets. Sensors monitor the collision, collecting clues about the structure of the universe. The research may, for example, help to answer questions about the existence of multiple dimensions, about the apparent asymmetry between matter and antimatter, and about what Dark Matter actually is.

Most importantly, perhaps, it may finally unify the two great scientific approaches to studying our universe: the theories of quantum mechanics, which study the particle-wave nature of matter and energy at a subatomic level, and the general theory of relativity created by Einstein to explain the workings of the universe at large.

Such joined-up understanding would enable the development of enormously powerful technologies that could endow our descendants with seemingly godlike powers. However, the future ability of our species to enjoy such benefits will depend on our efforts now to discover our place in the universe, and to develop harmonious relationships with one another. Despite all our efforts to live up to our Latin name *Homo sapiens* – "wise people" – we may never achieve the supremely godlike gift of always behaving wisely.

Looking to the future

The Romans worshipped an important yet often overlooked god called Janus. His role was pivotal,

Double vision This two-faced female figure from a medieval rood screen at Sancreed church, Cornwall, draws on the past- and future-facing symbolism of the Roman god Janus.

literally, in that he was god of doors – we may envisage him as the spiritual hinge upon which the door hangs to swing one way and then the other, opening and closing. We speak his name every time we mention the month January – Janus was the god responsible for the transition from the old year to the new.

Icons of Janus often show him with two faces on his head, one gazing to the left and one to the right – he sees into the past and into the future. Like Janus, we have looked long and deep into the past; now, at the end of this book, it is time to face the other way and consider the future.

One day, people will be surrounded with technology routinely achieving tasks in a way that would seem miraculous even to us. They will, when leisure provides and the mood takes them, think upon their ancestors – us – and perhaps they will shake their heads at how little we knew, yet how hard we tried to find the answers to life's enduring puzzles – riddles that may remain unresolved for all time, forming a bond between us all.

Our descendants may also seek to find ways to bridge the gap of centuries and connect with our mindset, seeking their roots – just as we, in our modern, often urban lifestyle, may seek to resolve our alienation from nature's rhythms by taking time out to investigate the cycles of life that were the everyday reality of our forebears.

Many of us live fragmented lives, with the days separated from one another as if they were appointments scheduled in a year planner. But even city dwellers may learn to sense the planet beneath their feet. The Earth spins on its axis once each day, and we may easily align ourselves to this motion. When we look east, we see the sun appear to rise from that side of the world. When we watch the moon and constellations as they seem to emerge over the horizon, we should try to think of the horizon as sinking away beneath these celestial bodies, rather than imagining them as rising.

Like Janus we also need to look the other way and face west, because at noon we will then gaze forward, along the path of our planetary orbit. As if standing on the prow of a ship, we stare into the slowly curving course of our annual journey around the sun.

One of the most satisfying ways of getting a feel for solar time is to make a note of where along the horizon the sun rises or sets on significant dates – birthdays, anniversaries or even on the traditional seasonal milestones of solstices and equinoxes. These occur at the same spot on the horizon each year, so we can set up an alignment of rocks in the garden or markers on the windowsill that point to the places on the horizon that commemorate events of special importance to us as individuals.

Extreme archaeoastronomy

Science fiction often takes us to visit other planets, to walk among ancient civilizations. It is possible that one day our descendants will follow the path that we have so far only travelled in imagination, and discover truly alien archaeoastronomy. In the meantime, we may still imagine how a different solar system might shape the lives of our distant neighbours in the universe, wherever they are.

The poles of a planet without the stabilizing influence of a large moon are prone to wander erratically, dramatically affecting the intensity of the seasonal cycle. The inhabitants may have to migrate almost continually, seeking warmer winters or avoiding summer heat. During this oscillating journey they may set up markers to track the sun's apparent movement, particularly when it is directly overhead. But they would never find order in the chaotic tumbling of its axis.

With no moon, the night would have only specks of cold stars. The whole natural world would be overwhelmingly dominated by the sun – the unchallenged presence around which everything else revolved. This could instill absolute devotion to a single divinity, and obedience extending into all aspects of a tightly unified society. Such a culture could create distinctive architectural remains enshrining their supremely focused view of reality.

On the other hand, a planet with numerous small moons would enjoy plenty of interest in the night sky. Enquiring minds would set to work puzzling out their orbital idiosyncrasies. Initially, each moon might have its own observatories or temples, but eventually they would coalesce into a unified system of knowledge.

Not satisfied with that achievement, the inhabitants of such a planet would turn their capacity for understanding complexity to investigate life's other intricate matters. Complicated and multifaceted

Alien landscape A culture making its home on a habitable moon (such as the one imagined here by an artist) would be dominated by the vast planet that sailed across the skies.

structures would be inspired by the appreciation of unity through diversity. These masterpieces of art and engineering would, in their basic alignments and dimensions, commemorate the astronomical truths that laid the foundation for their culture's rapid voyage of discovery.

The inhabitants of a moon would look up into the sky and see a planet apparently many times larger than the sun, with phases that change through the month. Eclipses of the sun would be relatively common, as this much larger planet would obscure more of the sky, and the frigid span of totality would last a long time. At the opposite monthly phase, though, the sunlight reflected by a "full planet" would illuminate the night into nocturnal day. At such times, when the eclipse cycle allowed, the moon's inhabitants would see their own world's shadow passing across the bright face of the planet.

How the inhabitants would conceptualize the difference between the warm sun and the larger but cold planet might depend on whether they lived in the temperate zone or closer to the poles or equator. In extreme cases, the range of ideas could be mutually exclusive, spawning intolerant competition. The ruins of ceremonial and secular buildings would reflect the cults' differing views, incorporating alignments to the favoured celestial object.

A new perspective

One thing is consistent in these descriptions of fictional alien worlds: local conditions condition local responses. Earth's particular arrangement (with a moon that perfectly complements the sun, and a string of planets that dance among the stars) inspired our ancestors to populate the sky with sun and moon gods and many other celestial deities, in a pantheon that surely is unique to planetary systems like ours.

One day our descendants will have the chance to communicate with beings from other star systems, and we can only hope to meet in peace if both we – and those aliens – have evolved a sense of freedom from our home planet. Fortunately, the present interest in global archaeoastronomy is a sure sign our planet is growing up.

A giant step Astronaut footprints on the moon. So far, just 12 humans have walked on Earth's nearest neighbour.

GLOSSARY

Acronychal rising/setting
The rising/setting of a star or planet at or just after sunset.

Asterism
Any grouping of stars. The International Astronomical Union has listed 88 asterisms that fill the entire sky, and these are officially regarded as constellations. Small asterisms may be inside a constellation (the Pleiades in Taurus, for example) but many ancient or ethnic asterisms are larger than the modern official constellations.

Axis of rotation
An imaginary line around which the Earth spins once each day. The axis runs through the body of the planet, from the north pole to the south pole (the magnetic north and south poles are different, being caused by magnetism generated by the planet's iron core).

Celestial equator
The Earth's equator projected out into space. The plane of the celestial equator is currently inclined at an angle of about 23.4° from the plane of the ecliptic (they intersect at the equinoxes). This angle does vary slightly over time. It is currently getting smaller and was, for example, 23.9° in 1800 BCE – which can provide dating evidence for sites with multiple solar alignments.

Celestial pole
The Earth's north or south pole projected into the sky. The illusion that the sky and all celestial bodies are revolving around the celestial poles is created by Earth's daily rotation. For the past millennia or so, the north celestial pole has been close to the brightest star in Ursa Minor, which has become known as the pole star – Polaris.

Circumpolar stars
Stars that never set. This term is slightly misleading because circumpolar literally means "around the (celestial) pole". The observer's latitude determines which stars are circumpolar (the closer the observer is to either of the Earth's poles, the more circumpolar stars will be visible).

Cosmical rising/setting
The rising/setting of a star or planet at or just after sunrise.

Declination
In astronomy, the shortest distance measured in degrees (°) between an object and the celestial equator.

Ecliptic
The imaginary plane centred on the Sun, on which the Earth performs its orbit. The ecliptic is also, by extension, the path of the sun's apparent motion against the background of stars. The planets and our moon keep close to the ecliptic as they travel around the sky.

Equinox
One of the two dates in the year when the length of daylight and night are equal – in the present era on or around 20 March and 22 September. Equinox literally means "equal night". At the equator, uniquely, all days and nights are of equal length all year round.

Greatest elongation
The point at which the orbits of Venus and Mercury appear farthest away from the sun (these planets lie between Earth and the sun, so always appear close to the sun). A greatest elongation is classified as eastern when the planet is in the evening sky, and as western when it is seen before dawn.

Heliacal rising
The first appearance of a star in the eastern sky before dawn (the word comes from Helios, Greek god of the sun). Each morning as the sun rises it outshines the stars, rendering them invisible. Every day the sun appears to move about 1° from west to east around the ecliptic, so each successive morning a new segment of the starry sky is visible before sunrise.

Heliacal setting
The last time in the year a star is seen to actually set (rather than be bleached out of view in the sky above the horizon), which takes place at or just after sunset. Every day the sun appears to move about 1° from west to east

around the zodiac, so each successive evening a slightly different segment of the starry sky disappears below the horizon.

Lunar standstills

The two dates each month when the moon reaches its maximum or minimum declination. Each day in its monthly orbit of the Earth, the moon usually rises at a slightly different point on the horizon, and reaches a different maximum altitude in the sky – but on the standstills this difference is practically imperceptible to the naked eye, so the moon is said to stand still. However, those events are usually ignored in archaeoastronomy because each month the moon's rising and setting points and declination on the standstills themselves change slightly over an 18.6-year cycle. When this long-term movement in the monthly standstills appears to stop (before turning back in the cycle), the standstills reach their greatest maximum (and minimum) declination – these are the major (and minor) lunar standstills. In the year of the moon's major standstill, its northernmost rising (and setting) point is at the maximum distance from its southernmost rising (and setting) point. In the year of its minor standstill, around nine years later, these points are at the minimum distance.

Megalith

Literally "great stone", an isolated standing stone (also called a monolith, or "solitary stone") or a component of a structure such as tomb or temple, which can then be described as megalithic.

Precession of the equinoxes

This is the cycle, which takes some 26,000 years to complete, in which the Earth slowly wobbles on its axis, like a spinning top, causing both of the celestial poles to trace an imaginary circle in the sky. Precession explains why our northern pole star today is Polaris (Ursa Minor), but was Thuban (Draco) around 2800 BCE and will be Vega (Lyra) in around 4000 CE. Precession is described in terms of the constellation behind the sun at the spring equinox, which is currently Pisces. The sun will enter Aquarius at the spring equinox around 2070 CE.

Season

Period marked by the relative length of day and night (long days and short nights, for example, typifying summer). The annual cycle of the seasons, from winter to summer and back again, is caused by the tilt of Earth's axis relative to the plane of the ecliptic, on which it orbits the sun.

Solstice

A longest or shortest day. This occurs at the points in the Earth's orbit where the tilt of its axis is in alignment with the sun. On two days of the year, one of the Earth's hemispheres will receive the maximum amount of sunlight (the summer solstice), while the other hemisphere will receive the minimum amount (the winter solstice). The word solstice literally means "sun standstill" and refers to the pause in the sun's apparent motion. Each day the sun rises at a slightly different point on the horizon and reaches a different maximum altitude in the sky – but on the solstices the difference is practically imperceptible to the naked eye, so the sun's movement is said to have stopped still (before turning back in the cycle).

Synchronous orbit

The gravitational pull between two orbiting bodies, such as the Earth and moon, tends to synchronize their rotation. This gravitational locking causes the moon to rotate on its axis in exactly the same period as it orbits the Earth. This means we never see the far side of the moon from Earth.

Zenith

The point in the sky directly overhead. In the tropics, as the sun oscillates between the solstice extremes, an observer will see the sun at its zenith on two days of the year. Observers north of the Tropic of Cancer or south of the Tropic of Capricorn can never see the sun at its zenith.

BIBLIOGRAPHY

Aveni, Anthony, *People and the Sky*, Thames & Hudson: London, 2008

Aveni, Anthony, *Stairways to the Stars*, Cassell: London, 1997

Belmonte, Juan Antonio and Shaltout, Mosalam (eds.), *In Search of Cosmic Order: Selected Essays on Egyptian Archaeoastronomy*, American University in Cairo Press: Cairo, 2009

Burl, Aubrey, *Stonehenge*, Constable: London, 2006

Chapman, Allan, *Gods in the Sky*, Channel 4 Books: London, 2001

Cornelius, Geoffrey and Devereux, Paul, *The Language of Stars & Planets*, Duncan Baird Publishers: London, 2003

Freke, Timothy and Gandy, Peter, *Jesus and the Goddess*, Thorsons: London, 2001

Harley, J.B. and Woodward, David (eds.), *The History of Cartography Volume 1*, University of Chicago Press: Chicago, 1987

Hutton, Ronald, *The Stations of the Sun*, Oxford University Press: Oxford, 1996

Kelley, David and Milone, Eugene, *Exploring Ancient Skies*, Springer: New York, 2005

Krupp, E.C., *Beyond the Blue Horizon*, HarperCollins: New York, 1991

Lockyer, J. Norman, *The Dawn of Astronomy*, Dover Publications: New York, 2006 (new edition)

Magli, Giulio, *Mysteries and Discoveries of Archaeoastronomy*, Copernicus Books: New York, 2009

Mannikka, Eleanor, *Angkor Wat*, University of Hawai'i Press: Honolulu, 1996

Milbraith, Susan, *Star Gods of the Maya*, University of Texas Press: Austin, 1999

Ponting, Gerald, *Callanish and Other Megalithic Sites of the Outer Hebrides*, Wooden Books: Glastonbury, 2007 (revised edition)

Ridpath, Ian, *Collins Stars and Planets Guide*, HarperCollins: London, 2011

Ruggles, Clive, *Ancient Astronomy*, ABC-Clio: Santa Barbara, 2005

Ruggles, Clive, *Astronomy in Prehistoric Britain and Ireland*, Yale University Press: New Haven, 1999

Ulansey, David, *The Origins of the Mithraic Mysteries*, Oxford University Press USA: New York, 1989

Van der Waerden, Bartel L. (ed.), *Science Awakening II: The Birth of Astronomy Book 2*, Oxford University Press USA: New York, 1974

Worthington, Andy, *Stonehenge Celebration and Subversion*, Alternative Albion: Wymeswold, 2005 (new edition)

INDEX

Page numbers in *italic* refer to illustrations

ACKNOWLEDGMENTS

Author acknowledgments

With thanks to ...
Kate Alvis, Robert Benfer, Ian Button, Chance Coughenour, Claire Cox, Sam Haddock, Lawrence Hutchings, Cath Mayer, Yana Nilsson, Dawn Witherspoon and, most especially, my irreplaceable researcher – Joules Taylor – who takes going the extra mile firmly in her stride.

Picture acknowledgments

The publisher would like to thank the following people, museums and photographic libraries for permission to reproduce their material. Every care has been taken to trace copyright holders. However, if we have omitted anyone we apologize, and will, if informed, make corrections in any future edition.

Page 1 ImageDJ; **2** Getty Images/Dollia Sheombar; **2 bkg** Science Photo Library/Eckhard Slawik; **3** ImageDJ; **4–5** Photolibrary.com/Peter Arnold Collection/Bernd Koch; **6** Science Photo Library/Laurent Laveder; **8** akg-images/De Agostini Picture Library; **9** Alamy/Stephen Emerson; **10bl** Marsyas (Creative Commons License)/National Archaeological Museum, Athens; **10br** Museum of Natural Sciences Brussels; **11** John Glover; **13** Adam Stanford; **16** Alamy/Michael Dunlea; **17** Science Photo Library/Babak Tafreshi; **20–21** Science Photo Library/Max Alexander; **23** AWL/Doug Pearson; **24–5** Photolibrary.com/Tom Mackie; **26** Photographers Direct/Terry Mathews Creative; **29** Corbis/Yann Arthus-Bertrand; **30–31** Science Photo Library/Patrick Landmann; **32** Art Archive/National Museum of Archaeology, Valletta/Dagli Orti; **33** Fotolia/Skiernan; **34** Dreamstime/Geza Farkas; **35** SuperStock/Flirt; **37** Landesamt für Denkmalpflege und Archäologie Sachsen-Anhalt; **38** Getty Images/AFP/Jens Schlueter; **39** Corbis Wire/Waltraud Grubitzsch; **40** R. Engelhardt (Creative Commons License); **41t** Alamy/LOOK Die Bildagentur der Fotografen GmbH/Heinz Wohner; **41b** David Lyons; **42** Elisabetta Marcovich; **43** AWL/John Warburton-Lee; **44–5** AWL/Michele Falzone; **46** Stephane Compoint; **48** Jeremy Marley; **50** Getty Images/Time Life Pictures/Henry Groskinsky; **52** Getty/Richard Susanto; **54l** Corson Hirschfeld; **55** Getty Images/Digital Vision/Karen Huntt; **56tr** SuperStock/Minden Pictures; **57** Alamy/Lonely Planet Images; **58** National Geographic Stock/Ira Block; **60** SuperStock/age fotostock; **61** Corbis Wire/Francisco Martin; **63t** Getty Images/Dollia Sheombar; **63b** SuperStock/Cosmo Condina; **64** Alamy/Lonely Planet Images/Jon Sweeney; **65** Clive Ruggles; **66** Alamy/imagebroker/Egmont Strigl; **67** SuperStock/age fotostock; **68 & 69** Alamy/Steve Mansfield-Devine; **70** Art Archive/Archaeological Museum, Ferrara/Dagli Orti; **71** Scala, Florence/Cathedral, Orvieto; **72** Alamy/Arco Images GmbH/J De Meester; **73** Getty Images/National Geographic/Chris Hill; **74** Getty Images/DeAgostini/G Dagli Orti; **75** Corbis/Adam Woolfitt; **76t** Alamy/Dynamic Light Ireland; **77** David Lyons; **78** Alamy/Norman Barrett; **79** Alamy/Vibe Images; **80** Corbis/Homer Sykes; **81 & 82–3** David Lyons; **84–5** SuperStock/Minden Pictures; **85tr** Alamy/Nick Cable; **86cr** SuperStock/age fotostock; **87** Getty Images/Amana/Sadayuki Makino; **89** akg-images/Bildarchiv Steffens; **90** Art Archive/Egyptian Museum, Cairo/Dagli Orti; **92** Werner Forman Archive/Egyptian Museum, Cairo; **93** Getty Images/Pete Turner; **94** Alamy/Lonely Planet Images; **95** Getty Images/Stephen Studd; **97tr** Corbis/Lowell Georgia; **97bl** Corbis/Xinhua/Wang Song; **98 & 99** Werner Forman Archive/NJ Saunders; **100** AWL/Gavin Hellier; **101** Alamy/James Brunker; **103** Alamy/Powered by Light/Alan Spencer; **104 & 105** Clive Ruggles; **106** Fotolia/Steeve Roche/National Anthropological Museum, Mexico; **109** Getty Images/Neil Beer; **110** AWL/Danita Delimont Stock; **112** Alamy/David Hilbert; **113t** Superstock/age fotostock/Leonardo Diaz Romero; **113b** Photographers Direct/Ryan Watkins Photography; **115** Art Archive/National Anthropological Museum, Mexico/Dagli Orti; **116** Corbis/Angelo Hornak; **117** AWL/Michele Falzone; **118c** akg-images/Interfoto/Ny Carlsberg Museum, Copenhagen; **118b** akg-images/Bildarchiv Steffens; **119** Bridgeman Art Library/Prado, Madrid; **120** Art Archive/Louvre, Paris/Dagli Orti; **121** akg-images/SMB, Kupferstichkabinett, Berlin; **122–3** Alamy/LOOK Die Bildagentur der Fotografen GmbH; **125** Fotolia/Witold Krasowski; **126** Anthony Murphy/Mythical Ireland; **127** SuperStock/Irish Image Collection; **129** Shutterstock/Alexey Stiop; **129inset** Shutterstock/J. Wohlfeil; **130tr** John Finch; **130bl** Ray and Barnaby Norris (www.emudreaming.com); **131** Dinodia Photo Library Pvt. Ltd; **132** Corbis/Christophe Loviny; **133** Mark Marek (www.travelingmark.com); **135** Science Photo Library/John Sanford; **136–7** Getty Images/National Geographic/Jim Richardson; **138** Billy Duncan/The Tartan Lens; **140** Photolibrary/Charles Bowman; **141** Getty Images/Macduff Everton; **142–3** Photolibrary; **144** Photolibrary; **145** Alamy/Jim Laws; **146 & 147cr** Alamy/Robert Estall; **148** David Lyons; **149** Alamy/Michael Sayles; **150** Art Archive/Museo del Templo Mayor, Mexico/Dagli Orti; **151** Werner Forman Archive/Schultz Collection, New York; **152** Bridgeman Art Library/Bildarchiv Steffens/Ralph Rainer Steffens; **153** akg-images/Bardo Museum, Tunis/De Agostini Picture Library/G Dagli Orti; **154–5** Getty Images/Oxford Scientific/Per-Gunnar Ostby; **157l** Scala, Florence/Luciano Romano – courtesy of the Ministero Beni e Att. Culturali; **157r** akg-images/De Agostini Picture Library/G Dagli Orti; **159** Bridgeman Art Library/Louvre, Paris; **160t** Scala, Florence/BPK, Bildagentur für Kunst, Kultur und Geschichte, Berlin; **161** © Trustees of the British Museum; **162–3b** Photolibrary.com/Panstock LLC Catalogue; **165** Tips Images/Cosmo Condina; **166** Werner Forman Archive/E Strouhal; **167** Corbis/epa/STR; **168** Corbis/Science Faction/Stuart Westmorland; **169** Superstock/Wolfgang Kaehler; **171** Getty Images/Flickr/Andrea Colantoni; **173** Alamy/Chad Ehlers; **174bl** Photolibrary.com/India Picture Library; **174br** John van Leeuwen; **175** AWL/Amar Grover; **176** Werner Forman Archive/NJ Saunders; **177** akg-images/De Agostini Picture Library; **178–9** ESO/Y Beletsky; **180** Alamy/Images Etc Ltd; **180 bkg** Getty Images/Oxford Scientific/Malcolm Park; **182t** Alamy/Bill Brooks; **182b** Alamy/Kevin Ebi; **183** Alamy/Travel Division Images; **184–5** Stephane Compoint; **186** Tips Images/Angelo Cavalli; **187** Corbis/Bob Krist; **188** Ray and Barnaby Norris (www.emudreaming.com); **189** Neil Andrew Duncan/The Buena Vista Project, courtesy Robert Benfer; **190–91b** Getty Images/First Light/Robert Postma; **192** Werner Forman Archive; **193** Science Photo Library/Eckhard Slawik; **194–5** Getty images/Britain on View/Guy Edwardes; **196** SuperStock/JTB Photo; **197bkg** Science Photo Library/Eckhard Slawik; **197c** Shutterstock/Motordigitaal; **199** Jonathan C K Webb (www.webbaviation.co.uk); **200** SuperStock/Photononstop; **201t** Corbis/Pierre Vauthey; **201b** Creative Commons Licence/PD; **202** Getty/AFP; **203** Alamy/Wild Places Photography/Chris Howes; **204** Werner Forman Archive/National Museum of Archaeology, Valletta; **205** Corbis/Danny Lehman; **206** Robert Strusievicz, Calgary; **207t** National Geographic Stock/Thomas W. Melham; **208** Corbis/Paul C. Pet; **209** Getty Images/Photolibrary/Tom White; **210** Axiom/Peter Rayner; **211** Corbis/John Stanmeyer/VII; **212** Art Archive/Musée Guimet, Paris/Gianni Dagli Orti; **213** Corbis/National Geographic Vintage; **215** Getty Images/The Image Bank/Philippe Bourseiller; **216l** Axiom/Mikihiko Ohta; **216–17** Getty Images/Image Bank/Ed Freeman; **218** AWL/Danita Delimont Stock; **219** SuperStock/JTB Photo; **221** Scala, Florence – courtesy of the Ministero Beni e Att. Culturali; **222** Scala, Florence/National Museum, Naples/Fotografica Foglia – courtesy of the Ministero Beni e Att. Culturali; **223** © Trustees of the British Museum; **224** Werner Forman Archive/Museum fur Volkerkunde, Berlin; **225** akg-images/De Agostini Picture Library/G Dagli Orti; **226** SuperStock/Stock Connection ; **227tl** AWL/Gavin Hellier; **227tr** Photolibrary.com/Aflo/Yoshio Tomii Photo Studio; **228** Corbis/epa/Martial Trezzini; **229** Corbis/Homer Sykes; **230main** Science Photo Library/Detlev van Ravenswaay; **230bkg** Getty/Peter Arnold Collection/Photolibrary.com/Bernd Koch; **232** Science Photo Library/Detlev van Ravenswaay